BAD
money

Praise for *Bad Money*

'Vivek Kaul is the most accessible commentator on the Indian economy. In this book, he explains with clarity and wit the origins and consequences of the non-performing assets that are bogging down the banking system. Anyone interested in the state of the Indian economy should read it.'

– **Srinath Raghavan**, historian and professor at Ashoka University.

'Vivek Kaul's book on the NPA crisis in the Indian banking sector provides a rare combination of incisive analysis with the readability of a gripping detective story. Kaul is one of the very few commentators on the Indian economy whose views rise above the usual chatter of "up and down" commentary on economic trends. He delivers real insight combining a thorough grasp of institutional detail, an eagle-eye for patterns in data others are missing out, all anchored in a clear understanding of economics. And he writes with such fluency and clarity!'

– **Maitreesh Ghatak**, professor of economics, London School of Economics.

'For or anyone who wants to understand the history behind the banking mess, particularly the build-up of non-performing assets (NPAs) in commercial banks that the government and the Reserve Bank of India are still trying to sort out, Vivek Kaul's book should be compulsory reading. It makes a complex issue simple, without making it simplistic. He keeps the reader engaged by darting into banking history, policy changes as well as economic theories. There are many books on the NPA crisis in the market but this is one of the best and most lucid.'

– **Prosenjit Datta**, senior journalist and former editor of *Business Today* and *Businessworld*.

BAD
money

Inside the
NPA Mess
and How It Threatens the
Indian Banking
System

VIVEK KAUL

HARPER
BUSINESS

An Imprint of HarperCollins Publishers

First published in India in 2020 by Harper Business
An imprint of HarperCollins *Publishers*
A-75, Sector 57, Noida, Uttar Pradesh 201301, India
www.harpercollins.co.in

2 4 6 8 10 9 7 5 3 1

P-ISBN: 978-93-5357-721-6
E-ISBN: 978-93-5357-722-3

Typeset in 10.5/13.7 Sabon LT Std at
Manipal Technologies Litimed, Manipal

Printed and bound at
Thomson Press (India) Ltd

'Most people think of economics as not just a dismal science but also a boring one. No more. Vivek Kaul, with simple language and clear thinking, brings out both the drama and the sheer importance of this subject. *Bad Money* reads like an unputdownable thriller. It is a riveting story of what went wrong with our banking system – and also what ails our politics and economics. It is both entertaining and essential.'

> – **Amit Varma**, writer and columnist, and host of the popular podcast, 'The Seen and the Unseen'.

'In *Bad Money*, Vivek Kaul presents a powerful, simple, and well documented explanation for why public sector banks in India are in the current crisis of mounting NPAs. With great simplicity and brevity the book details the incentives of entrepreneurs looking for loans, incentives of private banks, of politicians controlling public sector banks and the Indian banking regulators. Peppered with insights from Thomas Schelling to Genghiz Khan, Kaul's writing style makes even NPA crisis a fun read.'

> – **Shruti Rajagopalan**, senior research fellow, Mercatus Center, George Mason University.

To the teachers of St. Xavier's School, Doranda, Ranchi,
who taught me to read, write and
understand the power of compounding

*'Garib lehron par pehren bithaye jaate hain
samundaron ki talashi koi nahi leta.'*
– **Waseem Barelvi**

Contents

Introduction   xiii

PART I

1. Let's Say Thank You to Nirav Modi   3
2. Why Simplistic Explanations Don't Always Work   8
3. Stability Leads to Instability   12
4. In Public Sector Banks We Trust   16
5. The Birth of State Bank of India   19
6. How the Government Ended Up Owning Banks   23
7. The Banking Crisis of 1990s   28
8. The Rise and Fall of Industrial Finance   39
9. Of Harshad Mehta, Ketan Parekh and Bad Loans   50

PART II

10. Everybody Loves a Public Sector Bank Loan   57
11. Baby Step Subbarao   65
12. How Good Money Became Bad Money   79
13. When Loan Defaults Could Kill   88
14. All Are Equal but Some Are More Equal   91

15. The RBI Crackdown: Rajan and His Men   106

16. No Free Lunch   115

17. The Central Banker Who Knew Too Much   126

18. Privatization by Malign Neglect   132

19. The Big Fish Everyone Wants to Catch   138

20. Was the RBI Caught Napping?   155

21. What Did the RBI Do, Once It Woke Up?   164

22. The PARAchute That Did Not Open   175

23. No Borrowing, No Lending, No Problem   180

24. Merger Blues   190

25. What the Government Wanted to Do with Our
    Money but Didn't   198

26. The Insolvency and the Bankruptcy Code   201

27. The Power Trap   218

28. RBI's Final Countdown   234

29. The Backlash against Rajan   241

30. Why Interest Rates Are Not Falling   248

31. Personal Finance Lessons from the PMC Scam   256

32. A Good Crisis Gone Waste?   266

    Conclusion   287

    Notes   293

    Index   321

    Acknowledgements   337

    About the Author   339

Introduction

John Maynard Keynes, an oft-quoted but less-read economist, who lived in the first half of the twentieth century, is said to have remarked: 'If you owe your bank a hundred pounds, you have a problem. But if you owe your bank a million pounds, it has.'

The Economist, which likes to call itself a newspaper, but is actually a magazine, a few years ago came up with the modern-day version of what Keynes had said: 'If you owe your bank a billion pounds *everybody has a problem* [emphasis added].'

Over the last decade, Indian banks have seen a major growth in their non-performing assets, or bad loans as they are more popularly known. Bad loans are largely those which haven't been repaid for a period of ninety days or more.* As of 31 March 2018, the bad loans of Indian banks amounted to more than Rs 10,36,187 crore. The bulk of these bad loans was with the government-owned public sector banks (PSBs) and amounted to Rs 8,95,601 crore. As of 31 March 2019, the overall bad loans of

---

* The interesting thing is that the definition of a bad loan used to be much broader earlier. In 1998, the Second Narasimham Committee recommended that the definition be tightened in line with the international best practises. In March 2004, a bad loan was classified as a loan on which the interest or the principal remained unpaid for more than ninety days instead of the 180 days norm, followed up until then.

banks had fallen to Rs 9,36,474 crore and that of PSBs had fallen to Rs 7,89,569 crore.

These bad loans had accumulated because of large defaults made by corporate borrowers – the biggest of them being Bhushan Steel, which had defaulted on over Rs 56,000 crore. There were many other such borrowers who had defaulted on bank loans. Defaults on loans made to industry (also referred to as corporate defaults) made up for nearly three-fourths of the overall loan defaults. All this money, if it had been utilized well, could have been put to some good use. It could have helped build better physical infrastructure and more factories in the country. This would have created more jobs, which the country badly needs, given its burgeoning demographic dividend, and, in turn, benefited many individuals. The spending by these individuals could have benefited businesses and, in the process, unleashed a period of high and sustainable virtuous cycle of economic growth. This could have quickly pulled many millions of Indians out of poverty. But it ended up being wasted. In the process, good money of bank loans became the *bad money* of the Indian financial system.

And because of this *good money turning into bad money*, everybody had a problem. This book deals with precisely that point – of everybody having to face a problem because banks and, in particular, PSBs, ended up accumulating bad loans.

The book starts with how corporates ended up taking on massive amounts of loans in the years 2003 to 2008, when the going in the Indian economy was good and the assumption was that the fast economic growth would last forever.

But the financial crisis of 2008 played spoilsport. Nevertheless, PSBs were encouraged to lend in the aftermath of the financial crisis and corporates kept borrowing.

Sometime in 2011, the situation changed, from one of over-optimism to one of pessimism. Corporates had overborrowed and banks had overlent. Corporate projects did not start on time due to a whole host of factors – from a lack of environmental clearances to a lack of non-environmental clearances to problems with acquiring land to roadblocks on policy issues, as well as the inability of the promoters of projects to bring in their fair share of capital to the projects.

Very soon, the steel cycle had turned from positive to negative and steel companies were staring at massive overproduction. This was true of the power sector as well, which ended up with massive overcapacity, particularly in thermal power. Thermal power needed coal and Coal India, India's major coal producer, couldn't supply the required amount.

Banks could have carried out a mid-course correction at this point. They could have stopped lending to corporates and limited the amount of bad loans they would end up accumulating. But that did not happen. Banks, specially PSBs were happy to restructure loans by increasing the tenure of the loan or decreasing the interest rate charged on it. In some cases, new loans were also given so that corporates could repay the old loans which were due. The idea was to not recognize bad loans as bad loans, but simply kick the can down the road for someone else to deal with.

A major question that the book tries to answer is on crony capitalism and what sort of role it played in the accumulation of bad loans. Was it the main reason behind the accumulation of bad loans or is there much more to the issue than just this?

Meanwhile, as all of this was happening, the banking regulator, the Reserve Bank of India (RBI), simply looked the other way. This changed in mid-2015, when Raghuram Rajan, the RBI governor between September 2013 and September 2016, launched an Asset Quality Review of banks and, in the process, forced them to recognize bad loans as bad loans. But even this did not bring out in the open the correct picture of the bad loans of the banks.

Urjit Patel, Rajan's successor as the RBI governor, put out a circular on 12 February 2018, which quashed all the schemes banks were using to restructure bad loans, and this forced them to recognize more bad loans. But are the banks done recognizing bad loans as bad loans? The jury is still out on that.

In economics, there is no such thing as free lunch for someone has got to bear the cost. As the bad loans of PSBs accumulated and losses mounted, the government had to constantly invest more money in these banks to keep them going. Between 2011–12 and 2018–19, it invested Rs 2,91,504 crore to keep these banks afloat. The bulk of this, Rs 90,000 crore and Rs 1,06,000 crore, were spent in 2017–18 and 2018–19 respectively. It plans to spend another Rs 70,000 crore in 2019–20 to continue to recapitalize these banks and keep them going. Between April 2019 and mid-November 2019, the government had invested Rs 55,757 crore in these banks. If we include IDBI Bank, which is no longer a PSB, but used to be one, the number goes up to Rs 60,314 crore.

All this money, which is going into the banks could have easily gone somewhere else. Also, who is paying for this mess? The taxpayer and the investors of the Life Insurance Corporation (LIC) of India and, as you shall see in this book. It's happening in ways we don't even realize.

There are other costs that come attached to this as well. Banks have jacked up interest rates to levels which they wouldn't have if they were not facing this massive problem of bad loans. And this has made the monetary policy of RBI ineffective.

An important point discussed throughout this book is the faith that the Indian depositor has in PSBs. Despite a few banks having a bad loans rate of more than 20 per cent, which means more than a fifth of the loans they have given out have been defaulted on, a large chunk of depositors continue to maintain their deposits with these banks and have not withdrawn them. At least, theoretically, some of these banks should have seen massive bank runs, but they didn't. And this helped them to keep going. It also ensured that the problem did not turn into a massive financial headache for the government and it could deal with it on a year-to-year basis.

And of course, towards the end, the book also offers solutions on how to ensure that this problem does not happen all over again. That's what *Bad Money* is all about.

The book is divided into two parts. Part I sets the context of the book and deals with some of the history of Indian banking, which is important in order to understand the bad loan crisis. The history essentially explains government control over PSBs and how it has ended up hurting these banks over the long term. India's banking history also explains why depositors continue to have faith in PSBs, despite the high number of bad loans these banks have on their books. Part II deals with the actual crisis; the how and the why of it.

* * *

My favourite book on economics is *The Great Crash 1929*, written by John Kenneth Galbraith, who, other than being a famed economist and an author, was also the American ambassador to India in the early 1960s.

The book was published in 1955 and is 240 pages long. Throughout the book, Galbraith's idea is not to bombard the reader with numbers and impress them with his thorough and detailed research. The idea is to use all the research to write in simple English and explain to the reader what really happened when the New York Stock Exchange crashed in October 1929; something that ultimately led to the Great Depression, which started in the same year.

Authors and economists have continued writing and debating on the Great Depression, more than nine decades later. But Galbraith's little book remains the best introduction to it.

Having read a lot of Galbraith over the years, his style of writing is something I have tried to follow in all my work; though, unlike him, I do tend to throw a lot of numbers at my readers. Even with that, the idea is to make things simple without making them simplistic, as the differentiation between simple and simplistic is very important.

In that sense, this book is no different. I have tried to explain in straightforward English what caused this massive accumulation of bad loans.

There is another point that I would request the readers to keep in mind while reading the book. This is a big-picture book, which goes into some detail of how the situation evolved and the Indian financial system got filled up with bad money.

Let's take an example to understand this point in some detail. In the aftermath of the financial crisis of 2008, many books were published. I have three favourites among them: Satyajit Das's *Extreme Money: The Masters of the Universe and the Cult of Risk*, Andrew Ross Sorkin's *Too Big to Fail: The Inside Story of How Wall Street and Washington Fought to Save the Financial System—and Themselves* and Raghuram Rajan's *Fault Lines: How Hidden Fractures Still Threaten the World Economy*.

Each of these books tackles the financial crisis in a different way. Das deals with the nitty-gritty of the financial services industry, in particular, Wall Street and how it created useless derivatives that led to an increased financialization of the system, which was one of the major reasons behind the financial crisis.

Sorkin's book deals with the specifics of the time when Lehman Brothers, the fourth-largest investment bank on Wall Street, filed for bankruptcy in mid-September 2008. It has insider details of what the Federal Reserve of the United States was thinking, what the US Treasury Department was thinking and how they came together to rescue some of the biggest banks and financial services firms in the United States.

Rajan's book goes into the past to explain some of the factors that caused the financial crisis. It also goes into great detail in telling us that the negative effects of the crisis are not going to go away in a hurry, unless the basic economic model of growth in the United States and the Western world is fixed.

Sorkin answers the *how* of the crisis; Rajan answers the *why* of it. Das is somewhere in between. While, Sorkin's book reads like a thriller and was most fun to read, the learnings were clearly more from reading Das and Rajan, who did not miss the wood for the trees.

Bad Money is somewhere between Das's and Rajan's approach to writing. While, it does try and answer some of the *how* of India's bad loan crisis, it's more about the *why*. As far as the *how* is concerned, you won't find any chapters in the book where an industrialist in trouble is talking to his top management and telling them, 'Let's default on the bank loans now.' Further, you won't find any chapters on how the industrialist moved loans borrowed for one project to another project. That kind of book on India's bad loan crisis remains to be written.

Having said that, *Bad Money* is not just about the bad loans of banks. It also deals quite a lot with how banks fit into the overall financial and societal system and the impact they have on our daily lives, without most of us even realizing it.

* * *

In an ideal world, all data used in a book should be as of a certain date. But that's not how lucky we writers are. Different data have different release dates and some economic data are even released a few years after the specific time period has elapsed. I have tried using the latest data in the book, as far as possible. Most data used are as of March 2019. In cases where March 2019 data weren't available, March 2018 data points have been used.

* * *

When talking to students who have very small attention spans these days, I like to give an example comparing Hindi film director Rohit Shetty with Hollywood director Quentin Tarantino. There is one essential difference between the movies of Shetty and Tarantino.

Shetty's movies are true-blue masala flicks, where you can start watching the film at any point and more or less figure out the back story on your own. Also, the stories largely move linearly. Tarantino, on the other hand, makes non-linear films, where multiple storylines move back and forth, until they finally come together in the end. Of course, this requires a lot more attention on the part of the viewer than what is required while watching a Shetty movie.

The point I am hoping to make to students is that my essays are like Tarantino movies – they tend to go back and forth, and given that they need some attention, the Shetty approach won't work.

Why am I making this point here? In order to read *Bad Money*, you don't need to be a fancy MBA or require a degree in economics or finance. It's meant for an average reader who understands English and has some knowledge of basic, fifth-standard math. Having said that, it's not like a Shetty movie either, which does not require much attention and which you can begin anywhere and still follow the narrative.

The book, like a Tarantino movie, requires some attention.

Dear reader, I sincerely hope, you will give it that time and have as much fun reading it as I had writing it.

Vivek Kaul
22 April 2019 to 7 February 2020
Prabhadevi, Mumbai

PART I

PART 1

1

Let's Say Thank You to Nirav Modi

In early February 2018, I was at Symbiosis International University, on the outskirts of Pune, to address a batch of journalism students. The university is built on a hill and at the top of the hill is the guest house.

It was late in the evening and I was standing outside my room, looking at the setting sun and clicking pictures. A few peacocks were roaming around, adding to the beauty of the scenery.

I was at peace with myself, happy at having taken the three-and-a-half-hour drive from Mumbai, where I live and work amongst a lot of concrete and people I don't know.

The peace and quiet lasted for all of ten minutes, and then my mobile phone rang. The STD code that flashed on my smartphone (as the call was coming from a landline) told me that someone from Noida was trying to reach me. I reluctantly picked up the call and found myself talking to someone who spoke chaste Hindi, a rarity these days.

An editor from a large Hindi daily had called and he wanted to know if I could write a 600-word piece in simple terms on the fugitive diamantaire Nirav Modi and the problems of bad loans in PSBs. PSBs are banks largely owned by the government.

Nirav Modi had scammed the Punjab National Bank (PNB) of Rs 12,645.97 crore[1] and escaped from the country. His escape had made him the talk of the town and even a Hindi newspaper, which wouldn't have bothered about banking news and analysis

3

on most days, was now interested in a piece on the fugitive and the bad loans of PSBs.

What surprised me was that it took the newspaper so long to realize the significance of the issue at hand. I had been writing on the problem of bad loans at PSBs from early 2014, which, as we shall see, wasn't very early in any sense of the term. And it wasn't only this newspaper which had ignored the issue; more or less, the entire Hindi media had.

In fact, by March 2018, the total bad loans of PSBs were at Rs 8,95,601 crore. This formed 86.4 per cent of the bad loans of the Indian banking system, which stood at Rs 10,36,187 crore. This was the *bad money* of the Indian financial system.

As a proportion of the total bad loans of PSBs, Modi's fraud and default amounted just 1.4 per cent. When looked at this way, the diamantaire Modi seemed to be small fry in the overall scheme of things.

But things change when we look at Modi's fraud in the context of PNB, which, at that point, was the second largest PSB in the country, after the State Bank of India (SBI). The total bad loans of PNB as of March 2018 had stood at Rs 86,620 crore. Modi's fraud and default formed around 14.6 per cent of the total bad loans of the bank. Now it seems significant.

Let's look at this in another way. Between 2012–13 and 2016–17, the average size of a fraud in the case of Indian banking was around Rs 3 crore. In the case of PNB, the average size of a fraud amounted to Rs 9.6 crore. Of course, a fraud of Rs 12,645.97 crore was quite big in comparison to the average fraud at PNB.[2]

On that day in February 2018, as I watched the setting sun and the peacocks, I was left wondering what was it that got a Hindi daily, published through large parts of northern, eastern and central India, interested in bad loans of PSBs.

After some thinking, the answer finally came to me. The newspaper could finally put a human face to the entire bad loan crisis that PSBs were facing. Nirav Modi was a businessman who bought and sold diamonds, and who hobnobbed with the likes of former Miss World and international film actor Priyanka Chopra. At the end of the day, the media likes to build heroes and, given half an opportunity, to pull them down.

Interestingly, psychologists even have a term for such a situation; they call it the identified life. Nirav Modi became an identified life when it came to the problem of bad loans being faced by PSBs in India.

Nobel prize winning economist Thomas Schelling explains the term in his book, *Choice and Consequence: Perspectives of an Errant Economist*. He writes: 'Let a six-year-old girl with brown hair need thousands of dollars for an operation that will prolong her life until Christmas, and the post office will be swamped with nickels and dimes to save her. But let it be reported that without a sales tax the hospital facilities of Massachusetts [a state in the United States] will deteriorate and cause a barely perceptible increase in preventable deaths—not many will drop a tear or reach for their cheque books.'[3]

Schelling came up with this example of a six-year-old girl to essentially distinguish between a 'statistical life' and an 'identified life'. The sick girl dying is an identified life whereas the people dying in hospitals are 'merely' statistical lives because we do not know who they are and, hence, we don't relate to them or care about them. And so, people are ready to donate money in order to save an identified life, but do nothing about the statistical one.

As Richard H. Thaler, another Nobel prize winning economist, writes in *Misbehaving: The Making of Behavioural Economics*: 'We rarely allow an identified life to be extinguished solely for the lack of money. But of course thousands of "unidentified" people die every day for lack of simple things like mosquito nets, vaccines, or clean water.'[4]

A great example of an identified life in a context totally different from banking is Mukesh Harane. Harane died of oral cancer in October 2009. He was addicted to *gutkha**. After his death, he

---

*   A chewing tobacco preparation.

became the face of the anti-tobacco message which was delivered through an audiovisual clip, shown regularly in cinema halls. A print campaign was also run.

The audiovisual clip featuring Mukesh was fairly disturbing. Every time I saw a movie in a multiplex, I wondered why is the government hell-bent on spoiling what is essentially supposed to be fun for anyone who has come to the cinema hall to watch a movie. But then the idea of the clip was to disturb you and, to that extent, it achieved its aim.

It has been argued that it could have been less gruesome; nevertheless, it managed to convey the ill-effects of consuming *gutkha* very well. It showed a dying Mukesh talking about the ill-effects of eating *gutkha,* with a feeding pipe going through his nose.

Mukesh as a victim of *gutkha* consumption was an identified life, and the anti-tobacco campaign featuring him really worked and touched a raw nerve. It showed very clearly how dangerous eating *gutkha* can be. It also explains why many government campaigns which simply highlight data do not work at all because they do not have an identified life in them.

As Jean Tirole, a Nobel prize winning economist, writes in *Economics for the Common Good*: 'Psychologists have identified our tendency to attach more importance to people whose faces we know than to other anonymous people.'[5]

Take the case of the distressing picture of a three-year-old Syrian child (Alan Kurdi), who was found dead on a Turkish beach in 2015. This forced Europe to pay attention to the refugees coming in from Syria. As Tirole writes: 'It had much more impact on Europeans' awareness than the statistics about thousands of migrants who had already drowned in the Mediterranean.'

The point here is that an issue really becomes an issue in the minds of people once they can visualize it in terms and put a face to it. In this way, Nirav Modi became the poster boy for corporate India looting the PSBs. The surprising thing is that by the time Modi's shenanigans came to light in January 2018, the

PSBs already had bad loans of around Rs 8 lakh crore. But even this huge number did not have much of an impact on the minds of the people. In fact, very few were even aware of how large the bad loans were. Nirav Modi's Rs 12,645.97-crore fraud clearly brought the issue of bad money to the forefront. In the months that followed his escape from India, the common man was found talking about him in general and PSBs in particular.

To that extent we need to thank Nirav Modi. What the big grim numbers of PSBs couldn't achieve, he single-handedly did.

Before Nirav Modi, there was Vijay Mallya who defaulted on bank loans of around Rs 9,000 crore and escaped from the country. Then there were others, like Jatin Mehta of Winsome Diamonds, who owes the banks around Rs 7,000 crore, and Chetan Jayantilal Sandesara and Nitin Jayantilal Sandesara, who escaped from the country after defrauding the banks of around Rs 5,000 crore.[6]

Many other corporates have also defaulted on loans, though their owners did not run away from India. These defaults helped build the narrative of corporates being primarily responsible for the bad loans of PSBs over the years.

They were the villains of the piece; they were the ones who turned the good money of the Indian PSBs into bad money. In the simple binary world of WhatsApp University, this is 100 per cent true, but in the real analytical world, there are many nuances that need to be taken into account in order to explain the absolute truth, if there is a thing like that out there. And *Bad Money* is about these nuances and the search for the absolute truth.

2

Why Simplistic Explanations Don't Always Work

The trouble with the human brain is that it craves simplistic explanations because it suffers from cognitive limits, or what psychologists call a 'bounded rationality'. There is only so much information that we have access to, and even if we had access to all the information at the same time, our brains wouldn't be able to process and make sense of it.

To get over this basic deficiency, the human brain seeks simplistic explanations. Let's use an example here to understand this in detail. The RBI has a Monetary Policy Committee (MPC). The MPC decides which way the interest rates in the banking system should go in the days to come. It can't force banks to raise or cut interest rates, but it can *incentivize* them to do so.

Let's say the MPC feels that the interest rates in the banking system should come down. In this scenario, it can cut the repo rate and thus incentivize the banks to cut the interest rates on their deposits as well as loans. The repo rate is the interest rate at which the RBI lends to banks.

Between January 2019 and June 2019, the MPC had cut the repo rate thrice by 25 basis points each and in the process brought it down to 5.75 per cent from 6.5 per cent. One basis point is one hundredth of a percentage. As often happens, once the MPC cuts the repo rate, the media goes into an overdrive to tell the world at large that the equated monthly instalments (EMIs) on loans will now fall. This time was no different.

Having said that, the whole 'RBI cuts repo rate, EMIs to come down' is a very simplistic explanation of the entire situation. Of course, it satisfies the human brain's need for an explanation about what will happen now that the repo rate has been cut. The trouble is that this is not always true, especially not in the recent times.

Banks raise deposits by paying a certain rate of interest. These deposits they then give out as loans, by charging a certain rate of interest. Borrowing from the RBI happens only when there is a shortfall of money at the bank's end. As of 19 July 2019, the credit–deposit ratio was at 76.3 per cent. What does this mean? For every Rs 100 raised as a deposit, the banks have lent out Rs 76.3 as loans. Once we take into account a cash reserve ratio of 4 per cent, which banks need to maintain with the RBI and a minimum statutory liquidity ratio of 18.5 per cent that banks need to compulsorily invest in government securities,* these financial institutions have been lending out almost all the deposits that they have.

Take a look at Figure 2.1.

Figure 2.1

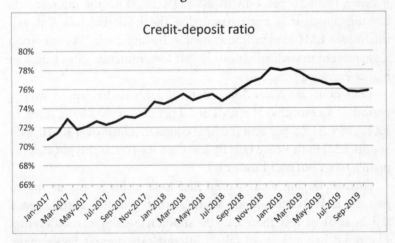

Source: Reserve Bank of India.

---

* Government securities are bonds issued by the Central government to raise money to finance the fiscal deficit. Fiscal deficit is the difference between what a government earns and what it spends.

Figure 2.1 tells us that in 2019, the credit–deposit ratio has been over 75 per cent. In this scenario, it has not been possible for banks to cut the interest rates on their deposits and, in the process, on their loans.

This means that the banks are already lending out all the deposits that they possibly could. In this scenario, they clearly need more deposits to continue giving loans. If they need more deposits, they need to keep offering a high rate of interest on them. Hence, it's not possible for them to cut the interest rates on their deposits, and, in turn, on their loans.

This is a simple explanation which overrides the simplistic explanation of an RBI repo rate cut leading to lower EMIs. Therefore, here is the difference between simplistic and simple.

Let's take this example a little forward. The idea is to show that what looks like a simple decision may have complex factors working for or against it.

Let's say a bank, in response to the repo rate cut by the MPC, cuts the interest rate on its car loans by 50 basis points and brings it down from 10 per cent to 9.5 per cent. With the interest rate coming down, it is but natural that the EMI will fall. But will this lower EMI lead to more people buying cars? The common logic offered in such situations is that lower interest rates lead to a higher consumption.

Let's consider a car loan of Rs 4 lakh to be repaid over a period of 48 months. The EMI at 10 per cent would have come to Rs 10,145. At 9.5 per cent the EMI comes to a little over Rs 10,049. So, the EMI in this case falls by less than Rs 100. Is this enough for people to go out and buy a car?

Anyone buying a car would first look at his or her ability to pay the EMI in the coming years. If that ability is there, then a fall in EMI of less than Rs 100 shouldn't make any difference. The point being, a small fall in interest rate doesn't really make any difference.

Now, what was the need to give these examples? First and foremost, the idea was that even the simple act of the RBI's

MPC cutting the repo rate has complex forces working behind it. Typically, we don't get to understand these things, because the media explains it away in a simplistic way. Further, the idea was to show that even though the topic might be complex, it can be explained in a simple way. This is the formula that I will try and follow through the book.

Finally, if even an act like the MPC cutting the repo rate can be so nuanced, a topic like the bad loans of PSBs is bound to be complex. As economist Alan S. Blinder, former vice-chairman of the Federal Reserve of the United States, the American central bank, writes in *After the Music Stopped—The Financial Crisis, the Response, and the Work Ahead*, in context of the global financial crisis that started in September 2008: 'It's hard to imagine how something as sweeping and multifaceted as the financial crisis could have stemmed from a single cause or had a single villain.'[7] Now, replace the phrase financial crisis in the above sentence with India's banking crisis, which is basically what the accumulated bad loans of Indian banks amounts to, and the logic stays the same.

India's banking crisis has stemmed from multiple causes and, hence, does not have a single villain, even though in our own simplistic way we have been blaming corporate honchos like Nirav Modi and Vijay Mallya for it. This is not to say that they are not to be blamed for the bad money problem. But there is much more to it than just their defaults and frauds. In short, it's complex.

3

Stability Leads to Instability

An old joke in the economics circle goes somewhat like this: 'Economists have predicted nine out of the last five recessions.' In fact, the record of economists predicting recessions and/or banking crises is terrible. While the economists do a fantastic job of explaining a crisis once it has happened, they rarely see it coming.

This even led the British monarch Queen Elizabeth II, while on a visit to the London School of Economics in late 2008, to ask: 'Why did no one see it coming?'[8] This was in reference to the financial crisis, which started in 2008.

One reason why economists fail to forecast financial and banking crises lies in the fact that their models rarely take banks and financial institutions, and the part they play in the general economy, into account.

One economist who did take the role of banks and financial institutions into account was Hyman Minsky. He died in 1996. But when Minsky was alive, his work was largely confined to the fringes and ignored by the mainstream economics establishment in the United States. His work was rediscovered in the aftermath of the financial crisis that broke out in 2008.

Interestingly, the RBI also managed to dig up Minsky in the Financial Stability Report published in December 2015. The idea, it seems, was to use Minsky's theory to explain India's banking crisis, though like a good central bank, the RBI did not say so directly. It just hinted at it.

Buried in this report was a very interesting box titled 'In Search of Some Old Wisdom', which said: 'When current wisdom does not offer solutions to extant problems, old wisdom can sometimes be helpful. For instance, the global financial crisis compelled us to take a look at the *Minsky's financial stability hypothesis* [emphasis added] which posited the debt accumulation by non-government sector as the key to economic crisis.'[9]

Actually, Minsky put forward the financial instability hypothesis and not the financial stability hypothesis as the RBI wrote.

How did Minsky define this hypothesis? As he wrote in *Stabilizing an Unstable Economy*: 'The way in which a speculative boom emerges and how an unstable crisis prone financial and economic system develops are of particular importance in any description of the economic process that is relevant for this economy. Instability emerges as a period of relative tranquil growth is transformed into a speculative boom. This occurs because the acceptable and the desired liability structures of business firms (corporations) and the organisations acting as middlemen in finance change in response to the success of the economy.'[10]

The basic premise of the financial instability hypothesis is that when times are good and people have seen a period of healthy economic growth, they want to take on more risk. Banks are willing to give riskier loans than they would usually do. Businessmen also want to take on more risk and expand their enterprises, and are happy to borrow more.

This leads to increased investment in the economy and is supposed to lead to higher profits for businesses in the years to come. At least that is how it's supposed to work in theory. Initially, banks only lend to businesses that are expected to generate enough cash to repay their loans. But as time progresses, the competition between lenders (i.e., the banks) increases and caution is thrown to the winds. An era of easy money is unleashed and money is doled out left, right and centre. Normally, it doesn't end well.

In fact, Minsky talks about the three stages of finance: hedge, speculative and Ponzi.

In order to understand Minsky, we need to refer to L. Randall
Wray's book *Why Minsky Matters: An Introduction to the Work
of a Maverick Economist*. Wray was a student of Minsky's and
knows his work very well.

As he writes: 'Minsky developed a famous classification for
[the] fragility of financing positions. The safest is called "hedge"
finance (note that this term is not related to so-called hedge
funds). In a hedge position, expected income is sufficient to make
all payments as they become due, including both interest and
principal.'[11] Hence, in the hedge position, the company taking on
loans is making enough money to pay interest on the debt as well
as repay it.

How do we define the speculative position? As Wray writes:
'A "speculative" position is one in which expected income is
sufficient to make interest payments, but [the] principal must be
rolled over.'[12]

Hence, in a speculative position, a company is making enough
money to keep paying interest on the loan that it has taken on, but
it has no money to repay the principal amount of the loan. In order
to repay the principal, the income of the company has to go up. Or
banks need to agree to refinance the loan, i.e., give a fresh loan so
that the current loan can be repaid. So, to that extent the position
is speculative. The banks can also reduce the interest rate on the
loan or increase its tenure. The third option is for the company
to start selling its assets in order to repay the principal amount of
the loan.

And what is the third stage? As Wray writes: 'Finally, a "Ponzi"
position [named after a famous fraudster, Charles Ponzi, who ran
a pyramid scheme—much like Bernie Madoff's more recent fraud]
is one in which even interest payments cannot be met, so that the
debtor must borrow to pay interest.'[13]

Charles Ponzi was a fraudster who ran an investment scheme
in Boston, United States, in 1919. He promised to double the
investors' money in ninety days and later in forty-five days. There
was no business model in place to generate returns. All Ponzi did

was to take money from new investors and hand it over to old investors whose investments had to be redeemed. His game got over once the money leaving the scheme became higher than the money being invested in it.

Along similar lines, once companies are not in a position to pay interest on their loans, they need to borrow more. This new money coming in helps them repay the loans as well as pay interest. Till they can keep borrowing more, they can keep paying interest and repaying their loans. The moment fresh borrowing stops, the company which has borrowed has no other option but to default. Hence, the entire situation is akin to a Ponzi scheme.

How does all this link to the Indian PSBs and the bad loans they have accumulated over the years? The banking crisis in India has evolved more or less in line with Minsky's financial instability hypothesis. A simple interpretation of Minsky's hypothesis would be that stability leads to instability, which is precisely how things unfolded in India.

There were years of stability and good economic growth. So banks were willing to lend more and companies willing to borrow. Eventually, the competition among banks led to falling lending standards. Finally, due to several reasons, the economy started to slow down. The high economic growth projections, which had led to companies borrowing more than they could possibly repay, went for a toss.

The companies entered a stage wherein they were not in a position to repay loans, unless their loans were restructured by the banks or they were given fresh loans to repay the earlier ones, in the hope that their business would recover in the years to come.

In the coming chapters, we shall see how PSBs and the companies that they lent to went through different stages of finance that Minsky talked about.

4

In Public Sector Banks We Trust

In April 2018, I was addressing a small audience in Hyderabad. At the end of the session, an old Bengali woman got up and asked me a simple question. 'Is my money safe?' I couldn't give her a general answer and so I asked her with which bank did she have an account. 'IDBI Bank,' came the answer.

IDBI Bank was one of the twenty-one PSBs at that point of time. (Since then, it has been taken over by LIC and has been declared a private bank.) Five associate banks of the SBI and the Bhartiya Mahila Bank had merged with it from 1 April 2017 onwards. This had brought down the number of PSBs from twenty-seven to twenty-one.

Among the twenty-one PSBs, IDBI Bank had the worst gross non-performing assets (NPA) ratio. Gross non-performing assets are those loans or advances, where: (1) interest and/or a part-repayment of principal of the loan (basically an instalment) remains overdue for a period of more than ninety days, in case of a term loan. A term loan is a loan which is repaid in regular instalments over a fixed period of time; (2) the instalment of interest or principal remains overdue for two crop seasons for short duration crops and one crop season for long duration crops; (3) the bill remains overdue for a period of more than ninety days in case of bills purchased and discounted.[14] This means that an organization has taken a loan against a receivable (i.e., a bill) which is due to be paid in some time. If the loan is not repaid to the bank for a period

16

more than ninety days from the date which it is due, it's considered to be a gross non-performing asset.

Also, a gross NPA in common parlance is referred to as a bad loan. Gross NPAs expressed as a percentage of total loans or an advance given by a bank is referred to as the gross NPA ratio, or, simply put, the bad loans rate.

As of 31 March 2018, IDBI Bank had bad loans amounting to Rs 55,588 crore against total loans of Rs 1,98,853 crore. This implied a bad loans rate of around 28 per cent.

The basic business model of a bank involves taking money in the form of a deposit from people and paying a certain rate of interest on it to the depositors. The bank then lends out that money at a higher rate of interest. If the money lent out by the bank is not repaid, it becomes difficult for the bank to repay its depositors.

Of course, it doesn't make sense for the depositors to wait for the bank to default on the deposits. Any sense of trouble at the bank should lead to the depositors lining up at the branches and taking their money out.

Here was a bank which had a bad loans rate of close to 28 per cent, but the depositors continued to have faith in it. In March 2018, the total deposits of the bank had stood at Rs 2,47,932 crore. They had fallen by around 8.3 per cent from March 2017, when the total deposits had stood at Rs 2,68,538 crore.

During the same period, the total advances of the bank had also fallen by 5.9 per cent to Rs 1,98,853 crore. They had stood at Rs 2,10,610 crore as of March 2017. The point being that the bank continued to have enough deposits to fund its loans. The depositors continued to have confidence in the bank, even though between March 2017 and March 2018 the bad loans rate of the bank had jumped from 21.2 per cent to 28 per cent. This was a massive jump.

By December 2018, the bad loans rate had jumped to 29.7 per cent. The deposits at the bank continued to be strong at Rs 2,29,966 crore. By March 2019, the bad loans rate had come down to 27.5

per cent, with the aggregate deposits going strong at Rs 2,27,372 crore.

Back in March 2018, IDBI Bank wasn't the only PSB which had a massive bad loans problem. There were other such banks as well.

The Indian Overseas Bank with a bad loans rate of 25.3 per cent came in next. UCO Bank with a bad loans rate of 24.6 per cent was third. Six PSBs had bad loans rates of more than 20 per cent. Fourteen PSBs had bad loans rates of more than 15 per cent. There were only two PSBs, Indian Bank and Vijaya Bank – with a bad loans rate of 7.4 per cent and 6.3 per cent, respectively – which had a bad loans rate in single digits. In fact, to be fair, the bad loans rate of the SBI, which was in single digits in March 2017 (at 6.9 per cent) had been pushed to double digits (at 10.9 per cent as of March 2018) due to its merger with the five associate banks and the Bhartiya Mahila Bank.

The overall bad loans rate of PSBs had reached a huge 15.6 per cent. Despite the massive problem of bad loans with the PSBs, the faith of the existing depositors in these banks remained intact. The total amount of deposits as of March 2011 had stood at Rs 40.2 lakh crore. By March 2018, this had jumped to Rs 76.5 lakh crore. By March 2019, the total deposits of PSBs had stood at Rs 79.2 lakh crore.

The question is, where does this confidence of depositors in PSBs come from? In order to understand this, we will have to take a brief detour and look at the history of PSBs in India. This is one of the key questions that the book will try answering.

5

The Birth of State Bank of India

The Imperial Bank of India was formed in January 1921 by bringing together the Presidency Banks of Bombay (now Mumbai), Calcutta (now Kolkata) and Madras (now Chennai). It was the predecessor to today's SBI.

The interesting thing is that the bank was privately owned (by both Europeans and Indians), even though it worked closely with the British government in India and was governed by it. The Governor General of the British Crown* had the power to issue instructions to the Imperial Bank in order to safeguard the financial policy of the British government in India, or its balances, for that matter. In fact, the Controller of Currency, who was appointed on to the Central Board of the Imperial Bank, had to act as the watchdog of the government when it came to the bank.[15]

It's worth remembering here that the RBI was formed only in 1935. Given this, the Imperial Bank of India carried out some central banking functions as well.

It managed the public debt of the British government in India. It also acted as a banker's bank, with most of the leading banks of the day maintaining a portion of their cash balance as a deposit with it (the modern equivalent being the cash reserve ratio that banks need to maintain with the RBI). One of the objectives of the Imperial Bank was to expand banking facilities across India and introduce a banking habit (something we are still trying to

---

* The title Viceroy was used more frequently in regular communication, but it had no statutory authority.

achieve nearly a hundred years later). Hence, the bank pursued a very aggressive policy when it came to opening branches across different parts of the country. By 1928, it had 202 branches against the seventy when it started. The interesting thing is that the private deposits of the bank (it had a lot of government deposits, given that it received all the government dues from the public) amounted to around one-third of the total deposits of the banking system in India. This confidence of the public came from the fact that despite being a privately owned bank, it worked closely with the government and was seen as the government's bank.[16]

As Bakhtiar K. Dadabhoy writes in *Barons of Banking: Glimpses of Indian Banking History*: 'The general confidence [arose] out of the belief that the government was deeply concerned in and could be trusted to take measures to ensure its stability and solvency.'[17]

It's this confidence that people had in the Imperial Bank of India (which later became the SBI) that rubbed off on the PSBs, as and when they came into the picture. And it's this confidence which continues to the present day, where people have let their deposits lie in banks, which have a bad loans rate of 15 per cent or more.

Calls for the nationalization of the Imperial Bank started as soon as India gained independence. On 4 February 1948, Mohanlal Saksena, a politician from Uttar Pradesh, who served as the Union minister of rehabilitation, became the first person to raise a query on the subject, to the finance minister, R.K. Shanmukham Chetty, in the Constituent Assembly. The query and the concerns around the Imperial Bank were genuine as the bank continued to be a British bank, with the top management of the bank being British personnel, with no Indian having broken through. Chetty gave a politically correct answer to Saksena's query and said that the government accepted the policy of nationalizing the bank, but it first needed to figure out the various technical questions that would come up if such a step were taken.[18]

One of the reasons why the government and most of the politicians of the day wanted to nationalize the Imperial Bank was to ensure that rural savings could also become a part of the banking system. At the same time, with increased deposits, these savings could then be made available as loans to a large part of the population which wanted to borrow money but was unable to borrow from banks.

The Rural Banking Enquiry Committee (RBEC), which submitted its report in May 1950, found that the extension of banking had been lopsided 'with heavy concentration in larger towns and cities'. The committee recommended that the Imperial Bank, along with other commercial banks, should be encouraged to expand to *mandis*, or market towns, and other towns which have commercial or industrial importance.[19]

After the RBEC, another committee, the All-India Rural Credit Survey Committee (AIRCS) was appointed in August 1951. The AIRCS took more than three years to submit its report, which it finally did in December 1954.

It recommended the nationalization of the Imperial Bank and the government accepted it. The committee, with a lot of help from the RBI, had carried out field enquiries, which covered 1,27,343 families in 600 villages across seventy-five districts across the country. These enquiries revealed that the professional moneylender, the agriculturist moneylender and the trader ruled rural credit and supplied close to 70 per cent or more of it.[20]

This would have been a major point that led the then government to nationalize the Imperial Bank of India and establish the State Bank of India (SBI). It was established on 1 July 1955, with all the assets and liabilities of the Imperial Bank being transferred to it. In fact, initially the idea was even to amalgamate ten more banks with the SBI. These banks were the Bank of Bikaner, the Bank of Jaipur, the Bank of Rajasthan, the Bank of Baroda, the Bank of Indore, the Bank of Mysore, the Travancore Bank, the Hyderabad State Bank, the Bank of Patiala and the State Bank of Saurashtra. This did not happen primarily because the RBI Governor Benegal Rama Rau was of the view that the SBI need not immediately be burdened with the responsibility of integrating these banks into it.

Over the years, eight of these banks became subsidiaries of the SBI, with the Bank of Bikaner and Jaipur being merged.[21]

The Imperial Bank was primarily nationalized to spread the banking habit in the country. It was stipulated that the SBI would open 400 branches within five years, which it did by 1 June 1960. By 1967, the bank had been reasonably successful in mobilizing the Indian savings by getting people to deposit them in the bank. Personal deposits accounted for 90 per cent of the total deposit accounts and 39 per cent of the total deposits in the bank.[22] The fact that the bank was government-owned helped.

The interesting thing is that until the SBI came along, when it came to industrial lending, the banks in India stuck to financing the working capital of industries. This was, of course, a very safe and a risk-free way of lending. But in a newly independent nation, just risk-free lending wouldn't help. The bank's lending to industry increased from Rs 49.3 crore in December 1955, a few months after its nationalization, to Rs 533.2 crore in April 1968. Also, much of this lending was carried out to basic industries like iron and steel, fertilisers, chemicals, cement and mining, engineering, etc. The bank gave out loans to other sectors as well, from the cooperative sector to small-scale industries to agriculture.[23]

This was how the first round of nationalization played out in India. The second round happened in 1969 and it had nothing to do with spreading the banking habit, but everything to do with politics.

6

How the Government Ended Up Owning Banks

Indira Gandhi was the Union minister of information and broadcasting in Lal Bahadur Shastri's cabinet. She became the Prime Minister of the country on 24 January 1966, after Shastri's sudden death in Tashkent, supposedly from a massive heart attack. Gandhi owed her position to senior Congress leaders, together referred to as the Syndicate.[24]

Her first year in office had proved to be a nightmare. As the third volume of the history of the RBI points out: 'For the next two years, drought persisted. Then a balance of payments crisis broke … Planning was put on hold for three years. In the 1967 general election, the Congress lost a large number of seats in Parliament. War, famine, political uncertainty, economic distress—the cup of misery was brimming over.'[25]

Over and above this, Gandhi also wanted to get out of the control of the Syndicate leaders and she felt she needed 'a dramatic gesture that would revitalise the hopes of the nation and put her firmly in control'. The election manifesto of the Congress for the 1967 Lok Sabha had also talked about bringing 'banking institutions under social control to serve the cause of economic growth more effectively and to make credit available to the producers in all fields where it's needed'.[26]

As it often happens in politics, things proceeded at a slow pace for few years and then everything happened in a matter of days. Things started to happen at a breakneck speed in July 1969.

On 9 July 1969, Gandhi sent a note to the Congress Working Committee. She suggested that banks be nationalized. In the note she said: 'There is a great feeling in the country regarding the nationalisation of private commercial banks ... Either we can consider the nationalisation of the top five or six banks or issue directions that the resources of banks should be reserved to a larger extent for public purposes.'[27]

The Syndicate still ran the Congress and they didn't think this was an important issue. Gandhi wanted to wrest control away from the Syndicate. She needed a dramatic issue to do that and nationalization of private banks fit the bill remarkably well.[28]

On 16 July 1969, three days after the AICC (All-India Congress Committee) session had ended, she relieved Moraji Desai of the finance portfolio and took over it herself. The history of the RBI suggests that the RBI Governor L.K. Jha hadn't been kept in the loop because he was not in favour of nationalizing private banks.

Jha was in favour of social control of banks. As the third volume of the history of the RBI points out: 'Bank managements were considered insensitive to the needs of society. These perceptions of the political class led to demands for state intervention. At first the idea was confined to "social control", *whatever that meant* [emphasis added], but soon it gave way to a call for outright nationalisation.'[29]

The history of the RBI suggests that Gandhi asked Jha to come to Delhi on 17 July. He came with a detailed note on social control of banks. She told him to leave the note he was carrying on her table and go into the next room to help draft the legislation on nationalization of banks. This story comes with the disclaimer that 'we will perhaps never know exactly what happened in those three days but one thing was certain' and that was 'Gandhi had decided to go ahead with immediate nationalisation'.[30]

On 18 July, Gandhi met I.G. Patel, who was then the Economic Affairs Secretary in the central government. She asked him if banking was under his charge. He said that it was. After this, as Patel recalls in *Glimpses of Indian Economic History*: *An Insider's*

View, Gandhi told him: 'For political reasons, it has been decided to nationalise the banks. You have to prepare within 24 hours the bill, a note for the Cabinet and a speech for me to make to the nation on radio tomorrow evening. Can you do it and make sure there is no leak?'[31]

Patel told her that what she wanted would be done. At the same time, he offered her two suggestions. The first being that foreign banks should not be nationalized and the second being that there was no need to nationalize all the banks – only banks which accounted for 85–90 per cent of the total banking business should be nationalized. Gandhi agreed, and told him that she would leave the details to him.[32]

Interestingly, the idea to nationalize private banks had actually come from P.N. Haksar, principal secretary to Gandhi, and also her confidant. He urged her to take some bold economic measures for political survival. He also convinced her that the people of the country would support her on the issue.[33]

The idea was to nationalize banks with deposits of Rs 100 crore or more. But it so turned out that Dena Bank, which was considered to be an important private bank, had deposits of only Rs 98 crore and would miss the cut-off mark. To avoid this, the limit was lowered to Rs 50 crore or more.[34]

Such was the hurry to nationalize banks that the government promulgated an ordinance on 19 July 1969, which happened to be a Saturday. In a speech to the nation the same evening, Prime Minister Indira Gandhi said, 'Control over the commanding heights of the economy is necessary, particularly in a poor country where it's extremely difficult to mobilize adequate resources for development and to reduce inequalities between different groups and regions.'

I.G. Patel makes a very interesting point in his book, where he says: 'On my own, I inserted a sentence in Mrs Gandhi's speech: "This is the culmination of the process which began with the nationalisation of Life Insurance and the Imperial Bank to occupy the commanding heights of finance." The idea was to link with

the past, to take away the revolutionary edge, and even more, to
assure that no more nationalisation would follow.'[35]

Not surprisingly, businesses were unhappy with the decision,
with many businessmen losing their banks to the government. The
president of the industry lobby FICCI, Ramnath Poddar, called it
a 'hasty step'. Both K. Kamaraj and Atulya Ghosh, who were the
Syndicate bosses trying to control Gandhi, had no option but to
welcome the decision. They even pointed out that the decision had
been accepted in principle by the AICC. The Young Turks in the
Congress party, led by Chandra Shekhar, welcomed the decision,
having campaigned for the nationalization of private banks. The
Lok Sabha met two days after the ordinance on the nationalization
of banks was promulgated. Atal Bihari Vajpayee 'raised the issue by
asking about the propriety of promulgating an Ordinance of such
significance when the Parliament was to meet within two days.'[36]

Another round of nationalization of banks happened in 1980.
But this round was nowhere as eventful as the one in 1969. Gandhi
wasn't trying to make a political point. The initiative this time
around came from I.G. Patel, who was the RBI governor at that
point of time.

As Patel later recalled: 'I had to recommend to Mrs Gandhi
... she should nationalise another swathe of private banks. The
Reserve Bank had the responsibility to supervise private banks
and to ensure their compliance with social control norms as well
as with law. Several small private banks had now grown to [a]
respectable size and it was not easy to control their activities in
practise. Some of them, like the Punjab & Sind Bank and the
Vijaya Bank, had become the personal fiefdoms of individuals
who disregarded all rules and advice with impunity. They, with
their shady dealings, were offering unfair competition to the
nationalised banks. I decided that the only practical way to tackle
the problem was to nationalise the banks ... *Mrs Gandhi readily
accepted the advice—going against her promise of no new wave of
nationalisation, strictly speaking* [emphasis added].'[37] An ordinance
to nationalize six more banks was issued on 15 April 1980. The

six banks that were nationalized were Andhra Bank, Corporation Bank, New Bank of India (which was merged into PNB after it ran into trouble later), Oriental Bank of Commerce, Punjab & Sind Bank, and Vijaya Bank. The cut off this time around was Rs 200 crore of deposits.[38]

What did the nationalization of banks achieve? As Patel put it: 'By all accounts, the nationalisation of major banks was a great success initially. Apart from the political dividends for Mrs Gandhi, *it greatly increased popular confidence in the banking system* [emphasis added] and thus increased the mobilisation of private savings through banks. The savings so mobilised were also used now for supporting public borrowing as well as for meeting hitherto neglected genuine credit needs.'

Nationalization increased the confidence in the banking system, which is why people continue to bank with PSBs. It explains how PSBs continue to have lakhs of crore of deposits, despite the fact that they are bleeding big time. The nationalization of banks essentially provided an explicit guarantee to depositors that 'all obligations of PSBs will be fulfilled by the Indian government in the event of a failure.'[39] Hence, it doesn't matter to people if they are banking with IDBI Bank, which has the highest proportion of bad loans among all PSBs, or Indian Bank, which has the least bad loans.

To conclude this chapter, there were multiple reasons for going into some detail on the nationalization of banks. First and foremost, it was to establish that much of what seems like economics is basically politics, which is why the subject of economics was originally called political economy. If Indira Gandhi wasn't so desperate to get rid of her image of a *'goongi gudiya'* and the control of the Syndicate bosses within the Congress party, the 1969 nationalization of private banks wouldn't have happened. The second point here is that after 1980, and until the 1990s, when the government started giving out licences for private banks, much of the Indian banking scene was controlled by PSBs.

7

The Banking Crisis of 1990s

The year was 1991, and India was facing an economic crisis, in general, and a foreign exchange crisis, in particular. The economic growth during the year was down to 1.1 per cent, the lowest since 1979–80 when the Indian economy had contracted by 5.2 per cent, primarily on account of the second oil shock of 1979.

In early 1991, India had more or less run out of foreign exchange. The country needed to mortgage gold in order to raise foreign exchange so as to be able to continue paying for essential imports including oil. Now gold, as we know, is a touchy thing among us Indians. As Sanjaya Baru writes in *1991: How P.V. Narasimha Rao Made History*: 'A family that mortgages gold to finance its daily needs is a family in despair.'[40]

When Cabinet Secretary Naresh Chandra told Prime Minister Chandra Shekhar about having to mortgage gold in order to pay for imports, 'his initial reaction was that of disbelief and anger'. 'I do not want to go down in history as the man who sold gold for buying oil,' Chandra Shekhar said to have exclaimed furiously.[41]

To which Naresh Chandra replied, rather coolly, 'But, sir ... you have to choose between going down in history as the prime minister who mortgaged gold or as the prime minister who defaulted.'[42] The prime minister wasn't left with an option.

Chandra Shekhar's government was a minority government, which was surviving on the outside support of the Congress party. Once the Congress party pulled the plug on the government, the elections to the tenth Lok Sabha followed. During the campaign period, Rajiv Gandhi, the leader of the Congress was assassinated and senior Congress leader P.V. Narasimha Rao became the next prime minister.

Rao knew the economy was in a bad shape. Under the previous regime, the foreign exchange reserves had fallen to a level which was enough to pay only for three weeks' worth of essential imports. In this scenario, India had to take an emergency loan of $2.2 billion from the International Monetary Fund (IMF). This was done by offering 67 tonnes of gold as collateral.

Rao realized that he needed a technocrat as his finance minister, someone who could open up the Indian economy and get rid of the licence-quota raj which was holding it back. I.G. Patel was approached first. He had been a part of the wave of nationalizing India's private banks. He had also been the fourteenth RBI governor, between 1977 and 1982. After retiring from the RBI, he served as the director of IIM Ahmedabad. Between 1984 and 1990, he was the director of the London School of Economics.

Patel refused Rao's offer and instead recommended Manmohan Singh. Singh had taken over from Patel as the governor of the RBI. He had a three-year tenure at the RBI. After that, he took over as the deputy chairman of the Planning Commission. In March 1991, Singh was appointed as the chairman of the University Grants Commission (UGC). And this was when Narasimha Rao came calling, and on 21 June 1991, the day Rao took over as the prime minister of the country, Singh was appointed as the finance minister.

Singh presented his first Budget on 24 July 1991, ending his speech with the following lines:

'As Victor Hugo once said, "No power on earth can stop an idea whose time has come." I suggest to this august House that the emergence of India as a major economic power in the world happens to be one such idea. Let the whole world hear it loud and clear. India is now wide awake. We shall prevail. We shall overcome.'[43] The interesting thing is that Hugo didn't exactly say what Singh attributed to him. Hugo is supposed to have originally said in French: '*On résiste à l'invasion des armées; on ne résiste pas à l'invasion des idées,*' a literal translation of which is, One resists the invasion of armies; one does not resist the invasion of ideas. What Singh said that day in July 1991 was one of the many paraphrased variants of what Hugo said, which have cropped up over the years.

The trouble was other than going through an economic crisis and a foreign exchange crisis, India was also facing a banking crisis at that time. By 1992–93, the bad loans rate of PSBs was at 23.1 per cent. In 1993–94, it jumped further to 24.8 per cent, which meant almost a fourth of the loans given out by PSBs hadn't been repaid.[44]

What was happening here? The nationalization of private banks, in 1969 and 1980, had given the government (basically, the politicians) more or less total control over the Indian banking system. In the 1980s, loan melas became the order of the day. A 1989 World Bank working paper describes a typical loan mela: 'Melas are public meetings where thousands of households are provided bank loans … at ceremonies presided over by politicians. Political operatives are often involved in selecting beneficiaries and submitting applications to banks.'[45]

One politician who really pushed for loan melas organized by PSBs was Janardhana Poojary. Poojary was the minister of state for finance between December 1984 and 1987. A magazine profile of him written in 1987 said: 'To watch Poojary at a loan mela is to see the actor merge with the politician.'[46]

The profile talked about Poojary at one particular loan mela appealing to the women present in the audience. He said, according to the article, that in India, the poor women either have to sell themselves or kill themselves. With tears rolling down his face, he added that in order to get rid of their poverty, the Congress party would offer them a loan (and not the bank which would actually offer them the loan). As he said this, the women in the audience were moved, while the PSB officers present with the minister allegedly squirmed at the thought of more unrecoverable money going down the drain.[47]

The loan melas were a part of the *priority-sector lending*, which the government wanted the PSBs to carry out. The concept and rationale of priority-sector lending came from economist D.R. Gadgil, who was the deputy chairman of the Planning Commission in the late 1960s. Gadgil set up a study group which submitted its report in October 1969, after the nationalization of fourteen major private banks. The report drew attention towards huge credit gaps prevalent in key sectors like agriculture.

As the report pointed out: 'The doyens of commerce and industry were, until recently, in substantial control of the management and policies of banks and hence commercial banks had a pronounced urban orientation in their development and did not encompass the rural areas to any significant extent.'[48]

The report of the study group found that lending carried out by banks was skewed in the favour of large-scale industries, wholesale trade and commerce, rather than agriculture, small-scale industry, retail trade and small borrowers. It even offered data to buttress its point. Bank lending to agriculture, excluding plantations, accounted for less than 1 per cent of outstanding bank loans. At the same time, bank lending to the retail trade, which meant small individual borrowers, accounted for less than 2 per cent of the outstanding bank loans.[49]

Banks were not interested in lending to small borrowers and in the process, they ended up borrowing from moneylenders charging an exorbitant rate of interest. And this had to be corrected.

At that point of time, the RBI wasn't trying to micromanage the newly nationalized private banks. In 1972, the RBI formalized the description of the priority sector, which included lending to different sectors like agriculture, small-scale industry, small road and transport operators, retail trade, education, self-employed professionals, etc.[50]

These components of the priority sector, which were set in 1972, remained virtually unchanged until the mid-1990s, except

for the addition of home loans and consumption loans.[51] The idea
was to direct credit to areas which banks would otherwise ignore.

But even with this, the RBI hadn't set any specific targets
for priority-sector lending. As the third volume of the history
of the RBI points out: 'The government, seeing in it a powerful
opportunity, decided to prescribe targets for lending. The Bank
had not, in the initial years, prescribed any specific targets to be
achieved. Whatever quantum of lending it suggested was more in
the nature of an indication ... After nationalisation, too, the Bank
sought to promote the same indicative approach. But the political
and social demands were such that apportionment of credit to the
priority sectors became unavoidable.'[52]

In 1974, the government set a priority-sector lending target. A
third of overall lending by banks had to be to the priority sector.
Also, the overall target had to be achieved by March 1979. With
this change, the advances made under the priority sector reached
33.3 per cent in March 1979, against 15 per cent in 1969.[53]

Other than directing credit towards areas where banks were
reluctant to lend earlier, this also gave the government great
control over banks, which they did not have earlier. Politicians like
Poojary exploited this control by taking priority-sector lending to
totally another level of standing on a stage and distributing loans
to everyone who turned up. As the minister of state for finance,
he personally ensured that thousands of loan applications were
distributed before he carried out his mofussil tours. This ensured
a mass audience to whom the loans could be doled out as a part
of a loan mela.[54]

There was no way that the banks and the bankers officially
giving out these loans could appraise the borrowing strength of
the huge number of borrowers in the short time they had at each
mela.[55] In fact, this point was made quite eloquently in the report
submitted by the 1991 Committee on the Financial System (better
known as the first Narasimham Committee; M. Narasimham, the
chairman of the committee, was a former governor of the RBI):

'Priority sector lending was supposed to be a means to the broader end of improving the economic condition of "the neglected sectors of the economy". However, the way the policy was interpreted and pursued, the means became the ends in lending. Banks were pulled up for not meeting their credit target; and what happened in banks down the line was that bank managers were interested in ensuring that they lent more money to these sectors ... the emphasis was on providing the credit and there was no equal emphasis on recovery of credit ... loan melas ... showed *an official blessing for the abandonment of the principal of credit appraisal* [emphasis added].'[56]

The message being sent across by the politicians to the people at large was that it was okay to default on the loans. The history of the RBI also acknowledges this. As the fourth volume of the history of the RBI points out: 'While the loan melas pushed by the Minister of State for Finance invited sharp criticism from many including the bank staff, on the grounds of heavy leakage, corruption, and partisanship, the political leaders tended to adopt a public posture which generated a feeling among borrowers that they did not need to worry about discharging their debt.'[57]

Given this, it wasn't surprising that the people chose to default on the bank loans they had taken on.

As the World Bank Working Paper of 1989 referred to earlier points out: 'By encouraging financial irresponsibility, they ultimately threaten those they are intended to help – the poor, who become defaulters and henceforward [get] debarred from the banking system. Although there are no published figures, bankers claim that recoveries on loans dispensed through melas are as low as 20-25 per cent.'[58]

Ultimately, the government decided to waive off these loans. The first nationwide loan waiver was announced by the then deputy prime minister, Devi Lal, who was himself a large farmer, in 1989.[59] It was done through the Agricultural and Rural Debt Relief Scheme (ARDRS), 1990.

In 1989, the National Front government, led by Vishwanath Pratap Singh, was sworn in. The ARDRS was the result of a promise made by the National Front in the run-up to the elections.[60] The primary constituents of the National Front were the Janata Dal, the Telugu Desam Party, Dravida Munnetra Kazhagam and Asom Gana Parishad. The government was supported on the outside by the Bharatiya Janata Party (BJP) and the Left Front (an agglomeration of different communist parties).

The total loans waived stood at Rs 7,825 crore, which doesn't sound like much in comparison to the recent loan waivers by state governments across the country, the total bill for which runs to over Rs 2 lakh crore. The waivers touched 3.2 crore borrowers and 52 per cent of the agricultural borrowers. The waiver was on debt of up to Rs 10,000, including on overdue interest. The objective of the move, like every waiver after it, was to provide relief to artisans, farmers and weavers, who were caught in the vicious circle of debt.[61]

**

Now why have we gone into such detail about the history of PSBs in India, as the book is about the bad loans they have accumulated over the last decade?

Here are the reasons. First and foremost, to show the kind of control the government had (and still has) over PSBs. It had reached a stage where a minister could openly dictate who to give out loans to while standing on a stage. The entire process of due diligence before giving out a loan went for a toss. This is something that did play out in the last decade as well, as the PSBs went about accumulating bad loans because their political masters wanted them to give out loans to the companies they favoured. What started out under the garb of social banking, where banks were supposed to lend to the weaker sections of the society and individuals instead of just corporates and large borrowers, ultimately also led to helping crony capitalists in its own way. This was perhaps one unintended consequence of the rise of public sector banking in India.

Second, the kind of control the government has over the PSBs in India is a rarity these days. As Ruchir Sharma writes in *The Rise and Fall of Nations: Ten Rules in the Post-Crisis World*: 'Despite several waves of free market reform in emerging economies over recent decades, the state still runs a large number of banks in many countries. If you want a loan, you ask the government. On average, state banks control 32 per cent of all banking assets in the twenty largest emerging nations. That figure is 40 per cent or more in Thailand, Indonesia, Brazil, and China (where the line between state and private banks is murky and the actual number is likely much higher). It's 50 per cent or more in Taiwan, Hungary, Russia, and Malaysia and a striking 75 per cent in India.'[62]

Sharma's book was written in 2016 and the control of PSBs over India's banking sector has come down since then. Despite this, the government continues to maintain total control over PSBs.

In theory, if loans are defaulted on, a bank will be unable to repay its depositors completely. In order to avoid that, the owner of the bank, which in case of PSBs primarily happens to be the government, has to invest more money in these banks to keep them going. This is referred to as recapitalization of the banks. Between 1985–86 and 2006–07, the government carried out a total capital infusion of Rs 22,092 crore in these banks. Of this amount, Rs 10,063 crore was provided in 1993–94 and in 1994–95, when the bad loans rate of the PSBs had almost touched 25 per cent.[63]

Over the next decade, between 2007–08 and 2016–17, the government invested a total of Rs 1,28,724 crore to recapitalize these banks in order to keep them going, even as bad loans kept increasing.[64] In 2017–18 and 2018–19, the government invested Rs 1,96,000 crore in order to recapitalize the PSBs (twenty PSBs plus IDBI Bank, which is now owned by the LIC). In 2019–20, it plans to invest Rs 70,000 crore in these banks, with the number of PSBs down to eighteen, with the merger of Bank of Baroda,

Dena Bank and Vijaya Bank. This, as we shall see, has its own set of repercussions, some of which are not very obvious in the first place.

Also, when a government (Central or state) waives off loans, they need to compensate the banks. In 1989, when total loans of Rs 7,825 crore were waived, the government had to compensate the banks which gave out these loans. In the recent years, farm loan waivers have become a hygiene factor for political parties while fighting state assembly elections. An estimate made by CARE Ratings in January 2019, puts the total amount of farm loan waivers since April 2017 at Rs 2.2 lakh crore.[65]

The state governments have to compensate the banks that have given out these loans. For this, they need to either borrow more or cut down on their expenditure in other areas.

If it borrows more, it leaves a lower amount of savings for others to borrow from. This pushes up interest rates to that extent, as lending to the government is viewed as the safest form of lending. If the government cuts down on expenditure in a particular area, then it hurts that area.

The bigger question is do these waivers actually help farmers in the long term, as is their aim? Or is it just a short-term gimmick that works well before the elections? In order to understand this issue completely, it's important to understand what economists call the fallacy of composition.

As Jonathan Tepper and Denise Hearn write in *The Myth of Capitalism: Monopolies and the Death of Competition*: 'If you are at a football game and stand to see the game better, you might get a better view. But if everyone stands, no one has a better view, and everyone is worse off.' The point being that what is true for a part or for an individual need not be true for the whole system.[66]

How does this apply in the case of farm loans being waived? The fact that a farm loan is waived works well for an individual farmer. It puts him financially in a better position. It probably also increases his propensity to spend on other things, and, hence, may benefit the economy in some way in the short term.

But it sends out the wrong signals for the system as a whole. First and foremost, it makes those farmers who were dutifully repaying their loans look very stupid. What will these farmers do the next time they take on a loan is a question well worth asking. So, to that extent it has a negative impact on the viability of future bank credit.

Secondly, there is evidence that shows that banks do not like to lend to people and in areas where loans have been waived. Hence, it has an impact on future access to bank loans.

Given this, what's good for an individual farmer does not work well for the system as a whole. Over and above this, it does nothing to solve the basic problem of an Indian farmer, which is to get a proper price for his produce and be able to repay the debt he has taken on to farm.

For that, we need agricultural markets to function properly. We need supply chains which ensure that a farmer's produce reaches the end consumer in the fastest and most profitable way. Currently, it's the supply chain (the agents who come in between the farmer and the end consumer) which makes the most money in the entire process.

Almost no reform has happened on this front. Also, these reforms will be messy because they will hurt a lot of people who are benefiting from the current system. Given their nuisance value, no politician wants to get into this mess.

In fact, politicians are not even ready to engage with farmers and explain the complexity of the situation to them. As Yascha Mounk writes in *The People Vs. Democracy: Why Our Freedom is in Danger and How to Save It*: 'Voters do not like to think that the world is complicated. They certainly do not like to be told that there is no immediate answer to their problems.'[67]

Hence, politicians do the easiest possible thing and take the populist decision of waiving farm loans. As Mounk writes: 'Glib,

facile solutions stand at the very heart of the populist appeal.'
A farm loan waiver makes a politician briefly popular, perhaps
translates into more votes, gets him elected, but does nothing to
solve the problem at hand.

8

The Rise and Fall of Industrial Finance

In 1947, a newly independent India faced many problems. A major problem that it faced was how to meet the medium-term and long-term credit needs of industry. A simple solution to this could have been to let the banks give loans to industry. But there was (and is) a basic problem with banks' lending to industry.

Banks borrow deposits from people who have savings and then lend that money out. They pay a certain rate of interest on these deposits and lend out this money at a higher rate of interest. If the rate at which they lend is reasonably higher than the rate at which they borrow, they make a profit and continue to be in operation without further investment of capital required (unless they want to expand rapidly).

The problem is banks draw a substantial portion of their deposits from small borrowers. The investment horizon of these borrowers is short and they like the money they have deposited with a bank to be relatively liquid. This means that they should be able to withdraw this money as and when they want to.

Banks largely have access to short-term funds. This limits their ability to lend for the long term. This was truer at the time India got independence than it's now. In fact, the banks at that point of time did not like the idea of financing even medium-term lending, forget long-term. The reason for it was that 'investment of short-term funds in long-term commitments wouldn't foster public confidence in the banking system'.[68] The logic being that if people saw banks' lending long term by borrowing short term, they were unlikely to deposit their savings in these institutions.

In fact, right after Independence, in February 1948, the central board of the RBI had rejected a proposal envisaging banks financing the long-term credit needs of the industrial sector. The RBI board reasoned: 'Given the nature of their liabilities, banks could not be expected to make long-term loans to industry. Apart from the risk arising from the relative illiquidity of such assets ... it was not appropriate for banks to extend long-term loans since their position would then be that of partners who shared "only the losses and not the profits" ... If ... industry makes profits, the banks only get the interest; should it suffer losses, banks could "lose their principal as well as ... interest".'[69] This summarizes the risk at the heart of industrial lending carried out by banks.

Also, it's worth remembering that Indian banks on the whole were not a very big part of the financial system. In 1951, there were 566 commercial banks in India, operating with 4,151 branches. The bank branches were largely limited to larger towns and cities. In fact, each branch served, on an average, a population of 1,36,000. But more than this, savings held in the form of bank deposits accounted for a little under 9 per cent of the total savings.[70]

What did not help was the fact that in the past commercial banks had tried to finance the industry and had bitten the dust. During the Swadeshi movement of 1906–13, several banks tried long-term financing of industry, mostly in Punjab, and failed at it. After World War I, a number of banks were started with the specific purpose of making long-term loans to industry. This didn't work out either.[71]

As the first volume of the history of the RBI published in 1970 points out: 'There was a general aversion on the part of the commercial banks to engage in industrial financing. This was due not only to the influence of British banking practises but also due to the lessons conveyed by the failure of certain banks, which had financed industrial enterprises on a long-term basis, *without being equipped for judging the business prospects of a concern or its commercial value* [emphasis added].'[72]

Given this situation, it was but natural that neither the banks nor the RBI were of the view that they should be meeting medium-term and long-term credit needs of industry. But then the question was if banks did not meet the credit needs of industry, who would?

* * *

The RBI came into existence on 1 April 1935. The British government in India had been thinking about how to finance the long-term credit and the medium-term credit to industries even before that. In 1916, the setting up of the Industrial Commission under Sir T.H. Holland was the first attempt in this direction. In 1929, another committee was set up under Sir B.N. Mitra to go into all aspects of banking in India. These commissions stressed on the necessity of setting up a specialized financial institution that could provide long-term finance to industry.[73]

At the end of World War II, the RBI started thinking about the subject of industrial finance all over again. As the first volume of the history of the RBI points out:'In a statement which the Government of India issued on April 21, 1945 ... it was stated that the question of the promotion of an Industrial Investment Corporation or a similar institution, for providing long-term funds for industry, was being examined by Government.'[74]

As a result, when the country attained independence in 1947, some thinking on the issue of providing long-term and medium-term finance to industry had already been done. To fulfil these financing needs, the Industrial Finance Corporation of India (IFCI) was set up by the government immediately after Independence. It started functioning from 1 July 1948.

IFCI at its inception was a developmental financial institution (DFI), and its basic function was to provide long-term finance of industry (or project finance, as the more technical term for the same goes) where the risks were higher and the ordinary financial system was unwilling to take on the same.[75]

The interesting thing is that DFIs had existed in Europe for more than a hundred years and had played a very big role in the industrialization of the continent. Many DFIs in Europe were started or sponsored by the government.[76]

The past success of DFIs in Europe had made their setting up in India an easier sell. In fact, at the time of the setting up of IFCI, the powers that be also realized that one single entity couldn't take care of the credit needs of small and medium enterprises all across the country.

While piloting the bill to set up IFCI, the finance minister, Shanmukham Chetty, had informed the Constituent Assembly (remember the first Lok Sabha elections happened only in 1952) of the government's intention to persuade state governments to establish institutions similar to IFCI in their respective states, in particular to finance small-scale industries. In March 1949, the Madras Industrial Investment Corporation Limited (MIIL) was established by the Government of Madras. MIIL was incorporated under the Indian Companies Act. Other states like Bombay wanted to set up institutions similar to MIIL.[77]

The question is instead of opening up firms similar to IFCI in every state, why couldn't IFCI simply open branches in different states? The RBI believed that the former was a better idea than opening branches because opening up state-level finance corporations would attract the support of the state government. It would also attract the resources of the local institutional investors, which otherwise might not have been available.[78]

The State Financial Corporations Act finally came into force on 1 August 1952. But even after this, India wasn't done establishing new DFIs. One reason for this lay in the fact that both IFCI and state finance corporations, given the risk involved, had gone slow on lending activities in the first few years after their inception.[79] Also, as the whole concept of development finance was new to India, it was but natural that institutions would take time to get up on their feet.

Two different proposals for DFIs were put forward in the early 1950s. The first proposal came in August 1953, from T.T. Krishnamachari, who was the minister for commerce and industry in the Indian government. The second proposal came a few weeks later, chiefly backed by the American government and Eugene R. Black, who was the president of the World Bank then.

It was still the early 1950s, and taking that into account, Krishnamachari's proposal was an unusual one. Nearly seven decades later, one can safely say that it was way ahead of its time. Krishnamachari felt that it wasn't enough to just have institutions which financed projects. He felt that any financial assistance was of use only after the entrepreneurs had finalized the project and were attempting to raise money to get it going.[80]

His view was that instead of sitting and waiting for entrepreneurship to pick up, the government should take initiative and encourage it. However, the ordinary machinery of the government wouldn't be able to execute anything like this. Hence, Krishnamachari proposed 'an industrial development corporation comprising government nominees, scientists and engineers, and industrialists of "proven reputation".' The vision behind this corporation was to 'plan and initiate projects, coordinate investments, provide technical and managerial expertise, and help raise resources for undertaking these investments'.[81]

Krishnamachari did not believe in the government continuing to hold on to the firms it created through this new DFI. He insisted that 'the assets created by this corporation should, in due course, be sold to the private sector'.

Krishnamachari's proposal had the echoes of a modern-day venture capital/private equity/angel investor sort of firm. A few weeks after Krishnamachari made a proposal for a new DFI, another proposal for a new DFI was made. This proposal came in October 1953, from Black. He mooted the idea of a privately owned and externally assisted DFI in India.

As the second volume of the history of the RBI points out: 'The precise antecedents of this proposal are not altogether clear. At a dinner meeting in Washington earlier the same year, the [RBI] Governor, B. Rama Rau, aired the idea of setting up in India an institution modelled somewhat along the lines of the Commonwealth Development Finance Company in the United Kingdom.'[82]

The interesting thing is that the Commonwealth Development Finance Company (CDFC) had commenced operations only in March 1953. The basic aim of CDFC was to promote investment activity among Commonwealth countries (or countries which were formerly a part of the British empire). In its first year of operations, the CDFC provided £1 million to the share capital of Sui Gas Transmission Company of Pakistan.[83] Black's idea was to set up a company along similar lines, which would invest and assist private corporations in India.

Nevertheless, misgivings were soon expressed about the idea of having three DFIs existing side by side. But the bureaucrats working in the economic departments of the government did not think so and believed that 'there was enough room for all three institutions to exist side by side, with the development corporation initiating and taking up new industries, the private bank assisting industrialists in their schemes, and the Industrial Finance Corporation financing existing industry.'[84]

The Government of India quickly accepted Black's proposal of a private institution which would finance private-sector investment. This institution came to be known as the Industrial Credit and Investment Corporation of India (ICICI) and came into existence in January 1955. The corporation initially issued shares worth Rs 5 crore. Of this, foreign investors in the United Kingdom subscribed to 20 per cent of the shares.[85] The CDFC also invested in ICICI. It also assisted in getting other British banking and finance companies to invest in ICICI.[86]

The investors from the United States subscribed to 10 per cent of shares in ICICI. The remaining 70 per cent of shares were subscribed by other institutions, which included banks, insurance companies and other corporates, as well as individual investors in

India. Shares worth Rs 1.5 crore were offered to the Indian public in February 1955. The issue was oversubscribed.

Interestingly, before ICICI was formed in early 1955, Krishnamachari's proposal for an industrial development corporation, along the lines he had envisioned, also saw light of day. The National Industrial Development Corporation (NIDC) was formed as a private limited company in October 1954, with an authorized capital of Rs 1 crore and paid-up capital of Rs 10 lakh provided totally by the government. The NIDC 'was authorised to issue shares and debentures, and to provide finance to industries related to planned development, in particular those manufacturing capital goods, machinery, and equipment'.[87]

Even after setting up these DFIs, the government wasn't done with establishing them yet. Krishnamachari became the finance minister of the country for the second time in August 1963. This is when he put forward a proposal for another developmental financial institution. His feeling was that the IFCI was hampered in its operations because it was government owned. To get around this, he felt that a new development financial institution owned by the RBI was needed. He felt that this bank would be free from political pressures.[88]

On 1 July 1964, the Industrial Development Bank of India (IDBI) came into existence. IDBI was formed as a 100 per cent subsidiary of the RBI. It had an authorized share capital of Rs 50 crore, with an option of raising it later to Rs 100 crore. The RBI subscribed totally to the issued share capital of Rs 10 crore. IDBI was also allowed to raise more money by selling its own bonds and debentures with or without a government guarantee, and also accept deposits from people for a tenure of not less than one year.

IDBI quickly became the main DFI in the country when it came to industrial financing. In 1966–67, Rs 134 crore in total was distributed by the several industrial finance institutions. Of this, over Rs 62 crore was distributed by IDBI. The dominance of IDBI was particularly in the area of rupee loans, where it gave out loans of Rs 48.6 crore.[89]

For nearly twelve years, IDBI was a subsidiary of the RBI. In February 1976, the ownership of IDBI was transferred to the Government of India. At the same time, IDBI was made the principal financial institution to coordinate the activities of 'institutions engaged in financing, promoting and developing industry in the country'.[90]

The idea behind setting up all these DFIs was to get the manufacturing and the industrial sector in a newly independent India up and running. As the Cambridge University economist Ha-Joon Chang writes in *Bad Samaritans: The Guilty Secrets of Rich Nations and the Threat to Global Prosperity*: 'History has repeatedly shown that the single most important thing that distinguishes rich countries from poor ones is their higher capabilities in manufacturing, where productivity is generally higher, and more importantly, where productivity tends to grow faster than [in] agriculture and services.'[91]

The problem was that while the government was busy setting up all these DFIs, it was also introducing laws, rules and regulations that made it difficult for businessmen to carry out their businesses. In fact, points around what we now call the lack of ease in doing business were made as far back as 1954, by the Shroff Committee in its report. The Committee on Finance for the Private Sector was led by A.D. Shroff and it made a detailed appraisal of the climate for overall private sector investment in India.

Some of the points made by the committee in the report, as mentioned in the second volume of the history of the RBI, were as follows: 1) the existence of irritants in the form of licensing requirements for starting, expanding or modernizing industry, issuing capital, importing machinery, securing foreign exchange, and their effect in delaying and retarding private investment; 2) the report offered examples to deplore the amount of time and resources entrepreneurs were required to devote to establishing and maintaining contact with government departments in order to secure various licences, and the scope for corruption in this situation; 3) it stressed on the enormous change in the labour market as a result of legislative measures adversely affecting employers' freedom to adopt flexible labour practises, rationalize to step up productivity, or even to discipline their workforce. The basic point that was being made here was to 'ensure that a rise in the rewards of labour does not run ahead of the increase in the productivity of labour'. This is something that Indian governments don't seem to have understood even six-and-a-half decades later; 4) in fact, the report did not spare the private-sector businessmen and said that they 'could inspire greater confidence in the public by observing a proper code of conduct and eliminating unhealthy practises';[92] 5) and most importantly, it said that unless the overall climate for private-sector investment and business was improved, multiple DFIs to supply finance to the industry is not going to produce any results.[93] And that is precisely what happened. The share of industry in the overall Indian economy was 16.2 per cent in 1950–51. It crossed 25 per cent only in 1975, even though multiple DFIs to provide finance were available.

* * *

Things started to change for the DFIs in the 1990s. In December 1997, the Committee on Banking Sector Reforms was appointed by the then finance minister P. Chidambaram. It was led by M. Narasimham, a former governor of the RBI.*

The Committee on Banking Sector Reforms came to be more popularly referred to as the Second Narasimham Committee, as an earlier Committee on Financial System was also led by him.

One of the important recommendations of the committee was around the idea of universal banking. As the committee said in its report: 'The Committee has taken note of the twin phenomena

---

*   Narasimham was the first Reserve Bank–cadre officer to be appointed as governor, having joined as a research officer in the economics division of the bank.

of consolidation and convergence which the financial system
is now experiencing globally. In India also banks and DFIs are
moving closer to each other in the scope of their activities. The
Committee is of the view that with such convergence of activities
between banks and DFIs, the DFIs should, over a period of time,
convert themselves to banks. There would then be only two
forms of intermediaries, viz. banking companies and non-banking
financial companies. If a DFI does not acquire a banking licence
within a stipulated time it would be categorised as a non-banking
financial company.'[94]

What the committee meant was that banks and the DFIs were
doing the same set of things and, hence, it did not make sense
for DFIs to continue existing in their scope. It made sense if they
converted themselves into banks. In the mid-1990s, DFIs like
ICICI had gone into the banking business (ICICI Bank). ICICI had
also entered retail finance business and working capital finance,
areas in which banks used to specialize.[95]

At the same time, banks were providing long-term finance to
industry. They had also gotten into other areas like mutual funds,
securities trading, etc. Specialization as used to be the case wasn't
the order of the day. Universal banking with its cafeteria approach
was ready to take on the role of a one-stop financial supermarket.[96]

Also, by the end of the 1990s, the business model of the DFIs
was no longer economically viable. Even in the 1990s, the DFIs
extended long-term credit to the industry. All the lending for
new industrial projects was done by DFIs. In fact, up until 1991,
the DFIs had access to low-cost funds from the RBI as well as
multilateral agencies. They could also issue bonds which banks
could buy and show as part of them maintaining the statutory
liquidity ratio mandated by the government. Post 1991, as India
opened up its economy, this special treatment of DFIs was done
away with. Their access to low-cost funds was withdrawn and they
had to raise money from the financial system, just like everyone
else did.

What did not help was the fact that banks started to get into the business of project finance, or long-term industrial lending, as well. Banks had access to cheaper funds than DFIs; hence, they could carry out project finance lending at lower interest rates. All this put a lot of stress on the financial situation of DFIs. They ended up with a lot of bad loans.[97]

DFIs went out of fashion post-2000. In October 2001, the boards of ICICI and ICICI Bank approved the merger of ICICI and two of its wholly owned retail finance subsidiaries, which were ICICI Personal Financial Services and ICICI Capital Services, with ICICI Bank. The shareholders of ICICI and ICICI Bank approved the merger (or rather, it was a reverse merger with the parent company merging with the banking subsidiary) in January 2002. The RBI approved the merger in April 2002.[98]

This left a gap in the financial system, which PSBs had to fill.

9

Of Harshad Mehta, Ketan Parekh and Bad Loans

In Chapter 2, we saw how the Indian media thrives on a simplistic explanation of the RBI cutting the repo rate leading to banks cutting their lending rates and this leading to a fall in EMIs.

But there is one factor which rarely gets reported or written about in the Indian media. Before cutting lending rates, banks need to cut their deposit rates. If deposit rates come down, they also impact a large section of population, which has a significant portion of their savings in bank deposits. When it comes to bank deposits, there are largely two kinds of savers. First are the elderly, who use bank fixed deposits to generate a regular monthly income. Second are those who are saving for the future education and weddings of their kids as well as for their retirement. This section of the population is negatively impacted by banks reducing interest rates on their deposits.

As economist Michael Pettis writes in the context of China in his 2013 book, *The Great Rebalancing: Trade, Conflict, and the Perilous Road Ahead for the World Economy*: 'Most Chinese savings, at least until recently, have been in the form of bank deposits ... Chinese households, in other words, should feel richer when the deposit rate rises and poorer when it declines, in which case rising rates should be associated with rising, not declining, consumption.'[99]

A similar sort of logic should apply to India as well, as a bulk of savings happens to be in the form of deposits, in particular bank deposits. Hence, any fall in interest rates should make a section of the population feel poorer and should, in the process, negatively impact consumption, at least from the point of view of such savers.

Further, when banks cut interest rates, people who are saving towards a goal will have to start saving more. Pettis explains this in his book through an example that a student of his shared with him. As he writes: 'According to my student, her aunt was planning to save a fixed amount of money for when her twelve-year-old son turned eighteen and was slated to go to university. She had a certain amount of money already saved, but not enough, so she needed to add to her savings every month to achieve her target.'[100]

A similar logic works in an Indian context. When banks cut interest rates on their deposits, senior citizens saving in fixed deposits to generate a regular income, need to save more in order to generate the same income as they earned in the past. If they are not in a position to save more, they need to cut down on their expenses, which, in the words of economists, means cutting down on their consumption. The same works for a family saving towards the education and weddings of their children. They need to save more.

The larger point here is that there are second-order effects, or indirect effects, in economics, which most analysts and economists tend to miss out on. As Jean Tirole writes: 'In economic matters too, first impressions can mislead us. We look at the direct effect of an economic policy, which is easy to understand, and we stop there. Most of the time we are not aware of the indirect effects.'[101]

So, the fact that banks are cutting interest rates doesn't necessarily mean a good thing always, at least not for everyone. And that is the secondary or indirect effect of a lower interest rate policy.

Table 9.1 lists out the various kinds of household financial savings and the proportion each forms of the whole. The household financial savings comprises currency, deposits, shares and debentures, insurance funds, pension and provident funds, units held in the Unit Trust of India (which was a government-owned quasi mutual fund) and something referred to as 'claims on government'. The 'claims on government' largely reflects of investments made in post office small savings schemes.

Table 9.1: Shares of Components of Household Financial Savings.

(In %)	1970s	1980s	1990–91	1991–92 to 1996–97	1997–98 to 2002–03	2003–04 to 2006–07
Currency	13.9	11.9	10.6	10.9	8.6	9.3
Bank deposits	45.6	40.3	31.9	33.1	38.5	44
Non-banking deposits	3	4.6	2.2	9.4	2.9	0.7
Life Insurance Fund	9	7.5	9.5	9.5	13.1	14.6
Provident and Pension Fund	19.6	17.5	18.9	17.6	19	11.4
Claims on Government	4.2	11.1	13.4	7.1	14.9	16.9
Shares and Debentures	1.5	3.9	8.4	8.3	3.7	3.9
Units of UTI	0.5	2.2	5.8	5	0.1	-0.8
Trade Debt (Net)	2.7	0.9	-0.8	-0.8	-0.7	0

Source: Report of the High Level Committee on Estimation of Saving and Investment, Ministry of Statistics and Programme Implementation, 2008.

What does Table 9.1 tell us? In 1990–91, deposits formed 31.9 per cent of the household financial savings. This jumped to 44 per cent between 2003–04 and 2006–07. This meant that in the mid-

2000s, the banks suddenly had much more money to lend than they had before.

And why is that? In 1990–91, the total share of household financial savings invested in shares and debentures was at 8.4 per cent. It fell slightly to 8.3 per cent between 1991–92 and 1996–97. After that, it fell to 3.7–3.9 per cent in the 2000s. The same happened with investments that people had in the Unit Trust of India, an indirect way of investing in the stock market. It crashed from 5.8 per cent of the total household financial savings in 1990–91 to close to 0 per cent in 2002–03.

Why did this happen? Between 1992 and 2000, the stock market saw three major scams. The first scam was the Harshad Mehta scam, which was exposed in 1992. The second scam was the Vanishing Companies Scam of 1994, in which companies came out with initial public offerings (IPOs), collected the money and then disappeared. Retail investors lost thousands of crore in this scam. The third scam was the Ketan Parekh scam of the late 1990s and early 2000s, when Parekh used borrowed money to run up the prices of stocks referred to as K-10 stocks.

In 2003, the Unit Trust of India (UTI), which ran many investment schemes including the famous US-64 scheme, was shut down largely due to mismanagement. Having burnt their fingers in these scams and due to the mismanagement of money by UTI, the household financial savings moved out of shares (in direct form and indirect form through UTI). This was the indirect effect of the scams with household financial savings moving out of shares and units of UTI, and moving into fixed deposits.

In fact, in 2007–08 and 2008–09, bank deposits formed 50.4 per cent and 57.5 per cent of household financial savings respectively. The point here being that the indirect effect of the stock market scams and the collapse of the UTI led to banks suddenly having a lot more money to lend than they had before. And pretty soon, they were falling over one another to lend money to whoever was willing to borrow it. This led to banks throwing caution to the winds and lending without proper due diligence.

This easy lending in an era of growth and stability ultimately led to instability, and finally to all the bad money accumulating on the books of banks.

The funny thing is that the situation wouldn't have turned out to be so bad if the stock market scams and the collapse of UTI hadn't happened. This also tells us that the indirect effects of what happens in the economy are likely to play out over a period of time.

PART II

PART II

10

Everybody Loves a
Public Sector Bank Loan

The banking crisis of the late 1980s and the early 1990s took a while to sort itself out. As mentioned earlier, the bad loans rate of PSBs in 1993–94 was close to 25 per cent. By the turn of the century, in 1999–2000, it was still at 14 per cent. In 2004–05, the bad loans rate was at 5.4 per cent and only in 2005–06 did it fall below 5 per cent – it was at 3.7 per cent. The larger point here is that the last public sector banking crisis took a while to sort itself out and a similar thing, as we shall see, seems to be happening in the current banking crisis as well.

Also, as the bad loans rate fell in the early to mid-2000s, banks decided to go easy on their lending. This time around the banks went easy on lending to industry. Let's take a look at Figure 10.1, which plots the growth in lending to industry as well as overall bank lending over the years.

The growth in banks' lending to industry peaked between 2004–05 and 2007–08, when it grew by more than 25 per cent in each of the years. This was also the period when the overall bad loans of PSBs had been falling. In 2000–01, the bad loans were at Rs 56,507 crore. By 2006–07, they had fallen to Rs 38,900 crore. The PSBs could finally put the banking crisis of the 1990s behind them and lend with a free hand.

Figure 10.1

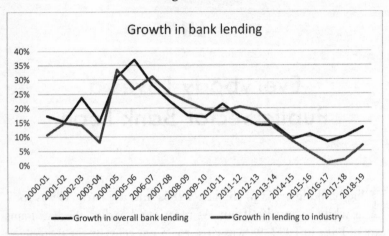

Growth in bank lending

— Growth in overall bank lending   — Growth in lending to industry

Source: Reserve Bank of India.

Also, to put it very simply, at any place and time there is a zeitgeist, or the spirit of the times. The spirit of the times globally during those days was that the happy days were there to stay. This applied to India as well. The Gross Domestic Product (GDP or the measure of India's economic size) grew at a rate higher than 9 per cent between 2005–06 and 2007–08 (real GDP growth which adjusts for inflation).* Such a high rate of economic growth was totally new in India's case, used as the country was to the so-called 'secular rate of growth', which was better known as the Hindu rate of growth.

The secular rate of growth averaged at around 3.5 per cent per year between 1950 and 1980. This was the time when countries in South East Asia like South Korea were making giant economic strides. As Shashi Tharoor writes in *India: From Midnight to Millennium*: 'Countries in South East Asia were growing at 8 to 15 per cent, or even more … India's share of world trade fell by

---

* As per the GDP series with a base year of 2004–05 which was being used at that point of time.

four-fifths. Per capita income, with a burgeoning population and a modest increase in GDP, anchored India firmly to the bottom third of the world rankings.'[102]

Nevertheless, things had improved since 1991; even then the GDP had grown by more than 8 per cent only once between 1991 and 2005–06. This was in 1999–2000 when the GDP grew by 8.5 per cent. The economy had then slowed down for a few years, primarily due to the American economic sanctions after India decided to test its nuclear bomb in 1998.

In this scenario, when the economy grew by more than 9 per cent for three consecutive years, banks went berserk. It was assumed that this sort of economic growth would continue forever.

With corporate profitability being one of the highest in the world, for the first time in the country's history, everything seemed to be going right.[103] The rewards of economic reforms initiated in 1991 were finally being reaped or so was the feeling at that point of time. It was expected that India would soon join China and grow at double-digit growth rates for decades to come. And given the prevailing zeitgeist, one couldn't expect corporates to stay out of it and not cash in on the situation. Big plans were made, and bank loans were taken to execute these plans.

As the Economic Survey 2016–17 points out: 'Firms ... launched new projects worth lakhs of crores, particularly in infrastructure-related areas such as power generation, steel and telecoms, setting off the biggest investment boom in the country's history.'

In 2003–04, the total bank lending to industry had stood at Rs 3.35 lakh crore. This jumped to Rs 26.16 lakh crore by 2013–14 in a decade. This was a jump of 681 per cent. Of course, this jump does not take into account the increasing size of the Indian economy. It's but natural for the overall bank loans to grow as the economy grows. Hence, we need to adjust for the increase in the size of the Indian economy. Take a look at Figure 10.2, which plots bank lending to industry as a proportion of the GDP (in this

case we take nominal GDP, or GDP which hasn't been adjusted
for inflation).*

Figure 10.2

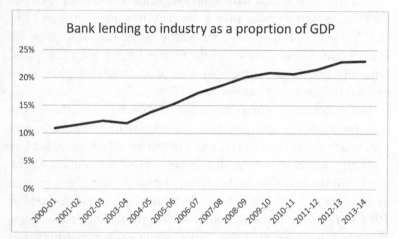

Source: Reserve Bank of India.

The interesting thing is that a bulk of the increase in bank
lending to industry happened between 2003–04 and 2007–08,
when it increased from around 11.8 per cent of the GDP to 18.6
per cent. In 2013–14, bank lending to industry was at 23 per
cent of the GDP.

There was a massive increase in bank lending to industry in a
period of a decade. Within that decade, a major increase came in
just four years. This was also reflected in the investment to GDP

---

*   As per the GDP series with a base year of 2004–05 which was
      prevalent at that point of time. Also, Figure 10.2 ends in 2013–
      14 because it's the last year for which the data for GDP series
      with a base year of 2004–05 are available. We cannot use GDP
      series with base year 2011–12, which is currently in use, simply
      because it has data starting from only 2004–05.

ratio (gross capital formation by industry) which was at 25.3 per cent in 2003–04 and had jumped to 37 per cent in 2007–08.

In fact, this was exactly the period which Minsky talks about in the financial instability hypothesis, where banks are ready to take on more risk and the competition among banks leads to falling lending standards. Companies bought into the so-called India growth story. They had expansion plans and were more than happy to borrow.

This is when a large number of the bad loans we see now originated, as the quality of lending fell. As Raghuram Rajan said: 'It's at such times that banks make mistakes. They extrapolate past growth and performance to the future. So they are willing to accept higher leverage in projects, and less promoter equity. Indeed, sometimes banks signed up to lend based on project reports by the promoter's investment bank, without doing their own due diligence.'[104]

In fact, Rajan even recounted a story that a business promoter had told him: 'He [i.e., the promoter] was pursued then by banks waving cheque books, asking him to name the amount he wanted.'[105]

* * *

Between 1989–90 and 1999–2000, the total lending to industry carried out by PSBs went up by 215 per cent to Rs 1.62 lakh crore. Over the next decade between 1999–2000 and 2009–10, the bank lending to industry went up by 582 per cent to Rs 11.02 lakh crore. The Figure 10.3, which plots the total loans given by PSBs to industry as a proportion of GDP between 1989–90 and 2013–14, shows this trend much better.[*]

---

[*]   There is a reason why we have stopped in 2013–14. The old GDP series has data only up to 2013–14. The new GDP series has data starting only from 2004–05. Given this, if one wants to look at the long-term trend one is forced to work with the old GDP series. Also, banking and industry at that point of time had access to only the 2004–05 GDP series and it's only fair that we use that.

Figure 10.3

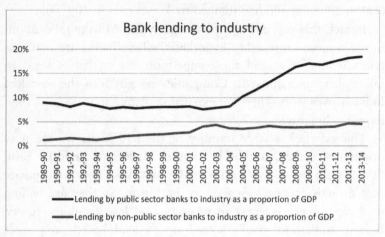

Source: Reserve Bank of India.

The lending by PSBs to industry as a proportion of GDP, between the late 1980s and the early 2000s, was flat at around 8 per cent, moving a few basis points here and there. But it really took off after 2003–04 and by 2009–10, it was at 17 per cent of the GDP. In absolute terms, the PSB lending to industry jumped from Rs 2.31 lakh crore in 2003–04 to Rs 11.02 lakh crore in 2009–10.

What did the non-PSB lending to the industries look like during the same period? Figure 10.3 also plots the lending by non-PSBs to industry as a proportion of the GDP. It went up from 1.3 per cent in 1989–90 to 4.6 per cent in 2013–14. The pace of increase in this case was faster than that of PSBs.

One reason for this superfast increase in lending to industry by banks in general and PSBs in particular was the death of DFIs, with banks moving into that space. Project finance had become an important part of lending. The other reason why PSBs got into project finance was the lack of a deep and liquid corporate bond market, where industries could raise money for the long term.[106]

It was also an era of the government trying to build better physical infrastructure across the country. This was done through public–private partnerships or directly through private players.

The idea was to improve infrastructure and, in the process, encourage the manufacturing sector to create jobs. The private players in these infrastructure projects relied on PSBs for loans. Obviously, it was in the interest of the government to get PSBs to give loans to private parties building infrastructure projects.[107]

This wasn't the only reason behind private players borrowing from PSBs. As mentioned earlier, India had seen a few years of greater than 9 per cent economic growth in the mid-2000s and this had led to the assumption that the country would continue grow at such rates in the years to come. Industrialists made this assumption and bankers bought into the story. Now, only if life was as simple as an excel sheet.

The high growth assumption led to the launch of new projects worth lakhs of crore, particularly in infrastructure-related areas like power generation, steel and telecom. Other than the government push towards better physical infrastructure, there was also the case of private players entering sectors like aviation, mobile telephony, etc., sectors earlier dominated by the government.[108]

Let's take a look at Figure 10.4, which plots the new projects launched over the years.

Figure 10.4

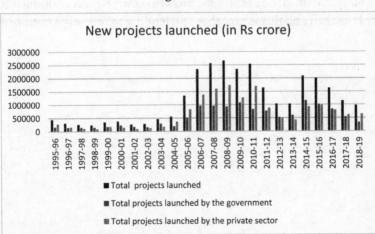

Source: Centre for Monitoring Indian Economy.

Figure 10.4 clearly shows us that the new projects launched (in Rs crore) went through the roof between 2003–04 and 2009–10. Total new projects worth Rs 4.7 lakh crore were launched in 2003–04. This had jumped to Rs 26.7 lakh crore in 2008–09. In fact, the launch of new projects remained strong even after 2008–09, after the global financial crisis began in September of 2008. New projects worth Rs 23.4 lakh crore were launched in 2009–10. This was followed by projects worth Rs 25.3 lakh crore being launched in 2010–11.

The global economic growth in 2007 had stood at 4.2 per cent. This had fallen to 1.8 per cent in 2008. The global economy contracted by 1.7 per cent in 2009. In this scenario, India's economic growth also fell to 3.9 per cent in 2008–09, but it recovered to 8.5 per cent in 2009–10 and 10.3 per cent in 2010–11.

The reason for this lay in the fact that the Government of India suddenly turned Keynesian and upped its expenditure in 2008–09 and 2009–10. The fiscal deficit, which had fallen to 2.6 per cent of the GDP in 2007–08, jumped to 6.1 per cent and 6.6 per cent in 2008–09 and 2009–10, respectively. As the government continued to spend money, this ensured that the economic growth continued to remain strong in India, while the global economic growth was subdued. With strong economic growth, new projects continued to be launched and this meant that PSB lending to industry continued.

11

Baby Step Subbarao

By doling out loans to industry, left, right and centre, the banks, in particular PSBs, had thrown caution to the winds. Not just the banks, even the industries which were borrowing did the same and ended up overborrowing. This started sometime in 2004–05, when the bank lending to industry jumped by 33 per cent in comparison to 2003–04.

A lot of this lending was happening to infrastructure projects. Take the case of three subsectors within infrastructure – construction, electricity generation and transmission, and iron and steel. Figure 11.1 plots lending to these sectors over the years.

Figure 11.1

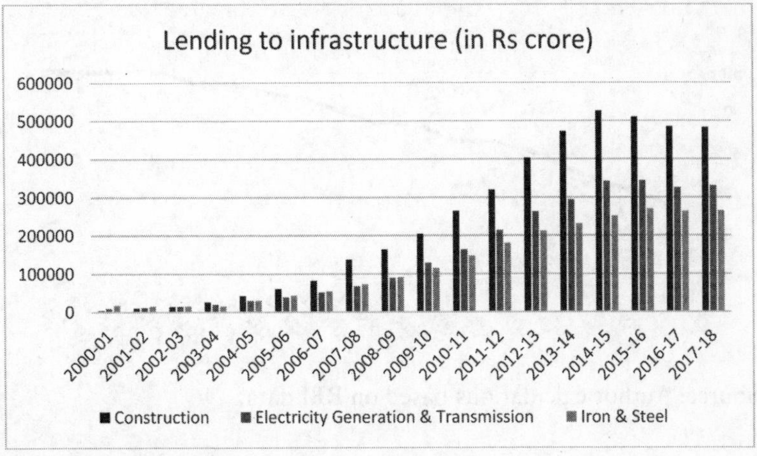

Source: Reserve Bank of India.

Figure 11.1 makes for a very interesting reading. Even without going into the specifics, it's clear that lending to the infrastructure sector zoomed up. The total lending to construction, electricity generation and transmission, and iron and steel in 2000–01 had stood at around Rs 29,817 crore. Of this lending to the iron and steel subsector had stood at Rs 17,129 crore in 2000–01. When it came to the construction sub-sector, a sum total of Rs 3,573 crore had been lent by PSBs. Rs 9,115 crore had been lent to companies operating in the electricity generation and transmission subsector. In total, these loans formed around 16.9 per cent of industrial lending carried out by PSBs. What this tells us very clearly is that before the turn of the century, the PSBs treaded very carefully when it came to lending to companies operating in these subsectors.

Now take a look at Figure 11.2, which plots the total lending to construction, electricity generation, and iron and steel subsectors as a proportion of total lending to industry carried out by PSBs.

Figure 11.2

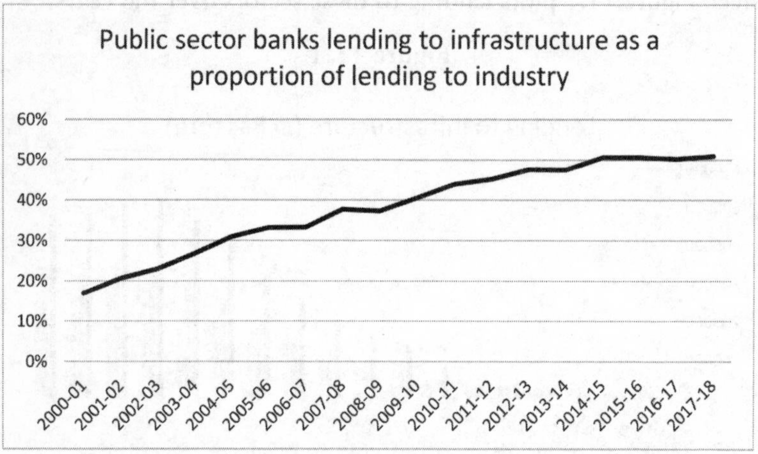

Source: Author calculations based on RBI data.

Figure 11.2 clearly shows that lending to the three infrastructure subsectors went up dramatically in the 2000s. It was at 16.9 per cent in 2000–01 and it had jumped to 37.3 per cent by 2008–09. In fact, if we go back as far as back 1989–90, lending to these three subsectors formed just 10.6 per cent of total lending to industry by PSBs.

There were reasons to why PSBs didn't lend to companies operating in these subsectors. First, they did not have the expertise required to lend to these companies. Secondly, this kind of lending led to asset–liability mismatches. People investing money in bank deposits have short investment horizons. On the other hand, many loans, including loans given to the industry in general and infrastructure in particular, are of a long-term duration. Let's try and understand this with some data from a random year. In 2007–08, 40 per cent of the term deposits (i.e., fixed deposits) of commercial banks had a maturity of one year or more, but less than two years. In an ideal world, banks should also be giving out loans which have a repayment period of one year or more and less than two years. But that, as we know, is not the case. Banks give out loans to industry, which in some cases have repayment periods running into more than two decades. They also give out home loans which have repayment periods of fifteen years or more. This situation is referred to an asset–liability mismatch and lending to infrastructure companies simply makes it worse.

How does this matter? A very long repayment period (or tenure of the loan, as it's technically called) essentially raises the risk of the loan not being repaid or being only partly repaid. The repayment in case of infrastructure projects largely depends on the cash flows generated by the project, and not on the collateral offered against the loan. The collateral can often be inadequate and does not cover for the loan that has been given.[109]

Over and above this, it's not easy to recover the loan if such a case defaults. It's easier to recover a loan defaulted against a cement factory than recover a default against bridge or a road.[110]

Nevertheless, this is something that banks know about. Hence, when a bank decides to lend to an infrastructure company, it's willing to take that risk. The same can be said about the Indian PSBs and their decision to lend big time to infrastructure firms.

But banks hadn't bargained on the infrastructure projects they had lent to on getting stalled. Or to put it a little more simply, as they had very little experience of lending to infrastructure projects, they did not know that delays could happen. The delays came from a lack of environmental clearances, a lack of non-environmental clearances, problems with acquiring land, roadblock on policy issues, as well as the inability of the promoters to bring in their fair share of capital into the projects.[111]

Basically, many projects which banks financed did not take off. If projects did not take off, there was no cash flow and without cash flow, there was no way the loan could be repaid. Take a look at Figure 11.3 – it plots the number of projects, abandoned/shelved/stalled every year over the years. A bulk of these projects were in electricity, construction and metals subsectors.

Figure 11.3

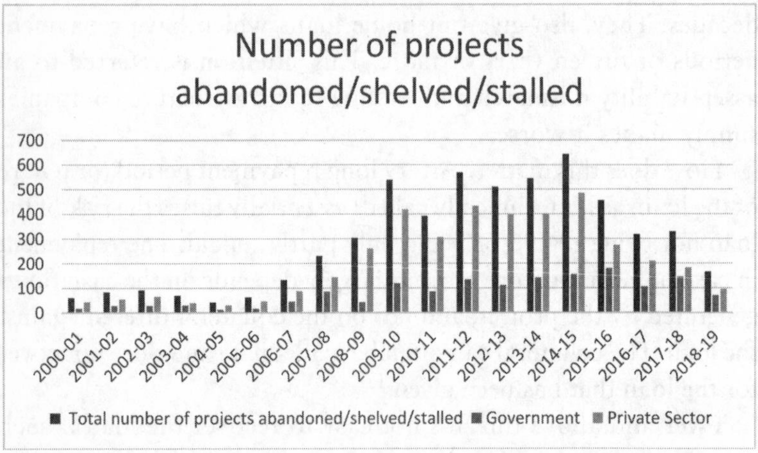

Source: Centre for Monitoring Indian Economy.

Figure 11.3 tells us that it must have been clear to banks by 2007–08 and 2008–09 that all wasn't well. In 2008–09, the total number of projects abandoned/shelved/stalled jumped to 303. Of these, 260 belonged to the private sector, and most were in the infrastructure sector. But PSBs didn't go slow on lending to industry in general, or to infrastructure in particular. In fact, they doubled down on it.

In 2009–10, the total lending to industry by PSBs had stood at Rs 9,18,975 crore. This increased to Rs 20,96,976 crore by 2013–14. When it came to lending to the subsectors of construction, electricity generation and transmission, and iron and steel, it jumped from Rs 3,42,506 crore to Rs 9,96,761 crore during the same period. Lending to these three subsectors formed 37.3 per cent of the total lending carried out by industry in 2008–09. This had jumped to 47.5 per cent in 2013–14 and touched 50.7 per cent in 2014–15 (see Figure 11.2).

The Lok Sabha elections were scheduled to take place in 2009. In this scenario, the incumbent United Progressive Alliance (UPA) government couldn't afford the economy slowing down because of the financial crisis. An election was around the corner and it had to be won. This is when the taps of PSBs were opened and they were encouraged to continue the flow of lending.

While the lending to industry and infrastructure companies increased, it wasn't as if the environment in which these companies operated had changed. There was no reason for projects to suddenly start taking off now, given that they hadn't in the past. Hence, the number of projects abandoned/shelved/stalled went up even further. As can be seen from Figure 11.3, it touched 543 in 2013–14 and a high of 643 in 2014–15. Of course, with this, more and more bank loans were getting stuck as well.

Take a look at Figure 11.4, which plots the value of projects abandoned/shelved/stalled.

Figure 11.4

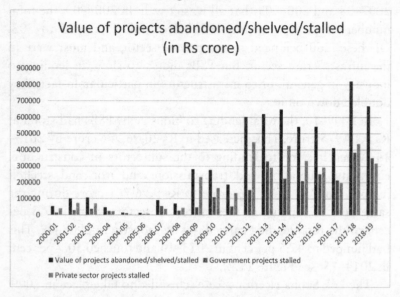

Value of projects abandoned/shelved/stalled (in Rs crore)

■ Value of projects abandoned/shelved/stalled   ■ Government projects stalled
■ Private sector projects stalled

Source: Centre for Monitoring Indian Economy.

In 2013–14, the value of projects abandoned/shelved/stalled stood at Rs 6,48,336 crore. It would reach a high of Rs 8,20,127 crore in 2017–18. Clearly, the huge burst in industrial lending, along with an increase in government spending, helped. India's economic growth, which had fallen to 3.9 per cent in 2008–09, recovered to 8.5 per cent in 2009–10 and 10.3 per cent in 2010–11.*

* * *

D. Subbarao took over as the RBI governor from Y.V. Reddy on 5 September 2008. As Reddy's tenure was coming to an end, inflation was going up. For a period of three months ending June 2008, the inflation, as measured by the Wholesale Price Index, stood at close

---

*   GDP with base year 2004–05, which was prevalent then.

to 9 per cent.* Of course, in order to tackle high inflation, Reddy had been raising the repo rate. Hence, by September 2008, the repo rate stood at 9 per cent – having gone up by 125 basis points from 7.75 per cent since the beginning of the year.

When Subbarao took over, the main aim of the RBI was to bring down the high inflation. Subbarao says so very clearly in *Who Moved My Interest Rate? Leading the Reserve Bank of India through Five Turbulent Years*: 'The only thing I could think of saying when I was ushered in front of the media for a sound byte minutes after signing on as the Governor, was that reining in inflation ... would be my top priority.'[112]

Just ten days after Subbarao took over, Lehman Brothers filed for bankruptcy on 15 September 2008. On 16 September 2008, AIG, the largest insurance company in the world, was nationalized by the American government. Before this, Fannie Mae and Freddie Mac, the two American government–sponsored enterprises in the home loan business, had been put under conservatorship. The world, as we knew it, had changed in a matter of a few days.

The first thing that happens in the aftermath of any financial crisis is that money in the financial system becomes scarce. Anyone who has any money keeps it with himself. In the process, interest rates on short-term loans start to rise. In India, the interest rates in the call money market went up dramatically. Call money market is the market where banks lend their surplus funds for one day (i.e., overnight).

---

* The RBI moved towards inflation, as measured by the Consumer Price Index, as a key measure of inflation only in April 2014, after Raghuram G. Rajan became the governor. Before that, the RBI gave more weightage to inflation as measured by the Wholesale Price Index in comparison. Here, we take the inflation as measured by the Wholesale Price Index with a base year of 2004–05, which was what was being used at that time too.

On 16 September 2008, a day after Lehman Brothers filed for bankruptcy, the interest rate in the call money market was at 13.1 per cent. By 10 October, this had jumped to 18.5 per cent. Moreover, the Indian version of the global credit crunch played out as well.

Meanwhile, many corporates up until then had been borrowing from abroad, because interest rates were lower. Now, they started to approach Indian banks to meet their funding needs. At the same time, corporates started withdrawing the surplus funds they had invested in money market mutual funds. Money market mutual funds are essentially mutual funds which invest money in financial securities that mature in a short period of time.

So when corporates started withdrawing their money from mutual funds, the funds had to do something in order to be able to repay corporates. They started to withdraw the money they had invested in non-banking finance companies. The non-banking finance companies, feeling the credit crunch, approached banks for loans. Banks at that point of time were struggling to cope with the additional demand for credit from corporates.[113] This wasn't something unique to India. It was playing out globally.

In the aftermath of the financial crisis, central banks around the world had decided to run an easy money policy. The RBI was no different on that front. It cut the cash reserve ratio and the statutory liquidity ratio. Cutting the cash reserve ratio immediately increases the total amount of money available in the financial system as banks need to maintain a lesser amount of money with the RBI.

In order to fight inflation, Reddy had raised the repo rate as late as July 2008. On 20 October 2008, Subbarao cut the repo rate by 100 basis points, to 8 per cent from 9 per cent. This was huge because when the RBI cuts the repo rate, it tends to do so in increments of 25-basis points each. Even a 50-basis point cut is huge. What Subbarao was telling the world was that financial stability had now become more important than tackling inflation.

He cut the repo rate very fast and by December 2008, it was at 5 per cent. It's worth mentioning here that it had taken Reddy five years to push up the rate from 5 per cent to 9 per cent. It took Subbarao just three months (from September, when he took charge, to December) to reverse that.

Of course, by cutting the repo rate rapidly and taking other measures, the RBI ensured that there was no credit crunch in the Indian financial system and there was enough money going around for banks to lend, which they did.

Take a look at Figure 11.5, which plots the inflation in India between 2007 and 2013 as well as the RBI repo rate.[*]

Figure 11.5

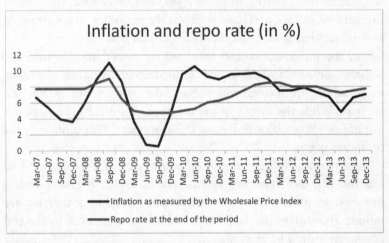

Source: Reserve Bank of India.

Subbarao started cutting the repo rate in October 2008, a few weeks after he took over as the RBI governor. The interesting thing is that inflation collapsed to almost zero in the months that

---

[*] Inflation as measured by the Wholesale Price Index (base year 2004–05) has been used, because this is the rate of inflation that the RBI would have taken into account at that point.

followed the financial crisis. This was primarily a reflection of the fact that economic activity had collapsed in the aftermath of the financial crisis. With buying and selling of things slowing down, it wasn't surprising that inflation collapsed. Inflation reached a low of 0.5 per cent in the period of three months ending September 2009. After that, all the government spending and bank lending started to have an impact, and inflation shot up.

The problem was that with bank lending and government spending increasing at a rapid rate, inflation was soon in double digits. As Milton Friedman wrote in *Money Mischief: Episodes in Monetary History*: 'Inflation occurs when the quantity of money rises appreciably more rapidly than output, and the more rapid the rise in the quantity of money per unit of output, the greater the rate of inflation. There is probably no other proposition in economics that is as well established as this one.'[114]

As the government and the banks pumped money into the Indian economy, and this money landed up in the hands of people, more and more money was chasing the same set of goods and services. While the supply of money went up quickly, the same did not happen when it came to goods and services. This ultimately led to higher prices.

In a period of three months ending March 2010, inflation had touched 9.6 per cent. It's worth remembering here that this is inflation as measured by the Wholesale Price Index that we are talking about. This means that the inflation experienced by the end consumer would be even higher.

Inflation stayed high for the next twenty-four months. The speed with which Subbarao and the RBI cut the repo rate in the aftermath of the financial crisis was missing when it was time to raise the repo rate. The RBI started raising the repo rate in March 2010. It raised the rate by 25 basis points to 5 per cent. This was done through an ad hoc policy announcement (meaning there was no meeting). By October 2011, the rate had been raised to 8.5 per cent.

Subbarao raised the rates thirteen times between 19 March 2010 and 25 October 2011, to get it to 8.5 per cent from 4.75 per cent. As he writes: 'We raised rates by 50 basis points on occasion [actually twice], but much of the time the increase was in steps of 25 basis points, earning me the moniker of Baby Step Subbarao.'[115]

A section of the analysts were of the view that as Subbarao had cut the repo rate by 400 basis points, from 9 per cent to 5 per cent in a matter of three months, he could have raised the repo rate at a faster pace if he was serious about tackling inflation.

With the benefit of hindsight, this view turned out to be correct. Subbarao himself admits to it in his book, where he says: 'I must admit in all honesty that the economy would have been better served if our monetary tightening [raising the repo rate] had started sooner and had been faster and stronger.' This was primarily because the economic growth after the financial crisis did not fall as much as experts thought it would. At the same time, the economic growth in the subsequent two years had revived at a faster pace and was stronger than it was believed it would be.[116]

Of course, this comes with much retrospection. At that point of time, the world economy was still not out of the woods and the crisis was still spreading through parts of Europe. In this scenario, discretion was a better part of valour and any RBI governor would have thought twice before raising the repo rate at a pace faster than Subbarao did.

This meant that an era of easy money in the Indian financial system, in the aftermath of the financial crisis, continued longer than it actually should have. In fact, Subbarao and the RBI were just doing what they should have done. Nevertheless, the politics of the day had a much bigger impact on how things eventually turned out (as it normally does).

In the aftermath of the financial crisis, the government, as a major owner of PSBs, had asked these banks to continue lending. This easy lending, as we saw, led to the accumulation of bad loans. But there were other reasons for it as well.

In February 2008, in his Budget speech, Finance Minister P. Chidambaram had announced a farm loan waiver, which eventually cost the nation around Rs 71,680 crore.[117] In the aftermath of the Mumbai terror attacks, Chidambaram was moved from the finance ministry to the home ministry. Prime Minister Manmohan Singh took over additional charge of the finance ministry.

In the original scheme of things, the government had aimed to achieve a fiscal deficit of Rs 1,33,287 crore, or 2.5 per cent of the GDP in 2008–09. This after the government had achieved a fiscal deficit of Rs 1,26,912 crore, or 2.7 per cent of the GDP in 2007–08. The actual fiscal deficit of the government in 2008–09 came in at Rs 3,36,992 crore, or 6 per cent of the GDP.

This happened because the government earned lower taxes than it had forecast. At the same time, it increased its total expenditure from the originally planned Rs 7,50,884 crore by around 18 per cent to Rs 8,83,956 crore.

The idea was that in a period of an economic slowdown, the government becomes the spender of the last resort and this pushes up economic growth. Along with increasing its overall expenditure, the government also cut taxes. On 7 December 2008, the government announced an across-the-board excise duty cut of 4 per cent (barring petroleum products). This cut was expected to lower the price of cars, textiles, cement, etc. In fact, car manufacturers were expected to cut prices ranging from Rs 8,000 to Rs 45,000, depending on the model. This was a part of a ten-point stimulus package worth Rs 30,700 crore.[118]

Another stimulus package was announced by the government on 3 January 2009. This included the incentivization of purchase of commercial vehicles, additional sops to exporters and small-scale industries, and raising the level of protection for cement and steel sectors.[119]

These fiscal stimuli from the government came on the back of the RBI flooding the system with a lot of money. Since November 2008, the central bank had pumped Rs 3,00,000 crore into the financial system.[120]

This is where things started to change. Manmohan Singh was supposed to undergo a coronary bypass surgery on 24 January 2009. This was Singh's second bypass surgery and he was expected to take four to six weeks to recover from it. Meanwhile, on the day of Singh's bypass surgery, Pranab Mukherjee was appointed as the finance minister.

When the government had announced the second stimulus on 3 January 2009, it had made it clear that there wouldn't be any more stimulus packages during 2008–09. Nevertheless, Mukherjee announced a third fiscal package on 25 February 2009. Service tax rate was cut to 10 per cent from 12 per cent.

The original excise duty cuts, which were supposed to last until March 2009, were extended. At the same time, the excise duty on all products which had an excise duty of 10 per cent was reduced to 8 per cent. In fact, 90 per cent of the tax collections came in from products which were on the 10 per cent excise duty slab. This included white goods, commercial vehicles and cement. Mukherjee also allowed the state governments to go beyond the fiscal deficit of 3 per cent of the state GDP during 2009–10. This meant that the state governments could also borrow and spend more money.[121]

This stimulus package was unveiled while Singh was still recovering from his bypass surgery. As Pranab Mukherjee admits in *The Coalition Years*: 'I and Manmohan Singh held differing views on economic issues.'[122] In fact, Manmohan Singh was the RBI governor between September 1982 and January 1985. Mukherjee was the finance minister through much of this period, between January 1982 and December 1984. So, Mukherjee was Singh's boss long before Singh became Mukherjee's boss as PM.

Meanwhile, the economic growth, which had fallen to 3.9 per cent in 2008–09,* had recovered to 8.5 per cent in 2009–10 and it jumped to 10.3 per cent in 2010–11. Despite the recovery, the stimulus wasn't withdrawn during the period Mukherjee was finance minister. In fact, the fiscal deficit in 2009–10 jumped even further, up to 6.6 per cent of the GDP.

---

*   As per the GDP series with base year 2004–05, which was being used at that point of time.

While all this government spending and the era of easy money helped revive growth, it also fuelled high inflation, which wouldn't go. This high inflation eventually slowed down the economy. It also led to high interest rates. This slowing economy along with high interest rates made many industrial projects for which banks had lent money simply unviable. As the government borrowed more for its spending, it left a lesser amount for others to borrow. Economists call this crowding out and this pushed up interest rates. The weighted average lending rate to industry, which had stood at 10.5 per cent in 2009–10, jumped to 12.8 per cent by 2011–12. Ultimately, all this came together to create a massive amount of bad loans on the books of PSBs and banks . This is how bad money in the Indian financial system peaked.

A former central bank governor once told me that *doing nothing* is never an option for a policymaker. He needs to be seen doing something. Also, there is tremendous pressure from lobbyists of industry associations to *do something*. And as big business ultimately finances politics in India, they need to be humoured even during bad times.

Given this, the fiscal stimulus from the government became a necessity once the financial crisis broke out. We can definitely debate whether the third stimulus which Mukherjee pushed through without even consulting the cabinet was required or not. But it's more or less clear that the government stimuli could have easily been withdrawn gradually once the economy was back on track in 2009–10. Clearly, Mukherjee is to be blamed for this.

As Subbarao puts it: 'As finance minister, he [i.e., Mukherjee] was criticised for being locked in the '70s mindset, not realizing that the world of finance had undergone a sea change in the three decades since.'[123]

12

How Good Money Became Bad Money

In the span of a few years, between 2003–04 and 2008–09, the bank lending to industry shot up from 11.8 per cent of the GDP to 20.15 per cent. Other than credit from banks, there were large inflows from abroad. The capital inflows in 2007–08 reached 8 per cent of the GDP. This added to the total amount of debt that companies had taken on, sending their debt to equity ratios beyond the conservative sphere. Everyone wanted to cash in on the greater than 9 per cent economic growth, which they believed would continue. But this dream soon started to unravel.[124]

What did not help was the fact that the economic growth fell to 6.7 per cent and 4.7 per cent in 2011–12 and 2012–13 respectively. The trouble was the revenue projections of projects had been built around the assumption of double-digit yearly growth. Now that wasn't possible once the economic growth collapsed to less than 5 per cent. Other than the economy going through a bad cycle, a part of the slowdown also stemmed from corruption scandals in the coal and telecom sector. This led to a policy paralysis at the government's end and, in the process, any major structural reforms which could have put the economic growth back on track took a back seat.[125]

As we saw in the last section, the RBI raised the repo rate to control inflation. This pushed up lending rates. Other than this, the borrowing costs also went up because the rupee lost value against the US dollar. One dollar was worth around Rs 40 at the beginning of 2008, before the financial crisis struck. As foreign investors withdrew money from India in the aftermath of the crisis, the rupee lost value rapidly against the dollar. By early 2009, one dollar was worth more than Rs 50. In mid-2013, the rupee lost value even further thanks to the taper tantrum in the United States, and one dollar crossed Rs 65.

This pushed up the borrowing cost of those firms which had borrowed in dollars pre-2008, because interest rates were lower abroad than in India. As the rupee loses value against the dollar, more rupees are needed to buy the total amount of dollars needed in order to repay the debt or even to keep paying interest on it. The Economic Survey of 2016–17 summarizes the situation well when it says: 'Firms that had borrowed abroad when the rupee was trading around Rs 40/dollar were hit hard when the rupee depreciated, forcing them to repay their debts at exchange rates closer to Rs 60-70/ dollar.'

To sum up, the following issues made things difficult for overleveraged companies and, in the process, for banks. These were: 1) assumptions of double-digit growth in revenues no longer remaining valid for projects; 2) interest rates on loans going up, thanks to efforts to control the burgeoning inflation in the economy; 3) delays in getting environmental and other clearances, as well as the land needed for the project, added to the budgeted cost; 4) the fall in the value of the rupee against the dollar, sent the borrowing costs in many cases soaring.

All this came together and wreaked havoc with the cash flows of the companies which had borrowed and their ability to keep repaying the debt. Even their ability to pay interest on it went for a toss.[126] This could be seen in the interest coverage ratio of the companies, which fell dramatically.

Interest coverage ratio is defined as the earnings before incomes and taxes (EBIT, or operating profit) of a company divided by the interest expense on its debt during a particular year. It tells us whether a company is making enough money to keep paying the interest on its debt.

For a company to be able to pay the interest on its debt during a particular period, its interest coverage ratio needs to be more than one. But it's generally said that if a company's interest coverage ratio is 1.5 or lower, its ability may be questionable at best.

This is precisely what happened in India. As the Economic Survey of 2016–17 points out: 'By 2013, nearly one-third of corporate debt was owed by companies with an interest coverage ratio less than 1 ("IC1 companies"), many of them in the infrastructure (especially power generation) and metals sectors.' The interest coverage ratio of power generation companies as a whole fell to 1.43 in 2013–14 from a high of 2.73 in 2006–07. This meant that their ability to keep paying interest on their debt came down dramatically. In fact, the ratio kept falling and fell to a low 1.17 in 2016–17, which meant that on the whole the companies were barely making enough money to keep paying the interest on their debt.

As the Economic Survey of 2016–17 further points out: 'By 2015, the share of IC1 companies reached nearly 40 per cent, as slowing growth in China caused international steel prices to collapse, causing nearly every Indian steel company to record large losses. The government responded promptly by imposing a minimum import price, while international prices themselves recovered somewhat, thereby affording the steel industry some relief. Even so, the IC1 share remained above 40 per cent in late 2016.'

As far as steel companies were concerned, their interest coverage ratio on the whole in 2015–16 fell to zero. This meant that their earnings before interest and taxes were in the negative territory. A ratio cannot be negative; hence, it was zero. This meant that steel companies on the whole were not making enough money from their business to be able to repay the interest on their debt. The situation couldn't have been more dismal than this.

Take a look at Figure 12.1, which plots the interest coverage ratio of several industrial subsectors to which banks had lent a lot of money over the years.

Figure 12.1

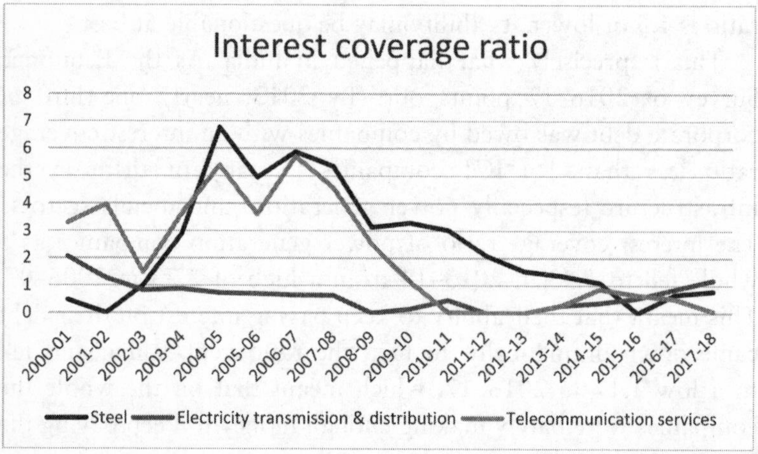

Source: Centre for Monitoring Indian Economy.

The telecom sector in particular has been in a bad shape over the years when it comes to paying interest on its loans from banks, with the interest coverage ratio being close to zero or less than one for several years. The steel sector also continues to be in a bad state.

When the interest coverage ratio of the companies with a huge amount of borrowed money had hovered around 1.5 to two, they were already in the speculative stage of Minsky's three stages of finance. And the moment the interest coverage ratio fell to around one or lower than one, they reached the Ponzi stage. The only way these companies could continue paying interest on their debt was by borrowing more money.

In this scenario, with many companies having taken on debt and being unable to pay interest on it, let alone repay the debt, the loan defaults should have happened left, right and centre, and bad loans of banks in general and PSBs in particular should have piled-up big time.

Take a look at Figure 12.2, which plots the bad loans of PSBs over the years.

Figure 12.2

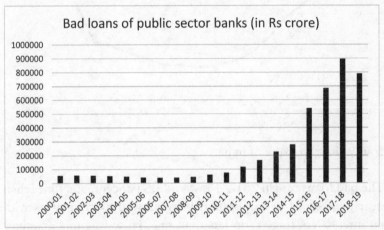

Source: Reserve Bank of India.

Figure 12.2 tells us that until 2012–13, the bad loans of PSBs hardly went up. In fact, in 2012–13, the total bad loans of PSBs had stood at Rs 1,64,500 crore. While this sounds quite a lot in isolation, it actually wasn't, once we take into account the total advances or loans given by PSBs up until then. Take a look at Figure 12.3, which plots the bad loans rate of PSBs (i.e., total bad loans divided by total advances or loans given out by PSBs expressed as a percentage).

Figure 12.3

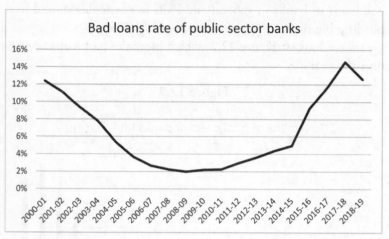

Source: Reserve Bank of India.

The bad loans rate in 2012–13 was at 3.6 per cent, at a time when nearly one-third of corporate debt was owed by companies with an interest coverage ratio less than one. How was this possible? In the normal scheme of things, the Indian banks should have forced bankruptcy, seized the assets against which the loans had been taken and sold them to recover their money. But that did not happen. This stemmed from the belief among banks that given the weak legal system in India, the process of seizing assets and selling them, would be extremely time consuming and wouldn't lead to a good recovery either.[127]

In 2001, the government had put in place a corporate debt restructuring (CDR) mechanism. This allowed defaulting companies to come up with turnaround strategies in consultation with the banks they had taken loans from. The steps that could be included under the CDR mechanism were: 1) extending the maturity of the loan, and thereby reducing the regular payment of interest and regular repayment of principal that needed to be made; 2) reducing the interest charged on the loan; 3) the debtors converting a part of the loan into equity. This way, the debt of the company would come down. Hopefully, this would help the company turn itself around in the years to come too. And when the stock market recognized the prospect of something like that happening, the stock price of the company would go up. The debtors (i.e., the bankers), who had converted their loans into equity, could then sell their stocks and recover the original loan (or so was believed at least in theory); 4) the bank could also provide additional financing to help the company, which is in a tricky situation when it comes to repaying its debt; 5) a combination of all these steps could also be taken.[128]

This strategy was referred to as *giving time to time* and had worked well in the bad loan crisis in the late 1990s and early 2000s. Other than giving time to the corporates to repay loans, it also worked at another level. The hope was that in the years to come, the economy would recover, the banks would give out more loans, the loan book would grow and the bad loans as a proportion of the total outstanding loans would come down. Given all this, the banks went for CDR.

In fact, considering the state of the economy and the fact that companies had borrowed beyond their capacity to repay loans, troubles for PSBs started as early 2011–12. When this happened, the RBI took recourse to *regulatory forbearance*. Forbearance means to hold back, to show restraint. In the normal scheme of things when companies were not able to pay the loan, the banks should have seized the collateral and sold it to recover the loan. The trouble with this strategy was that it hadn't worked in the past in India.

In this situation, the RBI came up with several restructuring programmes other than the CDR, which we have already seen. These were strategic debt restructuring, the 5/25 scheme, the Joint Lenders' Forum, etc. In total, the central bank came up with twenty-eight different circulars on various forms of loan restructuring.[129]

All these were ways to help banks restructure the outstanding loans which the corporates weren't in a position to continue repaying. Hence, the idea was that banks show forbearance to the corporate borrowers using programmes initiated by the banking regulator, the RBI.

In fact, by March 2015, the total corporate loans subject to restructuring had stood at Rs 5,28,538 crore. It had stood at just Rs 10,210 crore in 2006–07. Interestingly, the bad loans of banks as of March 2015 had stood at Rs 3,22,926 crore.

The fact that the restructured loans were greater than the bad loans told us that the banks were using the restructuring route to kick the bad loans can down the road. This also came to be referred as 'extend and pretend'. A favourite technique of bankers is what they call the evergreening of loans. This involves giving a new loan to the borrower so that he can pay the interest on the original loan or even repay it. And then everyone can just pretend that all is well.

If the projects had been carried out in the timelines that had initially been assumed, they would have turned out to be profitable ones. But that did not happen. The business promoter who had put the project together, and taken on a loan to complete it, had very little equity (or the money that he had invested) left in the project. And given this, it was but natural he lost interest in the project. It was at this point of time that the bank should have started recognizing bad loans.[130]

While the banks should have recognized bad loans for what they were, they should have also insisted on the promoters bringing in more of their money into the projects. Of course, forcing promoters to bring in more of their own money into the project would have been possible only if a bank could make a credible threat of taking over the project.[131]

At that point of time, before the Insolvency and Bankruptcy Code came into being, banks were really not in a position to threaten promoters – even incompetent or unscrupulous ones – to bring in more of their own money into the project.[132]

Stalled projects continued as zombie projects (i.e., alive on paper, but dead otherwise). Bankers gave fresh loans so that promoters could continue paying interest and the banks could pretend that things were fine. The trouble was that the interest on the loans coming in was basically illusory. It was the bank's money merely being returned to it – or what Minsky called the Ponzi stage or the third stage of finance. Promoters were able to pay interest only if the banks gave fresh loans to them. It was deceptive accounting at its very best, which postponed the problem to a future date for someone else to deal with.[133] This is how the good money of bank loans became the bad money of the Indian financial system.

In fact, to some extent this was also a case of what behavioural economists call *the sunk cost fallacy*. The fallacy shows up in many areas of life. Right from trying to finish a boring book to remaining in a bad marriage or an abusive relationship for that matter.

Nobel prize winning psychologist Daniel Kahneman in his book *Thinking, Fast and Slow* defines this fallacy as 'the decision to invest additional resources in a losing account'.[134] Simply put, one has invested (be it money, emotion or time) so much into something that one tries to make it work by investing more into it. In the case of Indian PSBs, good money continued to be thrown after bad money.

As Kahneman writes: 'The escalation of commitment to failing endeavours is a mistake from the perspective of the firm but not necessarily from the perspective of the executive who "owns" a floundering project. Cancelling the project will leave a permanent stain on the executive's record, and his personal interests are perhaps best served by gambling further with the organisation's resources in the hope of recouping the original investment—or at least in an attempt to postpone the day of reckoning.'[135]

In the case of Indian PSBs, it made sense for the top management to keep kicking the can down the road. Given their past experience, they knew that there was no point in trying to do the right thing. Also, most of the individuals who reach the top job at a PSB (except perhaps the SBI) up until then had had very short tenures and no one wanted to spoil that. They wanted to leave the problems behind for their successor to deal with.

13

When Loan Defaults Could Kill

India has had a long history of banking and moneylending, as have other parts of the world. Moneylending in India can be traced back to the Vedic period, between 2000 to 1400 BCE. As far as banking is concerned, it can be traced to 500 BCE. In fact, Kautaliya's *Arthashastra*, dating back to the second century BCE, contains references to creditors, lenders and lending rates.[136]

Interest-bearing loans have been around even before the invention of coins (one of the first forms of money). As Kabir Sehgal writes in *Coined: The Rich Life of Money and How Its History Has Shaped Us*: 'Around 5000 BC, in what is now known as the Middle East, various types of debt instruments emerged ... Interest bearing loans started with agriculture and farming: seeds, nuts, grains, and cows borrowed by destitute farmers who repaid the loan with interest–in the form of the surplus from their harvest.'[137]

In any debt contract there is a borrower and a lender. If the borrower, at some point of time, cannot keep his promise, he is in default. If the credit system needs to keep working smoothly, then those who default on their loans cannot be allowed to go scot-free. If they are allowed to go unpunished, it sends out the wrong message to borrowers. Future borrowers will also default on their loans because there are no negative consequences of defaulting on a loan. In this scenario, the system will break down and lenders will soon stop lending because they know that the money they lend won't be repaid.

If we look at human history, loan defaulters were never allowed to go scot-free and they had to face negative consequences. During mediaeval times in Barcelona, a defaulting banker was given time to repay his debt. During this period, however, he was put on diet of bread and water. If by the end of the period, he had still not repaid the debt, he was beheaded. With time, the punishments became less harsh. A default in Victorian England meant spending time in the debtors' prison.[138]

There are similar examples from other parts of the world. As Sehgal writes: 'Declaring personal bankruptcy wasn't an option, so there was some creative licence in making payments ... There were even instances of men giving up their wives or sons to avoid interest payments.'[139]

Dan Davies makes a similar point in *Lying for Money: How Legendary Frauds Reveal the Workings of our World*: 'For a large period of the history of debt, there was nothing which very much resembled a bankruptcy code, and the law was that – outside of occasional "jubilee" episodes of overall debt forgiveness – borrowers had to pay what they could and debts would never be extinguished.'[140]

The consequences of not paying could be very serious. As Davies writes: 'In ancient societies, defaulting debtors could be stripped of their citizenship and sold as slaves for the benefit of their creditors (Athens was considered quite liberal in limiting the period of debt slavery for five years).'[141]

In fact, debtors' prisons have been around through most of human history. As Sehgal points out, it was a fairly common practise even in ancient Rome. As he writes: 'During the Roman Empire, a creditor could arrest the debtor for debt delinquency and haul him into court. If guilty, the debtor could land in a private jail and after sixty days become a slave, a bonded labourer, or even be killed. Though uncommon, creditors were allowed to cut up a debtor's body into chunks commensurate with the debt owed.'[142]

Debtors' prisons were around up until the late nineteenth century. 'In 1830, more than ten thousand people were imprisoned in New York debt prisons. Many times the debts were minimal. In Philadelphia, thirty inmates had debts outstanding of not more than a dollar. There were five people imprisoned for debt delinquency for every one put away for violent offense,' writes Sehgal.[143] Of course, things have changed quite a lot since then, as debt has become a more central part of our lives over the last hundred years.

Having said that, there has to be some negative effect of defaulting on a debt simply to ensure that the credit system does not totally break down. The promoters of large Indian firms barely faced any negative consequences for defaulting on money they had taken from banks. In fact, India until very recently did not have functioning bankruptcy rules and this made it almost impossible to 'kick out owners at a failing company and sell of its assets', and recover some portion of the loan in the process.[144]

As R. Gandhi, who was a deputy covernor of the RBI, said in a speech in December 2014: 'The sanctity of debt contracts has been continuously eroded in India, especially by large borrowers. The system protected large borrowers and their right to stay in control, rendering bankers helpless vis-à-vis large and influential promoters.'[145]

Rajan put it even better when he said: 'In India, too many large borrowers insist on their divine right to stay in control despite their unwillingness to put in new money ... The promoter threatens to run the enterprise into the ground unless the government, banks and regulators make the concessions that are necessary to keep it alive. And if the enterprise regains health, the promoter retains all the up-side, forgetting the help he got from the government or the banks – after all, banks should be happy they got some of their money back! No wonder government ministers worry about a country where we have many sick companies but no "sick" promoters.'[146]

The point being that the large Indian promoters had to face no consequences of defaulting on PSB loans. In fact, forget seizing the collateral and selling it, in order to recover the loan, the banks even dilly-dallied in recognizing bad loans as bad loans. But as we shall see, somewhere in late 2014, all this started to be set right.

14

All Are Equal but Some Are More Equal

The bigger businessmen and promoters have enjoyed a privileged existence while dealing with the banking system in India. As George Orwell wrote in *Animal Farm*: 'All are equal but some are more equal than others'. When it comes to the bad loans of Indian banks, the businessmen epitomize the 'more equal'.

At the heart of the current bad loan crisis that the PSBs are facing are large loans given by a syndicate of different banks to big corporate groups.

Take a look at Table 14.1, which lists out the total bad loans accumulated from domestic operations of banks, across different sectors, as of 31 March 2018.

Table 14.1: Total Domestic Bad Loans of Banks.

(in Rs crore)	Total bad loans	Industry	Agriculture and Allied Activities	Services	Retail
March 31, 2018	9,61,962	7,03,969	85,344	1,23,520	38,039

Source: Rajya Sabha Unstarred Question No: 1492, Answered on 18 July 2018.

It's very clear that loans to industry formed around 73 per cent, or a little under three-fourths of the total bad loans of banks. PSBs make up for a large part of the Indian banking sector. Hence, what is true for banks on the whole is also true for PSBs, leading to the conclusion that most PSB bad loans were on account of defaults on loans given to industry.

Around 22.8 per cent of the bank loans given to industry had gone bad as of 31 March 2018. In case of PSBs, the bad loans rate was higher than 25 per cent. By March 2019, the bad loans rate for lending to industry carried out by PSBs was slightly lower at 23.6 per cent with the overall rate being at 17.5 per cent.

Given that the industry sector and the corporates are at the heart of India's bad loan crisis, it's worth asking, 'How important was malfeasance and corruption in the NPA problem?'[147]

Most armchair analysis on the issue of bad loans of PSBs suggests a nexus between politicians and businessmen. I have leaned towards this logic in my past writings in the mass media.

And there is a certain logic to it. The bad loans rate of Indian banks when it comes to retail lending has been around 2 per cent for a while. In fact, in some cases, the bad loans rate on retail lending is even lower. Take the case of the SBI. As of 31 March 2018, the bad loans rate on home loans disbursed by the bank had stood at 0.9 per cent. In case of auto loans and other retail loans, the rate stood at 1.1 per cent and 1.2 per cent, respectively. The bad loans rate on lending to industry stood at 21.9 per cent.

This means that the SBI does a terrific job at retail lending, but really messes up when it comes to lending to industry. What is happening here? Thomas Sowell, an American economist turned political philosopher, discusses the concept of separation of knowledge and power in his book, *Wealth, Poverty and Politics*.

How does it apply in this context? In PSBs, managers who have the knowledge to take the right decisions may not always have the power to do so. Take the case of retail lending. The manager looks at the ability of the borrower to repay a loan, and then decides whether to commission a loan or not. This explains why the bad loans ratio in case of retail lending is very low.

But when it comes to lending to industry and corporates, there are people out there who are trying to influence the bank manager's decision – from bureaucrats to ministers to politicians. In this scenario, the manager has to end up giving out loans even to those corporates who do not have the wherewithal to repay it.

The separation between knowledge and power led to a situation where loans were given to many crony capitalists, who have since defaulted. And what we are seeing now is a fallout of that.

While logically this makes perfect sense, how do you prove something like this beyond reasonable doubt, with solid evidence to buttress it? As Rajan put it: 'Undoubtedly, there was some [malfeasance and corruption], but it's hard to tell banker exuberance, incompetence, and corruption apart.' Take the case of R.P. Marathe, who was the managing director and CEO of Bank of Maharashtra, one of the smaller PSBs. In June 2018, he was arrested by the police for not following rules while lending to a real estate builder in the city of Pune. In October 2018, the police filed a closure report saying that the loans had been given as part of a 'normal banking transaction'.[148]

But even with this disclaimer, a few points can be made here:

1) The bankers were chasing industrialists to give out loans and they did very little due diligence beforehand. In fact, many did not even do their independent analysis and depended on SBI Caps and IDBI to do the necessary analysis. Any such analysis introduced a weakness into the system, and multiplied 'the possibilities for undue influence';[149]

2) In a survey carried out by the consultant EY, 64 per cent of the respondents believed that the bad loans of banks resulted primarily from the lapses in the due diligence carried out by the banks sanctioning the loans.* Further, the report citing the

---

*   The principal respondents of the survey were banking professionals working in the PSBs, private sector banks, foreign

survey also suggested that banks relied on many third-party agencies, like surveyors, financial analysts, engineers, etc., in order to carry out the due diligence. These third-party agencies played an important role in assuring the financial information of the borrower, the work completion status of a particular project, the application of funds, etc. The entire system was manipulated. In fact, in some situations, the borrowers even managed to get the reports drafted in ways it suited them;[150]

3) Eighty-seven per cent of those surveyed by EY believed that the diversion of funds to unrelated business through fraudulent means was one of the root causes for the bad loan crisis. This is something that the RBI believed as well. As S.S. Mundra, who was a deputy governor of the RBI, said in a speech in April 2016: 'Not all promoters/borrowers have had a clear conscience and some of them were out to dupe the system by using foul means … Some of the promoters have diverted borrowed funds for purposes other than for which the finance was availed. There are also occasions where some of the borrowers have siphoned off funds for personal gains and not created any productive asset. A section of the promoters have also disposed off [sic] movable fixed assets or immovable property given for the purpose of securing a term loan without the knowledge of the lender. The consequent defaults in such cases are intentional, deliberate and calculated and, hence, wilful. *It's this set of promoters that need to be singled out and quickly brought to justice* [emphasis added]';[151]

4) In fact, the point about loans being diverted to projects other than the ones they were meant for was made by several others as well. Raghuram Rajan recounts a story which is at the heart of the issue. A public sector banker had made a loan to a tycoon. The banker found out that the tycoon was diverting

---

banks as well as cooperative banks. In particular, these bankers worked for specific departments like vigilance, credit/operations, legal/compliance, audit/finance, asset recovery, etc.

money from an investment project. And what did the banker do? He cut the tycoon's credit line by 20 per cent. As Rajan puts it: 'I did not know whether to laugh or cry.'[152]

This was laughable indeed because despite knowing that the tycoon was stealing from the investment project for which the bank had given the loan, the banker chose to do almost nothing about it. And Rajan hits the nail on the head when he says: 'The worst thing this angry banker was willing to do was to cut future lending by a measly 20 per cent! Many promoters came from rich storied families, were well-connected and dominated the society pages. To ask the banker to get tough with the promoter was to ask him to take on an icon of the society. Some bankers could do this with ease, many could not;'[153]

5) Other than promoters diverting money from projects they had taken a loan for, there were cases of gold plating. This is how it worked. Let's say a business promoter approached a bank for a loan of Rs 20,000 crore to build a steel mill. Of the total project cost, the bank would give a loan Rs 15,000 crore and the promoter would bring in Rs 5,000 crore. So far so good. The thing is that the promoter knows that the mill can be built for as low as Rs 10,000 crore. This is the gold plating. The promoter has passed off a project which costs Rs 10,000 crore at best as something which costs Rs 20,000 crore. He gets a loan of Rs 15,000 crore against it. The difference between the loan amount and the actual cost of the project is the amount that the promoter can pocket.[154] In this case, it works out to Rs 5,000 crore. This Rs 5,000 crore is also his investment in the project. By pocketing Rs 5,000 crore of the loan amount, the promoter basically has not invested any of his money in the project. Hence, the risk that he has in the project is zero.

Rajan made a similar point in a speech he gave in November 2014: 'The reason so many projects are in trouble today is because they were structured up front with too little equity, sometimes borrowed by the promoter from elsewhere. And some promoters find ways to take out the equity as soon as the project gets going.'[155] At some level this became possible because banks were outsourcing their due diligence to others;

6) In fact, the promoters and businesses also made use of the lack of information sharing and coordination among banks. The lack of information sharing was used to pull a version of the scam explained just above.

As per the textbooks of financial management, the ideal debt to equity ratio (i.e., the ratio of the money borrowed by the promoter to the promoter's money invested in the business) should not be over 2:1. This means that for every one rupee that a promoter puts into the business, he shouldn't borrow more than two rupees. The promoter putting money into the business, which is his equity or capital, is important because it ensures some 'skin in the game' from his end. Also, it makes banks comfortable because if something goes wrong then the equity portion of the investment in the project can take the first losses.[156]

In some cases, the promoters barely had any equity in the project. Let's consider a project, X, in which the promoter was supposed to invest his fair share. He does that. The trouble was that the money he put into project X as equity was money borrowed from another bank for another project, Y. So this meant that the money was moved from project Y to project X. The banks financing projects X and Y did not know about this and the promoter ended up putting very little of his own money into the project. Hence, if any of these projects got delayed or lost money in any other way, there was no or very little equity to act as the first line of defence and soak the losses. Given this, the banks were then on the line almost immediately.[157]

In fact, often the promoters would even divert money borrowed for an investment project into real estate or the capital market. As Mundra said in a March 2015 speech: 'There are several instances of borrowers diverting money to real estate or capital market for short-term gains without deploying them for purposes borrowed.'[158]

7) Over the years, there has been a lot of talk about political and bureaucratic influence, about phone calls being made to bankers by politicians and bureaucrats to favour certain corporates and give them more loans than their financial situation should have allowed them to receive. But how does one establish this beyond doubt?

There is one company in which case political influence may have played a hand: Lanco Infratech. As on 31 March 2014, the company had total loans amounting to Rs 34,877 crore. Against this, the company had a shareholders' equity of Rs 1,457 crore. This meant that the company had a debt-to-equity ratio of around 24:1. Now, compare this to the reasonable debt-to-equity ratio of 2:1.

What the debt to equity ratio clearly tell us is that the banks giving loans to this company didn't carry out due diligence or were simply under pressure to hand out the loans.

Before we continue with this, let's make a small deviation. On 13 February 2014, the Lok Sabha was rocked by MPs from erstwhile Andhra Pradesh, protesting against the creation of the Telangana state. There were also those who were in favour of the creation of the state. One such MP, in the heat of the moment, pulled a bottle of pepper spray out of his pocket and started firing its contents into the air. The 'pepper spray MP' happened to be a gentleman called Lagadapati Rajagopal.

Other than being a Lok Sabha Member of Parliament from Vijayawada on a Congress Party ticket, between 2009 and 2014, he also happened to be the founding chairman of Lanco, the company we are talking about here. Rajagopal was a part of the new high-flying Andhra entrepreneurs who had soared post the rise of Y.S. Rajasekhara Reddy, who was chief minister of undivided Andhra Pradesh between May 2004 and September 2009.

Senior journalist Shekhar Gupta wrote in the *Indian Express* in February 2014 that Rajagopal's companies got new loans of Rs 3,500 crore against an equity of Rs 239 crore, with a leverage of around 14.7:1. Twenty-seven banks were involved in bailing Rajagopal out.[159]

The leverage of 24:1 is suggestive of potential political influence. Lending in groups was a standard operating procedure when it came to Indian banks. The idea was to limit losses by spreading out the risk. But it made things difficult when the company and the promoter defaulted on the debt.

An excellent example here is that of former airline tycoon and liquor baron Vijay Mallya. Mallya's debt was spread across seventeen banks. When he defaulted on his debt and moved to Great Britain, the seventeen banks had to come together and agree on how to get the money back. With so many banks having to work things out together, it became an excuse for inaction.[160]

8) There is one final point that needs to be made here. When it came to seizing assets of a defaulter vis-à-vis restructuring the loan, the banks treated different borrowers differently. The small borrowers who defaulted on their loans felt the full force of the Securitisation and Reconstruction of Financial Assets and Enforcement of Securities Interest (SARFAESI) Act of 2002 (the legal route available to banks before the Insolvency and Bankruptcy Code came into being). As Rajan put it: 'Its [i.e., SARFAESI Act's] full force is felt by the small entrepreneur who does not have *the wherewithal to hire expensive lawyers or move the courts* [emphasis added], even while the influential promoter once again escapes its rigour. The small entrepreneur's assets are repossessed quickly and sold, extinguishing many a promising business that could do with a little support from bankers.'[161]

* * *

On most days, the Indian business press *largely* reports what the corporates it covers want it to report. This stems from the fact that the business model of the newspapers and news channels in the country has largely become advertisement-driven over the years. The consumers of news across different news platforms rarely pay for it any more. This can be made out from the fact that the newspaper prices in India have just about doubled in the last three decades.

In this scenario, expecting the press to ask even the most basic questions from the corporates they cover shouldn't be expected. As the old saying goes, you don't bite the hand that feeds you.

Let's consider the interesting case of the top management of the SBI, the country's largest bank, and their comments on bad loans over the years.

In May 2010, O.P. Bhatt, the then-chairman of the bank, said, 'The worst is over' when he was asked about the non-performing assets, or bad loans, of the bank.[162]

In February 2012, Pratip Chaudhuri, the then-chairman of the bank, said: 'We think the worst is over with regard to NPAs. NPAs have plateaued.'[163]

In August 2016, Arundhati Bhattacharya, the then-chairman of the bank said: 'The worst is behind us when it comes to stressed assets.'[164] Stressed assets or loans are the sum of bad loans and restructured loans. Bhattacharya was technically right here to some extent, as, by 2016, PSBs had stopped using the restructuring route to *extend and pretend* to not recognize bad loans for what they were. Having said that, they were still not done with recognizing the bad loans as bad loans. Bhattacharya repeated the statement in 2017 as well, when she said: 'Worst is over. A few chunky accounts remain.'[165]

For many years, three different chairpersons of the SBI told the world that as far as they saw it, the bad loan crisis was over. This was even as the bad loans of the bank went up multiple times. In March 2010, the bad loans of the SBI and its associate banks stood

at Rs 23,529 crore. By March 2018, the bad loans of the SBI (with
its associates and the Bhartiya Mahila Bank having merged with
it) had jumped to Rs 2,23,427 crore. This, despite its chairpersons
saying over and over again that the worst was behind us.[*]

While the comments of the chairpersons of only the SBI have
been shared here, they were not the only ones making such
remarks. A simple Google search will tell you that bankers across
the spectrum were saying similar things.

The business media went with what the chairpersons of the
SBI and various others banks said over the years. They rarely
questioned them on the fact that if the worst was truly behind us,
why did the bad loans just keep going up year on year?

In this scenario, hoping that the business media would come up
with a defining story exposing the sad state of PSBs in India was a
tad much to expect. The defining exposé on the sad state of Indian
PSBs, in particular, and banks, in general, happened through a
report titled 'House of Debt', authored by analysts at the stock
brokerage Credit Suisse.

Ashish Gupta and Prashant Kumar were the two research
analysts who had authored the original report. Other than
crunching numbers, which lead to insights, another essential
part of any analyst's job, working for a stock brokerage based in
Mumbai, is to pick up the soft insider information that keeps going
around all the time. '*Kya lagta hai?*'[**] is a question oft repeated in
these circles.

As Gupta spoke to those who mattered, the executives he met
at various companies were saying that all was not well. As Gupta
puts it: 'I decided I needed to do a deeper dive.'[166] The result of
this deep dive, along with Kumar, was the research report, rather
poetically titled 'House of Debt'. The original report was published
on 2 August 2012.

---

[*]   To be fair, as of March 2019, the bad loans of the State Bank of
       India came down to Rs 1,72,750 crore.

[**]   What do you think?

The basic point that the report made was the *high concentration risk* of Indian banks when it came to the loans they had given. It pointed out that the loans given out by Indian banks had grown at the rate of 20 per cent per year for the last five years. Nevertheless, this increase was driven by lending to a few select corporate groups. The total debt of these ten groups had jumped five times in the five year period up to March 2012. It also amounted to 12.6 per cent of all loans given by these banks. The borrowing concentration of Indian banks was even higher than countries like Russia, Indonesia and Korea.[167]

The ten groups were Adani, Essar, GVK, GMR, Lanco, Vedanta, Reliance ADAG, JSW, Videocon and Jaypee. In March 2007, these groups owed the Indian banking system a total of Rs 99,300 crore, or around 5.7 per cent of the total loans given out by the Indian banking system. In March 2012, the loans had jumped to around Rs 5,39,500 crore.[168]

Of course, there was no problem in companies borrowing from banks; the major issue was whether these companies were in a position to repay the loans they had taken on.

The overall interest coverage ratio of these groups was 1.5. This meant that on the whole they were just about making enough money to be able to pay the interest on the loans. The problem is averages often hide more than they reveal. Some groups like the Adani group and the Vedanta group were well placed, with an interest coverage ratio of 2.5 and 2.8, respectively.

On the other hand, the Videocon group, Essar and GMR were already in trouble, with an interest coverage ratio of 0.3, 0.6 and 0.6, respectively. With an interest coverage ratio of less than one, this meant that the operating profit of these groups was not enough to be able to pay the interest due on the debt they had taken on.[169]

Of course, as we have seen earlier, there was a huge sense of *irrational exuberance* among promoters. New steel projects were being launched on the assumption that the demand for steel would continue growing forever. It seems promoters and analysts did not take the China factor into account. Other than being the world's largest steel producer into account, it was also the world's largest consumer of steel. The assumption was that China would also continue to grow at the breakneck speed that it was. But that didn't turn out to be the case. In the years to come, the Chinese growth would slow down and the country would take to dumping the steel it produced in other parts of the world.

Other than steel mills, there was also the case of power plants. Again, the assumption made here was that the coal imports would continue to remain cheap. This explains why many power plants were built along India's western coast, far away from the eastern part where the main coal mines are – in the states of Odisha, Jharkhand, West Bengal and Chhattisgarh.[170]

The PSBs, while giving loans to corporates, were not looking at the overall debt levels of the group. They were just looking at the overall debt of the particular company within the group they were lending to. Arundhati Bhattacharya admitted as much to the *Financial Times* in 2013, when she said: 'We really weren't monitoring the overall group gearing.'[171] Gearing is another term for leverage or the total amount of debt taken on by a company or a corporate group vis-à-vis the equity it has in its line of businesses.

Not surprisingly, once the 'House of Debt' report was published in August 2012, companies were furious. Companies which had stalled projects claimed that the projects would soon be back on track. The bankers who had been caught with their pants down accused Gupta and Kumar of needlessly exaggerating the scale of the problem.[172] They had become victims of the ostrich syndrome, where they assumed that not dealing with a problem would make it go away.

This also shows the stigma that came with recognizing bad loans. As Rajan said in an August 2015 speech: 'The stigma as well as the provisioning (and the associated fall in profitability) attached to a loan being labelled "non-performing" makes banks eager to avoid the label.'[173]

Gupta and Kumar (along with Kush Shah) weren't done with the 'House of Debt' series. Two more reports were published in August 2013 and October 2015. By March 2015, the total debt of the ten groups mentioned above stood at Rs 7,33,546 crore.

The interest coverage ratio of these groups as a whole stood at 0.8. This meant that taken together they were not making enough money to be able to pay the interest on the debt they had taken on. The situation of the Andhra entrepreneurs had gone from bad to worse, with the interest coverage ratio of the GMR, GVK and Lanco groups standing at 0.2, 0 and 0.2, respectively. The JSW Group was best placed with an interest coverage ratio of 1.9. The Videocon Group was the worst placed, with operating losses of Rs 1,649 crore.[174] To cut a long story short, most of these groups were in a financial mess.

These highly indebted business groups tried to repair their balance sheets by selling assets in order to repay their debts. This didn't help much. In certain cases, the assets that they had to sell were essentially the ones bringing in money for the company in the first place.

In fact, the Credit Suisse analysts put out an update on the debt situation of the ten groups in February 2017. As of 31 December 2016, the interest coverage ratio of eight out of these ten companies (the calculation did not take the GMR group and the GVK group into account because their consolidated numbers were not available) was 0.9 – again not enough as a whole to be covering the interest on their outstanding debt.[175]

In another update put out in February 2019, the interest coverage ratio of the ten groups had improved slightly to 1.1. But if we considered only eight of these companies (and left out JSW Steel and Vedanta), the interest coverage ratio was 0.6.[176] Hence, most of the 'House of Debt' companies continued to remain in a bad state.

What the 'House of Debt' reports told us was that the Indian bad loans problem was largely a problem of large Indian corporates.

In fact, as of September 2018, there were 568 borrowers who had bad loans of Rs 6,28,560 crore. Of this, ninety-five borrowers had bad loans of more than Rs 1,000 crore each, which totalled up to Rs 5,57,110 crore.[177]

A May 2019 study carried out by the well-respected business newspaper *Business Standard* took the top 1,000 companies by market capitalization into account. After leaving out banks and other financial firms, the sample had 964 companies left. Of these 964 companies, the interest payments on outstanding debt for 217 companies exceeded their operating profit from April to December 2018. This meant that these companies were not making enough money to be able to pay the interest due on their debt. The interesting thing is that these companies accounted for 29 per cent of all corporate borrowings among listed companies as of March 2014.[178]

In fact, the Economic Survey of 2016–17 called this situation a twin deficit, where both banks which had lent to companies and companies which had borrowed from banks were in a mess. As the survey pointed out: 'Typically, countries with a twin balance sheet (TBS) problem follow a standard path. Their corporations over-expand during a boom, leaving them with obligations that they can't repay. So, they default on their debts, leaving bank balance sheets impaired, as well. This combination then proves devastating for growth, since the hobbled corporations are reluctant to invest, while those that remain sound can't invest much either, since fragile banks are not really in a position to lend to them.'[179]

On a broader note, it's also worth mentioning here that the owners of a company no longer in a position to continue paying interest on its debt have no real incentive in acting in the best interests of the company. This is a point that the Nobel prize winning economists George Akerlof and Robert Shiller make in their book, *Phishing for Phools: The Economics of Manipulation and Deception.*

As they write: 'If the owners of a solvent firm pay themselves a dollar out of the firm, they diminish the amount they can distribute to themselves tomorrow by that dollar plus its earnings.'[180] Hence, owners of a solvent firm have some incentive to not take out money from it. But that is not the case with the owners of an insolvent (or bankrupt) firm.

The economists continue: 'In contrast, if the owners of a bankrupt firm take an extra dollar out of their firm, they will sacrifice literally nothing tomorrow.'[181] And why is that? 'Because the bankrupt firm is already exhausting all of its assets paying all those Peters and Pauls. Since there will be no leftovers for the owners, they have the same economic incentives as Genghis Khan's army as it marched across Asia: *what they do not take today, they will never see tomorrow* [emphasis added].'[182]

The Genghis Khan comment might be a little bit of an exaggeration in the modern sense of the term, but unless there is a threat of their company being taken away from them, the Indian business promoter has no real interest in cooperating with the bank to ensure that it recovers a good portion of its loan. Of course, as we shall see, things started to change once the government put the Insolvency and Bankruptcy Code, 2016, in place.

15

The RBI Crackdown: Rajan and His Men

We have clearly seen that the PSBs were reluctant to recognize their bad loans. One was the stigma attached to recognizing a loan as a bad loan. But there were other incentives at work as well. When a bank fears losing its deposit base or has to face the wrath of its shareholders, it's likely to recognize bad loans in a timely manner.[183] But that hasn't been the case with India's PSBs.

The fact that the PSBs are owned by the government has essentially ensured that depositors and other creditors of these banks have not lost confidence in them and pulled out their money. The depositor has seen in the past that whenever a bank (New Bank of India and the Global Trust Bank come to mind here) has got into trouble, a merger with a bigger and more stable bank has been organized by the RBI. In this situation, the belief is that in the future if any of the current PSBs is in a bad situation, it will be suitably rescued (like when LIC took over IDBI Bank). This is an unintended consequence of the nationalization of banks in 1969 and 1980.

Take a look at Figure 15.1, which plots the total deposits with PSBs over the years.

Figure 15.1

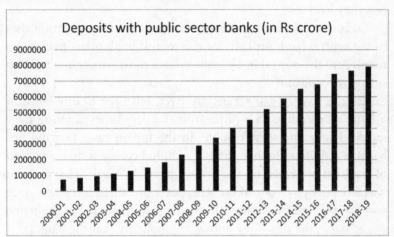

Source: Reserve Bank of India.

The total deposits of PSBs have gone up over the years. They were at Rs 23.2 lakh crore in 2007–08 and have since jumped to Rs 76.5 lakh crore as of 2017–18. This, despite the fact that the bad loans of the PSBs have gone through the roof during this period.

Of course, depositors invest money in the form of deposits for a certain period of time. In order to redeem deposits, it's important that loans given by the bank continue getting repaid.

If a good chunk of the loans given by the bank is not repaid, then its ability to redeem deposits in full goes down. Of course, the depositors are not going to wait for this situation to arise. They will start withdrawing their money as soon as they figure out that a bank is in danger.

If more than a few depositors turn up at different branches of a bank wanting their deposits back, it leads to what is called as a bank run. And any sustained bank run can bring the best banks down. Why is that the case? All banking works on the assumption that all or a large number of depositors will not turn up at the bank at the same time wanting their deposits back. Hence, banks only have a very small portion of the deposits lying with them; the rest they lend out.

Of course, in this day and age, any bank in such a situation goes to the central bank for help (or the central bank offers help on its own). And the central bank lends money to the struggling bank to satisfy its depositors.

So, the days of bank runs are over, but even a semblance of a bank run leading to a portion of the depositors wanting their money back can create trouble. In the Indian case, that did not happen – despite the bad loans – simply because a major section of banking is owned by the government. As Viral Acharya, who was a deputy governor of the RBI, put it in a 2016 interview, once you have the name of the country 'or a state's name in the name of the bank, the depositor knows … implicitly that the bank is … very safe'.[184]

This belief, among other things, led to banks not cleaning up their bad loans. As of March 2015, the bad loans of PSBs stood at Rs 2,78,468 crore. This clearly did not reflect the total amount of actual bad loans in the system.

Meanwhile, Raghuram G. Rajan had taken over as the governor of the RBI in September 2013. It was only towards late 2014 that he started talking about the fact that banks were not recognizing bad loans and how the corporates had taken the banks for a ride.

Rajan had at his disposal a small army of RBI inspectors. He asked these inspectors to look very carefully at the books of PSBs. The idea was to figure out how big the bad money hole was. The findings revealed a distressing picture of the state of Indian banks.

Many big loans were officially in good shape, but in reality had gone bad, with very slim chances of being repaid. At the same time, many industrial projects for which debt had been taken and which officially were supposed to be in good shape, actually weren't. The debt taken for these projects was never likely to be repaid. As Rajan admitted: 'I got a sense that the numbers were hiding a darker problem.'[185]

The banks had taken recourse to the various restructuring schemes that were on offer.

If the banks recognized the bad loans on time, they would have to make provisions for it, i.e., set aside money to meet these losses. Once they did that, their profit would come down.

Given this, and the fact that the 'banker horizon [was] excessively short until end of the CEO's term',[186] no one wanted to get into the messy bit of recognizing bad loans. Also, the restructured loans were exempted from provisioning. This also had incentivized restructuring, rather than recognizing bad loans as bad loans.

All this came to an end once the RBI launched the innocuously titled Asset Quality Review in July 2015. This involved RBI inspectors working with banks and going through their books and identified loans 'that were of concern, as well as loans that had potential weaknesses'.[187]

The dirt that came out of this exercise was huge. As Rajan put it: 'It was at least two or three times what I expected.'[188]

This can clearly be seen in the bad loans number of PSBs. As mentioned earlier, it was at Rs 2,78,468 crore as of March 2015. It jumped to Rs 8,95,601 crore as of March 2018. For banks as a whole, the bad loans had jumped from Rs 3,22,926 crore as of March 2015 to Rs 10,36,187 crore as of March 2018. The total amount of bad money in the system crossed Rs 10 lakh crore.

The first step towards solving a problem is recognizing that it exists. By forcing an Asset Quality Review on PSBs, the RBI did precisely that. With the benefit of hindsight, it can clearly be said that this exercise should have been initiated at least three to four years earlier. But the thing is that until Rajan took over, the RBI did not seem to understand the gravity of the situation, or perhaps it simply ignored it.

There is a simple reason why recognizing a bad loan on time makes sense. It's good accounting. Bad loans usually remain on the balance sheet of a bank for four years. After that, they are recognized as a loss asset and written-off, (We shall deal with this in detail in Chapter 17.)

A bad loan remains a substandard asset for a year and a doubtful asset for three years. As the number of years of a bad loan increases, the provisioning carried out against the bad loan keeps increasing as well. By the end of four years, a 100 per cent provisioning has been made against the bad loan. Hence, the bank has set aside enough money over a period of four years to write-off the bad loan.

Now take a situation where a bank has Rs 1,000 crore of outstanding loans from a corporate. The corporate stops paying interest on the loan and it is then categorized as a bad loan. In the first year, when the bad loan is a substandard asset, Rs 150 crore (or 15 per cent of the outstanding loan amount) will be provisioned against the loan. If it continues to remain unrecovered in the second year, it will become a doubtful asset. Between the start of the second year and the end of the fourth, another Rs 850 crore will be provisioned against the loan. At the end of the fourth year, the bank would have set aside Rs 1,000 crore to set off the losses against the loan.

If at the end of the fourth year too the loan remains unpaid, then the bank has set aside enough money to face losses on the loan, categorize it as a loss asset and write it off.

Now imagine a situation where a bank postpones the recognition of the same Rs 1,000 crore loan as a bad loan. One fine day, after the RBI crackdown, the bank will have to recognize Rs 1,000 crore as a loss asset and write-off 100 per cent of the loan. In this situation, the bank wouldn't have set aside Rs 1,000 crore as a provision against this loan. This Rs 1,000-crore loss would have to be recognized against the most recent profit or, if the bank is not making any profit, against the bank's capital. In the earlier case, the provisioning happened gradually over a period of time. Here it happens all at once and, hence, hurt the bank more.

Other than being bad accounting, it shows that the bank was not prepared, which isn't good in a business as sensitive as banking. As Rajan put it: 'We can postpone the day of reckoning with regulatory forbearance. But unless conditions in the industry improve suddenly and dramatically, the bank balance sheets present a distorted picture of health, and the eventual hole becomes bigger.'[189] This is how things played out in case of Indian PSBs.

Therefore, recognizing a bad loan as a bad loan on time is about doing the right thing and, in the process, preventing the problem from becoming bigger in the future.

PSBs did not recognize bad loans on time; hence, their provisioning went up big time as they went through the RBI's Asset Quality Review. Take a look at Table 15.1; it lists out the provisioning carried out and the losses incurred by PSBs between 2015–16 and 2018–19.

Table 15.1: Bleeding Public Sector Banks.

Year	Provisions and Contingencies (in Rs crore)	Losses (in Rs crore)
2015–16	1,52,930	(17,992)
2016–17	1,70,410	(11,388)
2017–18	2,40,956	(85,371)
2018–19	2,35,580	(81,724)

Source: Indian Banks' Association and the investor presentation of IDBI Bank.

In total, PSBs have set aside Rs 7,99,876 crore for provisioning, between April 2015 and March 2019, thanks primarily to the Asset Quality Review. The trouble was that a good chunk of the restructured loans had already gone bad, and the banks were merely extending and pretending. Not surprisingly, an estimate made by CRISIL ratings suggested that around '40 per cent of [the] assets restructured during 2011-14 [had] slipped into NPAs'.[190]

In a research note published in June 2015, analysts at Morgan Stanley pointed out: 'The current managements' policy of "extend and pretend" is causing banks to move further into problems.'[191] The analysts also said that they expected 65 per cent of the restructured loans to turn into bad loans.

That is precisely what happened. The Asset Quality Review forced PSBs to recognize bad loans as bad loans. And given this, the total amount of restructured loans came down dramatically. By March 2019, the total corporate loans subject to restructuring stood at Rs 1,64,535 crore.

One consequence of this was that as the PSBs recognized bad loans rapidly, their provisions and contingencies went up (as can be seen in Table 15.1). Hence, the losses ate into the capital of these banks. In this scenario, the government – the major owner of these banks – had to recapitalize them, which means it had to invest more money into these banks to keep them going.

In August 2015, a few weeks after the RBI initiated the asset quality review of PSBs, the government initiated the Indradhanush reforms, which was a plan to revamp PSBs. An important part of these reforms was to infuse more capital into these banks. As the Indradhanush document points out: 'The capital requirement of extra capital for the next four years up to 2018–19 is likely to be about Rs 1,80,000 crore.'[192]

Of this, the government planned to pump in Rs 70,000 crore and the remaining Rs 1,10,000 crore, the banks had to raise on their own. Take a look at Table 15.2, which lists the details.

Table 15.2: Indradhanush Bank Recapitalization Plan.

Year	Total amount of money the government planned to invest in PSBs (in Rs crore)
2015–16	25,000
2016–17	25,000
2017–18	10,000
2018–19	10,000

Source: Indradhanush Document, Ministry of Finance.

What is interesting is that the government's estimate of the amount of capital needed by the banks over the next few years turned out to be extremely conservative. Take a look at Table 15.3. It lists out the total money that the government has invested in PSBs over the years to recapitalize them. Between 2015–16 and 2018–19, the government wanted to invest Rs 70,000 crore in PSBs. It ended up investing Rs 2,45,997 crore, which was considerably more than what it had planned for.

Table 15.3: Government Investment in PSBs.

Year	Amount (in Rs crore)
2010–11	6,000
2011–12	12,000
2012–13	12,517
2013–14	14,000
2014–15	6,990
2015–16	25,000
2016–17	24,997
2017–18	90,000
2018–19	1,06,000

Source: www.indiabudget.nic.in.

As the bad loans kept piling up, the PSBs kept provisioning for it. They ultimately reached a stage where they were not making enough profit to keep provisioning the bad loans against their profits.

They had to provision the bad loans against the capital of the bank. The burgeoning amount of bad loans obviously led to a situation where the total amount of provisioning that the banks needed to do against these loans would go up. The provisions would first be made against profits and then against capital. Hence, the total capital of the banks would come down in the process and the PSBs would reach a stage where they wouldn't have had the minimum amount of capital required by the RBI for the banks to continue in business.

Of course, the government couldn't let this happen. And this explains why it invested Rs 1,96,000 crore in banks in 2017–18 and 2018–19. The thing here is that while the PSBs are owned majorly by the government, they are not totally owned by the government. They are listed on the stock market and have public shareholding as well. Given this, they can sell new shares and raise capital to continue being in business. But this formula doesn't work, because selling new shares would lead to the dilution of the government's ownership – something that the Indian government over the years hasn't been comfortable with.

More than that, as the PSBs are in trouble, the private investors are more than likely to stay away from these banks. This is primarily because the feeling is that the moment you give new capital or new money to these banks, they will end up provisioning even more bad loans against this new capital. This means that the government has ended up being the only rescuer of these banks, even though they are listed entities. And this means that what was basically a banking problem morphed into a fiscal problem as well.

16

No Free Lunch

As of 31 March 2019, PSBs had bad loans amounting to Rs 7,89,569 crore (including IDBI Bank, which was recategorized as a private bank as of 21 January 2019, after being taken over by LIC). These banks had a bad loans rate of 12.6 per cent. This, of course, was the average rate across banks. There were banks which were in a much worse situation than the average. Take the case of IDBI Bank, which had a bad loans rate of 27.5 per cent. The bad loans rate of UCO Bank was at 25 per cent.

The other banks with very high bad loans rate at that point of time were Indian Overseas Bank and Central Bank of India, both with a bad loans rate higher than 20 per cent.

As these banks had such a high bad loans rate, they should have been in some trouble when it came to redeeming fixed deposits at their maturity. But nothing of that sort happened. The banks managed to keep repaying their deposits. To keep these banks going, the government, as the major owner of the PSBs, invested fresh money or capital in the banks every year.

Now where did the government get the money to recapitalize PSBs? Between 2013–14 and 18 November 2019, the government spent Rs 3,28,301 crore. Of this around, Rs 1,96,000 crore was spent in a two-year period, 2017–18 and 2018–19. Indeed, that is a lot of money.

The question is where did this money come from? A lot of it was a simple allocation in the yearly budgets which was used to recapitalize the PSBs. Take the years 2016–17 and 2017–18,

115

when the government spent Rs 25,000 crore and Rs 24,997 crore, respectively, from budgetary allocations. It had to actually earn this money through taxes and then use it to recapitalize the banks.

But this changed in October 2017, when the government announced that it would use recapitalization bonds to recapitalize the PSBs. The idea came around a year after the government had demonetized Rs 500 and Rs 1,000 notes, leading to banks sitting on a lot of deposits, which they had been unable to lend.

The government issued bonds which were bought by the PSBs. The government then used this money to invest in the PSBs. Basically, this is how government borrowed the deposits of banks and invested in the banks.

Let's look at the entire idea pointwise:

1) The recapitalization bonds were supposed to have a tenure of 10-15 years and till date have paid anywhere between 7-8 per cent interest to the PSBs buying these bonds. In 2017–18 and 2018–19, the government issued recapitalization bonds worth Rs 80,000 crore and Rs 1,06,000 crore, respectively. Between the announcement in October 2017 and 30 September 2019, the government had issued recapitalization bonds worth Rs 2,50,814 crore. Banks had bought these bonds using their deposits. The government had reinvested this money in the banks and helped them recapitalize. This had kept the banks going.

2) Before October 2017, whatever money the government had invested in the PSBs, came from budgetary allocations. This meant that the government had to earn or borrow this money from somewhere. The money that was used to recapitalize the PSBs could have been used somewhere else, which it was not. Also, higher the amount of money that the government invested in PSBs to recapitalize them, the higher was its expenditure. The higher the expenditure, the higher its fiscal deficit would be.

3) By issuing recapitalization bonds, the government took the problem of the increase in the fiscal deficit, simply out of the equation. This way of recapitalizing government banks was what economists called budget neutral. The government was taking money from banks by issuing bonds and then using that money to recapitalize the banks. Hence, to that extent, it wasn't spending money earned from taxes or borrowing money, to recapitalize the PSBs. And given that, its expenditure wasn't going up because of this. Hence, there was no impact on fiscal deficit at this point of time.

4) Having said that, the government has to pay PSBs buying these bonds, a regular rate of interest. This interest adds to the government expenditure as well as the fiscal deficit. Over and above this, the bonds will have to be repaid, as and when they mature in the years to come. Even this money, will have to come out of the government coffers. Also, the public debt of the government goes up because of this. Someone will have to pick up the tab for this in the years to come.

As Arun Jaitley said in his first budget speech as the finance minister, in July 2014: 'Fiscal prudence to me is of paramount importance because of considerations of inter-generational equity. We cannot leave behind a legacy of debt for our future generations. We cannot go on spending today which would be financed by taxation at a future date.' Clearly, more than Rs 2,50,00 crore has been added to the public debt of the country, thanks to these bonds and this number will only continue to go up in the years to come. In that sense, this is not a free lunch, as it might seem.

5) The last time the government did this was when PSBs faced a bad loan crisis in the 1990s. It sold bonds to PSBs and then used that money to recapitalize them. Back then, the government recapitalized banks to the extent of Rs 20,446 crore between 1985–86 and 2000–01. It issued non-marketable bonds (the banks couldn't sell these bonds). It later converted these

bonds into marketable bonds. Of course, the idea is to help banks come out of the crisis and then flourish in the years to come. In total, the interest that the government paid to the banks on these bonds amounted to Rs 7,888 crore. During the period, the banks paid the government Rs 15,222 crore as dividend.[193] The government is hoping to achieve something similar this time around as well. Whether that happens, only time will tell.

6) Also, recapitalization bonds allow the government to go slow on PSB reform simply because it's not paying for recapitalization from its own pocket. The PSBs are financing their own recapitalization. Given that, the government can continue to go easy on PSB reform. Any PSB reform will hurt the status quo, something that no government wants. The status quo in this case being the 3,89,956 officers, 2,95,380 clerks, and 1,21,647 sub-staff who work for PSBs.[194]

This means that the bad performance of PSBs will continue in the years to come and as we shall see, they will continue to lose share to the private banks. As the Economic Survey of 2019–20 points out: 'In 2019, every rupee of taxpayer money invested in PSBs, on average, lost 23 paise. In contrast, every rupee of investor money invested in "New Private Banks" (NPBs)—banks licensed after India's 1991 liberalization—on average gained 9.6 paise.' Over and above this: 'PSBs account for 85 per cent of reported bank frauds while their gross nonperforming assets (NPAs) equal Rs 7.4 lakh crores which is more than 150 per cent of the total infrastructure spend in 2019.'[195]

This is an excellent example of that old adage: there is no free lunch in economics. Talking about free lunches, we also need to talk about LIC buying IDBI Bank, the junkiest PSB, from the government. LIC completed the acquisition of a 51 per cent stake in the bank in January 2019. How did it help the government?

Up until then, in order to keep the bank going the government had to constantly make fresh investments in it every year. Between 2015–16 and 2017–18, the government invested a total of Rs 16,600 crore as fresh capital in the bank. In fact, Rs 12,471 crore was invested just in 2017–18. This meant that the money that the government was spending on the bank couldn't be spent somewhere else.

Now, with the change of ownership, this is LIC's headache. As of March 2019, IDBI Bank had bad loans worth Rs 50,028 crore. The bad loans rate was 27.5 per cent. This means that the bank would continue to need fresh capital to survive. Six months after LIC's acquisition of IDBI Bank, the market capitalization of IDBI Bank had fallen by more than half.[196]

It's worth remembering here that LIC, unlike the government, has no money of its own. It only has the money that it collects as premium from policyholders every year by selling life insurance policies. This is not the government's money. It's the money that the average Indian has handed over to LIC because he or she trusts the organization of doing a good job of managing it by investing it in the safest possible way. By investing in IDBI Bank, LIC essentially abused the faith that the average Indian has in it. Of course, this is not the first time something like this has happened. In the past, LIC has been used to rescue the initial public offerings as well as further public offerings of those public sector enterprises the stock market wasn't interested in.

Another point that needs to be made here is that once one junk bank has been sold to LIC, what is the guarantee that this is where it will stop? Obviously, individuals who buy LIC policies will have to pay for this and other such disastrous decisions in the form of lower returns. There has been a lot of talk about how every LIC policy comes with a sovereign guarantee. But the guarantee is on the capital and not on the returns. Also, if the situation does arise, it's worth asking how will the government fulfil the sovereign guarantee? Either by printing money or by borrowing more; and both come with costs attached to it. So, a sovereign guarantee doesn't mean much if it has to be encashed.

When it comes to 'no free lunches', another point needs to be made here. The PSBs responded to the bad loan stress in another way. They increased their interest margins. This means that the difference between the interest they charged on their loans and the interest that they paid on their deposits has gone up.

As the Economic Survey of 2016–17 points out: 'For example, December 2016, the gap between the average term deposit rate [interest rate paid on borrowing] and the average base rate [interest rate charged on lending] had grown to 2.7 percentage points, from 1.6 percentage points in January 2015.' In fact, the difference was at 3.24 per cent as of October 2019. (See Chapter 30 for details.) What this really meant was that the borrowers who continued to repay their loans had to pay a higher rate of interest. In that sense, they had to also pay for those who were defaulting, which again brings us back to the point about there being no free lunch in economics.

This is a point that Rajan made in a speech in November 2014 at the Institute of Rural Management in Anand: 'The promoter who misuses the system ensures that banks then charge a premium for business loans. The average interest rate on loans to the power sector today is 13.7 per cent, even while the policy [repo] rate is 8 per cent. The difference, also known as the credit risk premium, of 5.7 per cent is largely compensation banks demand for the risk of default and non-payment. Since the unscrupulous promoter hides among the scrupulous ones, every businessperson is tainted by the bad eggs in the basket. Even comparing the rate on the power sector loan with the average rate available on the home loan of 10.7 per cent, it's obvious that even good power sector firms are paying much more than the average household because of bank worries about whether they will recover loans.'[197]

One point that comes out clearly is that the banks trust an individual taking on a home loan to repay the amount far more than they trust a power company. What does this really mean? It means that in case of a home loan default, the bank has the confidence of seizing the asset (the home against which the loan has been given) and selling it to recover the amount. It does not have the same confidence when it comes to power companies and, hence, the higher rate of interest.

* * *

One of the sectors which actually came under a lot of pressure due to the changing economic scenario both globally and within the country was the iron and steel sector. The PSBs, having lent to companies operating in this sector, also had to face the pain. As of 31 March 2016, the total stressed loans of the total loans given to the sector stood at 53.2 per cent. This meant that a little over half the loans lent by PSBs to the iron and steel sector had either gone bad or had been restructured. This figure jumped to 60 per cent as of March 2017.[198] If we just look at the overall bad loans of the sector, they stood at Rs 1,65,661 crore as of March 2017.[199]

This primarily was on account of a massive overcapacity in the sector. Steel is a very important element of increasing industrialization. The global demand for steel had stood at just 200 million tonnes in 1976. By 2015, it had grown to 1,000 million tonnes. Of this, a bulk of the demand came between 2000 and 2008, increasing at the rate of 9 per cent per year, effectively doubling during the period.[200] This was primarily on account of the fast rise of China and the country's unending demand for steel.

The Indian promoters assumed that this unending demand would continue forever and started setting up new factories. Take a look at Figure 16.1; it plots the total production and consumption of finished steel in India over the years.

Figure 16.1

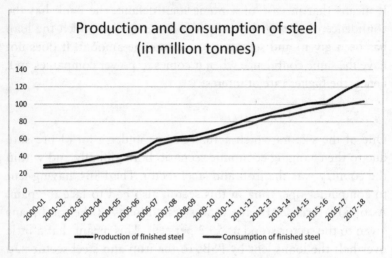

Source: Centre for Monitoring Indian Economy.

As can be seen, the gap between the two curves (production and consumption; basically supply and demand) has been increasing over the years. This means that as a nation India has been producing more steel than it consumes. This is primarily because between 1999–2000 and 2007–08, when the production increased at the rate of 10.7 per cent per year, faster than the global average of around 9 per cent.

The demand for steel in China peaked in 2013 and then went down by 3.3 per cent in 2014. A further decline was experienced in 2015, primarily on account of a slowdown in construction as well as a drop in overall infrastructure requirements. A part of the demand fall from the infrastructure sector was made up for by an increase in demand for steel used in automotive manufacturing. Nevertheless, China ended up with a steel overcapacity of 400–450 million tonnes, which was more than the total steel that India was producing at that point of time, or still produces for that matter. A similar overcapacity was estimated in Japan and South Korea.[201]

This created a problem for Indian steel manufacturers. China started dumping steel into the Indian market. And given the cheaper price, it made sense for Indian companies consuming steel to buy Chinese steel. Take a look at Figure 16.2, which plots the monthly import of steel from China over the years.

Figure 16.2

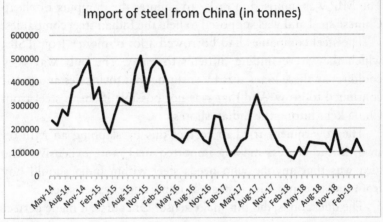

Source: Centre for Monitoring Indian Economy.

Figure 16.2 shows that the import of steel from China into India jumped up majorly in 2014 and 2015, until it started to fall. A major reason for this was the Chinese dumping steel at a lower price. The price of Chinese imports to India fell to as low as $442 per tonne on an average in March 2016, against $825.9 per tonne on an average in May 2014.

This falling price became a worry for Indian domestic producers, especially those who had taken on debt from PSBs to start new steel factories. If this dumping had continued, it would have made sense for Indian steel consumers to buy steel directly from China. This would have meant that the demand for Indian steel would have collapsed and Indian steel manufacturers would have found themselves in an even bigger hole. And this would have meant more bad loans for PSBs and more good money would have turned bad.

Of course, the government couldn't be seen sitting around doing nothing. It had to act and that's exactly what it did.

On 5 February 2016, the Directorate General of Foreign Trade imposed a minimum import price (MIP) on 173 steel products. The prices ranged from $352 per tonne to $752 per tonne of steel. The MIP was imposed in order to counter the dumping of cheap Chinese steel and was supposed to help the Indian steel companies.

The steel companies had borrowed a lot of money from PSBs, which they were finding difficult to repay. The only way they could repay these loans was by ensuring that their sales and profit continued to grow. And that was not possible if cheap steel from China kept hitting the Indian shores.

The government tried to correct this by slapping an MIP on steel, in the process making imported steel more expensive. The idea was that anyone who needs steel within India should buy from Indian companies instead of importing cheaper steel.

The question is, did this make sense? Of course, it made perfect sense for the steel companies. But not for the overall Indian economy.

When we are analysing economic issues, we tend to look at the seen effects while ignoring the unseen effects. In the case of MIP being fixed on steel imports, it means looking only at the benefits that this would bring to the Indian steel companies (the seen effect) and not looking at the harm it would cause to the consumers of steel (the unseen effect).

Not surprisingly, stock analysts had labelled this move of the government as a 'game changer' for the steel companies.

As Henry Hazlitt writes in *Economics in One Lesson*: 'The tariff has been described as a means of benefiting the producer at the expense of the consumer. In a sense this is correct. Those who favour it only think of the interests of the producers immediately benefited by the particular duties involved. They forget the interests of the consumers who are immediately injured by being forced to pay these duties.'[202]

A tariff is essentially a tax or a duty that is paid on imports. In the case of the MIP on steel imports, no duty was fixed and no tax had to be paid. The MIP would force consumers of steel to buy the product at a higher price from Indian steel companies; it meant that the companies were being forced to pay more than they would have if this move had not been made. Hence, to that extent, even an MIP is basically a tariff.

Steel is an input in many different sectors, from automobiles to real estate to engineering to construction and infrastructure. Thus, when the price of steel goes up, companies operating in these sectors need to pay more while buying it. And this in turn impacts the prices of the consumer goods that these companies produce and the physical infrastructure that they create. This was the unseen negative of imposing an MIP on steel imports to ensure that steel companies don't default on their bank loans.

Take the case of the impact it has on engineering goods exports. As T.S. Bhasin, chairman of EEPC India, an engineering goods exporters' body, said at that point of time: 'The MIP will raise the cost of raw materials for engineering products by about 6–10 per cent.'[203] This is another example of how there is no free lunch in economics.

17

The Central Banker Who Knew Too Much

Even as PSBs were busy pushing their bad loans down the road, they also wanted to ensure that they did not end up accumulating more such loans. One way this happened was through write-offs. Another way was with PSBs going slow on lending, in particular to industry.

First, let's take a look at write-offs in detail.

A loan is an asset for a bank. The interest that is paid on it is the income that the asset generates. The loan will keep generating an income as long as the borrower keeps paying the required interest on it. If the payment of interest on the loan, or the part-repayment of principal of the loan, is overdue for more than ninety days, it becomes a bad loan.

The non-performing assets or bad loans of banks are essentially categorized as substandard assets, doubtful assets and loss assets. Let's take a look at each of these kinds of bad loans:

1) Substandard assets: These are bad loans which have remained bad loans for a period of less than or equal to twelve months. A key feature of this category of bad loans is that the bank will suffer some loss and will not be able to recover 100 per cent of the loan. Hence, it needs to set aside some money from its accumulated profits or capital as a provision to compensate for a probable loss. Given this, a provision of 15 per cent of the loans categorized as substandard assets needs to be made.

2) Doubtful assets: Bad loans which have remained in the substandard category for a period of twelve months are categorized as doubtful assets. A key feature of this category of bad loan is that on the basis of currently known facts, conditions and values, the bank's chances of recovering such a loan are highly questionable and improbable. But there is still some chance of doing so, at least in the initial years.

The banks need to set aside more money in this case – than they need to do in case of substandard assets – for the possibility of non-recovery of loans. For doubtful assets of up to one year, a provision of 25 per cent of the loans categorized as doubtful assets needs to be made. Between the first and third year, a provision of 40 per cent of the loans categorized as doubtful assets needs to be made. For a period of more than three years, a doubtful asset can be categorized as a loss asset and a 100 per cent provision needs to be made.

3) Loss assets: These are assets where there is almost no hope or very little hope of recovery. Such bad loans need to be written off, which means that they need to be dropped from the balance sheet of the bank. Of course, before doing this, a 100 per cent provision needs to be made for these bad loans. Basically, loans which have been bad loans for four years (a year as a substandard asset and three years as a doubtful asset) can be dropped from the balance sheet of banks by way of a write-off. In that sense, a write-off is an accounting practise.

Also, this does not mean that a bank has to wait for four years before it can write off a loan. If it feels that a particular loan is unrecoverable, it can be written off before four years.

So, does that mean that once a loan is written off it's gone forever and is no longer recoverable? In India things work a little differently. In fact, almost all the bad loans written off are technical write-offs. The RBI defines technical write-offs as bad loans which have been written off at the head office level of the bank, but remain as bad loans on the books of branches and, hence, recovery efforts continue at the branch level. If a bad loan which was technically written off is partly or fully recovered, the amount is declared as the other income of the bank.[204]

Another advantage of a technical write-off for a public sector banker is that no one can ever directly accuse him of just writing off a loan. As long as the loan is a technical write-off, by its very definition it means that the bank will continue to make efforts to recover the money. Now whether banks do that to their best possible extent, as we shall see, is rather debatable.

We need to take a look at the total amount of bad loans written off by the PSBs during the course of a year and the total amount of loans previously written off that were recovered during the same year. Take a look at Figure 17.1, which plots this between the years 2000–01 and 2012–13.

Figure 17.1

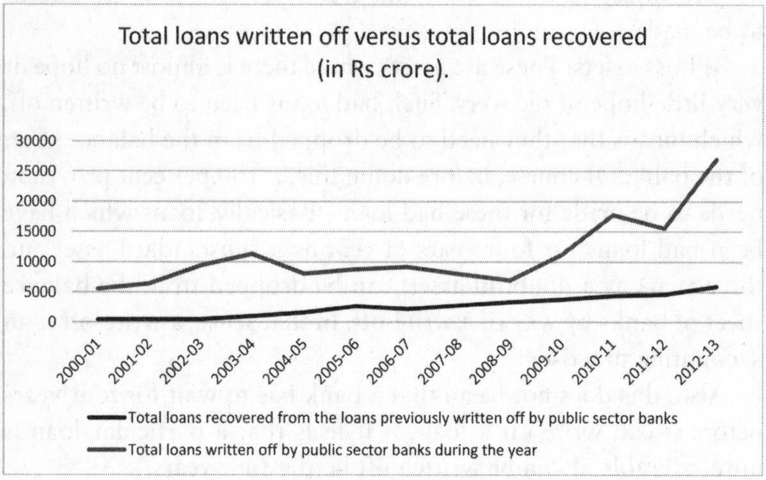

Total loans written off versus total loans recovered (in Rs crore).

━━━ Total loans recovered from the loans previously written off by public sector banks
━━━ Total loans written off by public sector banks during the year

Source: 'Two decades of credit management in banks: Looking back and moving ahead' (Address by Dr K.C. Chakrabarty, deputy governor, Reserve Bank of India, at BANCON 2013, 18 November 2013).

We can see from Figure 17.1 that while the total loans written off by PSBs have kept moving upwards, over the years, the total recovery from loans written off previously has barely moved. Between 2000–01 and 2012–13, PSBs recovered around 23.4 per cent of what they wrote off.

Dr K.C. Chakrabarty, who was a deputy governor at RBI then, came out against this very strongly in November 2013, when he said the poor recovery of loans written off was 'a clear sign of poor standards of credit and recovery administration, as well as a certain amount of apathy on the part of banks in expending efforts to revive accounts'. He further said that write-offs have 'emerged as a tool for banks to manage their reported gross NPA numbers'. This meant that without this *accounting eventuality* being available to PSBs, where bad loans were written off after four years, their bad loans would have grown even bigger than they eventually did.

How have things been since November 2013? Between April 2014 and March 2018, the total loans written off by PSBs stood at Rs 3,16,515 crore. Of this, around Rs 44,900 crore of loans previously written off, or around 14 per cent, has been recovered.[205] Hence, in the recent years, the rate of recovery of the loans written off has been even more disappointing than was the case in the past.

While a write-off is not a loan waiver, the data does show very clearly that it more or less functions like one. Also, there is an essential contradiction at the heart of it all. For a write-off to happen, a loan must be deemed as unrecoverable and, hence, dropped from the balance sheet of a bank. But in India we have the facility of technical write-offs, where a bad loan is written off over a period of time, but still can be recovered.

The RBI has mandated that 'banks should disclose full details of write-offs, including separate details about technical write-offs in their annual financial statements'.[206] But beyond this, there is nothing more a bank needs to do when it comes to disclosing information regarding its write-offs. Hence, there is a great opaqueness in how banks handle their technical write-offs.

Also, given the fact that the banks are not able to recover much of what they write off, the question is then why is the RBI encouraging such an opaque system? Given that the PSBs are ultimately owned by the public (i.e., the people of India), more information regarding write-offs and their recovery, should be freely available in the public domain.

In the past, whenever the RBI has been asked about specific bad loan details, it has cited the provisions of Section 45E of the Reserve Bank of India Act, 1934, wherein the RBI is prohibited from disclosing credit information. As per the section, the loan information submitted by different banks to the RBI shall be treated as confidential and is not to be published or otherwise disclosed.

** *

In the last section, we saw what proportion of written-off loans is recovered by banks. Now we will see the total amount of recovered loans through various mechanisms, like Lok Adalats, the Debt Recovery Tribunals, the SARFAESI Act and the Insolvency and Bankruptcy Code.

Table 17.1: Rate of Recovery of Bad Loans.

	Amount recovered (in Rs crore)	Total bad loans (in Rs crore)	Rate of recovery
2012–13	23,300	1,93,200	12.1%
2013–14	32,000	2,63,021	12.2%
2014–15	30,800	3,22,926	9.5%
2015–16	22,800	6,11,609	3.7%
2016–17	38,500	7,91,995	4.9%
2017–18	40,352	10,36,187	3.9%
2018-19	1,26,085	9,36,474	13.5%

Source: Report on Trend and Progress of Banking in India.

In 2012–13, the total amount of loans recovered by banks through various mechanisms stood at Rs 23,300 crore. The Rs 23,300 crore worth of recovered loans included loans which had been written off and, hence, were no longer a part of the overall bad loans number. The recovered loans also included bad loans which the borrower was no longer repaying, but which hadn't been written off up until then.

If we look at the rate of recovery (which is the recovered loans divided by the total bad loans of the banking system), we see that it was going down for many years. In 2012–13, the rate of recovery had stood at 12.1 per cent. By 2017–18, it had fallen dramatically to 3.9 per cent. In 2018–19, the rate of recovery improved to 13.5 per cent, thanks to a slightly better recovery under the Insolvency and Bankruptcy Code (as we shall see in Chapter 26).

The more loans banks are able to recover, the less capital the government needs to invest to recapitalize them. But even with a rate of recovery of 13.5 per cent, it seems that the government in the years to come, will have to invest more money into the PSBs than it has probably bargained for.

18

Privatization by Malign Neglect

Over the years, politicians in India have referred to public sector enterprises as 'family jewels'. This has often been offered as an excuse to not sell public sector enterprises, which includes banks.

As any family in possession of heirlooms will tell you, these jewels need to be handled with care. But that doesn't seem to have happened in India. Excellent examples of this are the telecom and airline sectors. Both sectors were dominated by public sector enterprises at one point of time. As the government opened up the economy, it refused to privatize the companies operating in these sectors. Over the years, private companies began dominating these sectors. So while the government did not privatize the companies it owned, the sectors got privatized on their own. This has been referred to as privatization by stealth. Something similar is playing out in the banking sector now. Private banks are gradually taking over a larger segment of the banking business in India.

As mentioned earlier, one of the ways PSBs prevented further accumulation of bad loans was by going slow on lending. The RBI also put many banks under the Prompt Corrective Action Framework (which we shall discuss in Chapter 24) and in the process slowed down the overall lending by PSBs.

As of 31 March 2019, the total outstanding deposits in the Indian banking system amounted to Rs 125.6 lakh crore. PSBs had 63.1 per cent of these deposits. On the other hand, the private sector banks had around 28.7 per cent of these deposits. So PSBs continue to have the most deposits among the different kinds of banks operating in India. Nevertheless, they have lost market share over the years. As on 31 March 2011, when the total deposits in the Indian banking system amounted to Rs 53.9 lakh crore, the PSBs had a share of 74.6 per cent in it. The private sector banks had a share of a little over 18 per cent. Clearly, private banks have gained at the cost of PSBs over the years.

A similar story has played out in case of loans as well. As of 31 March 2019, the total loans given out by Indian banks had stood at Rs 98.2 lakh crore. Of this, the PSBs had a dominant market share of 58.8 per cent. The private banks, on the other hand, had 33.6 per cent of the overall market share of bank loans. Of course, the situation a few years back was very different. On 31 March 2011 the total loans of the Indian banking system amounted to Rs 40.8 lakh crore. In this, the PSBs had a share of 74.9 per cent. The private sector share was around 17.8 per cent. This tells us that private banks have done a lot of catching up with their public sector counterparts over the last few years.

When it comes to overall deposits and loans in the Indian banking system, the private sector banks have rapidly gained market share. But this still doesn't tell us how bad the situation has been in case of PSBs in the same timeline.

In 2018–19, private banks raised Rs 7.1 lakh crore worth of deposits. PSBs raised just Rs 2.7 lakh crore. In 2010–11, PSBs had raised deposits worth Rs 6.4 lakh crore; private banks had raised deposits worth Rs 1.7 lakh crore during the year. Take a look at Figure 18.1.

Figure 18.1

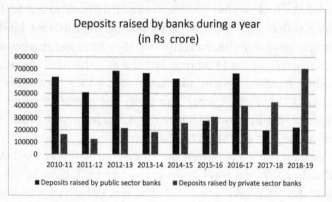

Source: Reserve Bank of India.

Between 2015–16 and 2018–19, in three out of the four years, private banks raised more deposits than PSBs. The difference was the largest in 2018–19.

On the loans front, in 2018–19, private banks gave out total loans of Rs 7.4 lakh crore. PSBs gave loans worth just Rs 3 lakh crore. If we compare this to 2010–11, PSBs had given loans worth Rs 5.4 lakh crore. Private banks had given loans worth Rs 1.4 lakh crore. Take a look at Figure 18.2.

Figure 18.2

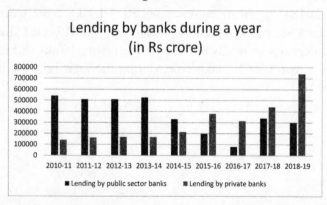

Source: Reserve Bank of India.

What this tells us is that the privatization of the banking sector is well and truly on. Ruchir Sharma, the head of Global Macro at Morgan Stanley, calls this phenomenon, *privatization by malign neglect*. As he writes in *The Rise and Fall of Nations*: 'India ... has adopted a de facto policy of what I can only describe as *privatization by malign neglect* [emphasis added]. The political class can't bring itself to sell off the old state companies, or to reform them either. Instead, it simply watches as private companies slowly drive the state behemoths into irrelevance.'[207]

The interesting thing here is that even though the overall lending of PSBs came down, the lending to the retail sector (housing loans, vehicle loans, credit cards, etc.) remained strong. It was only the lending to the industry which contracted big time, and this was perhaps understandable. This was happening from early 2014 onwards because of defaults on loans given to industry.

Another point that has been made is that the lack of capital has held back PSBs from lending. Is that right? Let's take a look at Figure 18.3. This plots the growth in total outstanding retail loans of PSBs and private banks over the years.

Figure 18.3

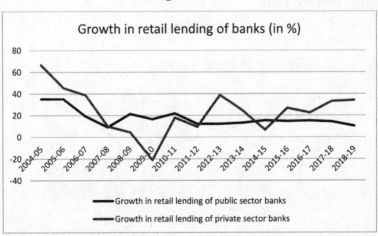

Source: Reserve Bank of India.

As can be seen from Figure 18.3, the total outstanding retail loans of PSBs have grown at around 12–15 per cent over the last few years at a very stable rate. Of course, the outstanding retail loans of private sector banks have grown faster than that of PSBs. One reason for this is that their base is lower. As of 31 March 2018, the outstanding retail loans of PSBs had stood at Rs 11.4 lakh crore. The outstanding retail loans of private banks stood at Rs 6.5 lakh crore as of the same date. Hence, it's but natural that the outstanding retail loans of PSBs will grow at a slower rate, given the higher base. But that does not explain the entire situation. In 2017–18, the PSBs gave out retail loans worth Rs 1.4 lakh crore. The private banks did much better by giving out retail loans worth Rs 1.6 lakh crore. Many PSBs had been put under the prompt corrective action framework by the RBI. Under this framework, limitations were placed on the lending as well as deposit raising of PSBs. In 2018–19, the PSBs gave retail loans worth Rs 1.2 lakh crore. In comparion, private sector banks did much better by giving out loans worth Rs 2.2 lakh crore and in the process capturing a greater section of the market.

Now let's take a look at Figure 18.4, which plots the growth of total outstanding loans to industry by PSBs as well as private banks over the years.

Figure 18.4

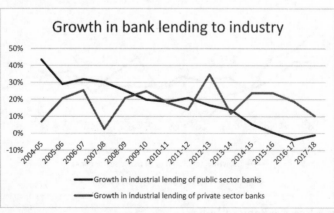

Source: Reserve Bank of India.

This tells us very clearly that the growth in PSBs' lending to industry has been coming down over the years. Between 2016–17 and 2018–19, the lending to industry actually shrunk. This means that the total outstanding loans to industry given by PSBs actually came down.

This fall in lending growth was often been used to conclude that PSBs are not lending because the government isn't infusing enough capital in them. This is not the right conclusion to draw simply because if that was the case, PSBs lending to the retail sector wouldn't be growing at a healthy rate of 10–15 per cent.

This is more a case of PSBs avoiding lending to industry because they were once bitten and twice shy. As the bad loans from industry grew, the less interested PSBs became in lending to industry.

Also, it's worth noting that the growth of private banks lending to the industrial sector has also come down during the recent years. What this tells us is that many corporates in India are heavily leveraged and are not in a position to currently take on new loans. Hence, it makes sense for banks to not give fresh loans to the industrial sector in many cases.

What this also means is that the while the PSBs have managed to hold on to the existing deposits and depositors, the new depositors seem to prefer the private sector banks. The same is true about bank lending that has happened over the last few years.

19

The Big Fish Everyone Wants to Catch

Arvind Subramanian, who was the chief economic adviser of the ministry of finance between October 2014 and June 2018, paraphrases Shakespeare in his book, *Of Counsel: The Challenges of the Modi–Jaitley Economy,* to say that '"something is rotten in this state of Indian banking" for having allowed stigmatized capitalists to survive and thrive for so long'.[208]

While the top brass of the RBI openly talked about big industrialists diverting money from the project they had borrowed money for to other projects, nobody was ever named.

The irony is that even though these things are well known and openly talked about, there is not one estimate available on what proportion of bad loans were because of large industrial borrowers diverting money to line their own pockets in comparison to loans which were genuine defaults.

The only industrialists/businessmen who have been openly named are those who have defaulted/defrauded on their bank loans and escaped from the country. And this list of names is a long one. In an answer to a question raised in the Lok Sabha, the ministry of external affairs, using information provided by the Enforcement Directorate, listed the following people to be involved in financial irregularities, facing criminal investigation and who fled the country or were living abroad: Vijay Mallya, Christian Michel James, Nirav Modi, Mehul Choksi, Ashish Sureshbhai Jobanputra, Priti Ashish Jobanputra, Ramachandran Viswanathan, M.G. Chandrasekhar,

Sanjay Bhandari, Nitin Jayantilal Sandesara, Chetan Jayantilal Sandesara, Dipti Chetan Sandesara, Hiteshkumar Narendrabhai Patel, Deepak Talwar, Deepa Talwar, Sunny Kalra, Aarti Kalra, Sanjay Kalra, Varsha Kalra, Jatin Mehta, Lalit Modi, S. Harpal Singh Dutta, Ritesh Jain, Mugundhan Gangam, Pushpesh Kumar Baid, Nitish J. Thakur, Purvi Modi, Mihir Rashmi Bhansali, Aditya Nanavati, Sunil Varma, Neeshal Deepak Modi, Nehal Modi, Mayank Mehta, Jayesh Indravardan Shah, Deepak Krishna Rao Kulkarni, Deepak Modi, Subhash Shankar Parab, Rajiv Saxena, Rajesh Gajera, Carlo Valentino Fernando Gerosa and Guido Ralph Haschke.[209]

Of course, this is a long list of people. The two famous names here are Nirav Modi and Vijay Mallya. We will talk about their stories here. Let's start with Nirav Modi.

The Punjab National Bank (PNB) filed a complaint with the Criminal Bureau of Investigation (CBI) on 29 January 2018, alleging that Nirav Modi and his co-conspirators had carried out a massive fraud against the bank. Two days later, on 31 January the CBI filed a first information report (FIR), which said that Modi and his co-conspirators had cheated PNB and caused it a wrongful loss.[210] The RBI later revealed that the PNB had reported the fraudulent issuance of a letter of undertaking worth Rs 12,645.97 crore, or around $2 billion.[211]

Nirav Modi started trading diamonds in 1999. In a little over a decade's time, he had entered the branded diamond business. But that is not important here. What is important is for us to understand how Modi scammed a PSB of close to $2 billion. As per the CBI, the scam started in or before 2011.[212]

Let's try and understand how he carried out the scam pointwise.

1) Modi was in the business of importing and exporting diamonds. In order to import diamonds he needed money. For this, he approached the Brady House branch of PNB in Fort, Mumbai, for a loan.

2) This started sometime in 2011. It's very likely that at that of time, the bank would have agreed to give Modi a loan at the rate of around 10 per cent, given the prevailing interest rates. Borrowing at an interest rate of 10 per cent would have made things expensive for Modi. At the same time, he couldn't buy diamonds using Indian rupees. He needed American dollars for it. After borrowing in rupees from an Indian bank, he would have had to convert those rupees into dollars. That would have entailed a cost of conversion as well. Therefore, it made sense for Modi to borrow in dollars. This had two advantages. One, the rate of interest would be much lower on a dollar loan, and, two, he wouldn't have to incur any cost of conversion.

3) The problem was that Modi didn't have a banking relationship with a foreign bank and, hence, a foreign bank wouldn't give him a loan in dollars. But there was a way around this problem. While the foreign bank didn't know Modi, PNB did have a banking relationship with him – in particular, the Brady House branch. So Modi went to the Brady House branch and the bank issued a letter of undertaking to him. Modi took this to a foreign bank, or a foreign branch of an Indian bank, and got the dollar loan. The letter of undertaking was essentially a guarantee offered by the PNB for the loan that Modi had taken on. In case Modi defaulted, PNB promised to repay the dollar loan. This is how it was supposed to work.

The dollar loan didn't go into Modi's bank account. It went into the bank account that PNB maintained with the foreign bank. From this account, the firm from which Modi was importing diamonds was paid off. Let's say Modi was importing diamonds from a firm based in the United States. In this situation, the dollar loan amount would be deposited into the account that PNB maintained with a local American bank. And from this account, the American firm from which Modi was importing diamonds would be paid off.

4) In the normal scheme of things, the moment PNB issued a letter of undertaking, it should have insisted on collateral from

Modi or his firm. But that is something that did not happen. This was primarily because a few employees of the Brady House branch were also involved in the scam. This included the deputy manager Gokulnath Shetty and Manoj Kharat, who happened to be a clerk. Between them, they ensured that the details of the letter of undertaking were not recorded in the Core Banking Solution of the bank. Interestingly, between 2011 and 2017, 1,208 letters of undertaking (as can be seen in Table 19.1) were fraudulently issued by the PNB to Diamonds 'R'Us, Stellar Diamonds and Solar Exports – three firms controlled by Nirav Modi.

Table 19.1: Fraudulent Letters of Undertaking.

Year	Number of letters of undertaking opened fraudulently
2011	43
2012	115
2013	236
2014	123
2015	185
2016	356
2017	150
Total	1,208

Source: Report of John J. Carney, Examiner, United States Bankruptcy Code, Southern District Court of New York, 25 August 2018.

5) It has been established that a part of the money that Modi took on as a loan for importing diamonds from American firms, which were in fact fronts for him, was siphoned off to, in part, fund a fancy apartment in New York, worth $6 million. This was for the sole use of Modi and his family.[213]

In the normal scheme of things, Modi would import diamonds, sell them to his customers, and pay off PNB. In case Modi defaulted on the payment, the bank should have had access to a collateral, which it could then sell and make up for the default. The trouble was that PNB did not have any collateral. Also, it turned out that the firms from which Modi was importing diamonds were also linked to him. The question is how did this scam go on for so long? In very simple terms, the money coming in from the issuance of new letters of undertaking was used to pay off the letters of undertaking which needed to be paid off.

Let's try and understand this through an example. A letter of undertaking was issued in February 2017 to Solar Exports. This was for a loan to import diamonds from Hong Kong. Three firms, Auragems Company Ltd, Sunshine Gems Ltd and Pacific Diamonds FZE, from which diamonds were being imported, had to be paid. It so turned out that these firms were also linked to Modi. Money that was supposed to go to these firms was diverted into four bank accounts at Allahabad Bank and was used to pay off four outstanding letters of undertaking. The first payment of $2.7 million repaid a letter of undertaking dated 11 April 2016. The other payments of $1.4 million, $1.4 million and $1.3 million were used to pay off three letters of undertaking dated 2, 6 and 7 April 2016.[214]

Hence, in the end, Nirav Modi's scam degenerated into a Ponzi scheme, where money being brought in by a new letter of undertaking was used to pay off earlier letters of undertaking.

6) In fact, the round-tripping of diamonds also happened. The same diamonds were bought and sold by firms controlled by Modi in different parts of the world at varying prices. The prices at times would be wildly inflated above the market prices. This was done in order to create the appearance of legitimate transactions and then use that as an excuse to move funds across different parts of the world. Over and above this, there were also instances of firms in the United States controlled by Modi, creating sham transactions of back-office work for firms

controlled by him in other parts of the world. This was also used to move money around.[215]

Of course, by the time the PNB figured out what was happening, it had been robbed of close to $2 billion. Modi had figured out that his Ponzi scheme would be coming to an end soon and conveniently left the country in January 2018. As is often the case, the Indian system reacted after the horse had already bolted, with the CBI and other investigative agencies getting involved. The Enforcement Directorate conducted 247 searches across the country and seized/ attached assets worth Rs 7,638 crore until February 2018. The Income Tax department attached thirty-two immovable properties in the names of Modi, his wife, Amy, and various group concerns. Over and above this, 141 bank accounts and fixed deposits with Rs 145.74 crore in them, along with 173 paintings and artworks, were attached by the Income Tax department.[216] Some of the money that Modi scammed PNB of has been recovered through the sale of paintings and cars owned by him.

It's interesting that despite so many businessmen defrauding banks or defaulting on loans, and then leaving the country, Nirav Modi's name caught the attention of the people. There were multiple reasons for it. First and foremost, the fact that Nirav Modi's surname was the same as the country's prime minister, Narendra Modi, led to his name registering in the minds of people (although there is no relationship between them) more easily than that of others.

Secondly, Modi operated in the glamorous business of selling high-end diamonds. His designs were worn by celebrities like Priyanka Chopra, Amy Adams and Kate Winslet. He also sold his speciality diamonds at well-known auction houses, like Sotheby's and Christie's.[217] This ensured that the media had a lot to talk about him.

After escaping from India, Nirav Modi managed to avoid the authorities for more than a year. The law finally caught up with him in London in March 2019. As of end 2019, he was lodged in

Wandsworth Jail in London, charged with allegations of fraud, money laundering and criminal intimidation of more than six employees to prevent them from cooperating with investigative agencies. It remains to be seen whether he will be extradited back to India and whether he will face the courts here.

The interesting thing is that while the Indian media has managed to keep track of both Vijay Mallya and Nirav Modi, the same cannot be said about the many other Indian businessmen who have escaped the country. The government has given some updates on these businessmen when MPs have asked questions in parliament. But beyond that, there isn't much interest in them.

It's important that along with Mallya and Modi, other businessmen are also extradited back to India. This will go a long way in controlling the bank fraud menace that seems to have grown in the last few years. In fact, as the RBI Master Circular on frauds points out: 'It has been observed that frauds are, at times, detected in banks long after their perpetration. The fraud reports are also submitted to the RBI, many a time, with considerable delay and without the required information. On certain occasions, the RBI comes to know about frauds involving large amounts only through press reports.'[218]

Take a look at Table 19.2, which lists the details of frauds of Rs 1 lakh and above reported by the banks in India.

Table 19.2: Frauds of Rs 1 lakh and Above.

	Total number of frauds	Amount involved in frauds (in Rs crore)	Average fraud amount (in Rs crore)
2015–16	4,693	18,699	3.98
2016–17	5,076	23,934	4.72
2017–18	5,917	41,168	6.96
2018–19	6,801	71,543	10.52

Source: Lok Sabha Unstarred Question No. 918, answered on 14 December 2018 and an RTI filed by the Press Trust of India.

The RBI classifies frauds largely into following categories:

1) Misappropriation and criminal breach of trust;
2) Fraudulent encashment through forged instruments, manipulation of books of account or through fictitious accounts and conversion of property;
3) Cheating and forgery;
4) Irregularities in foreign exchange transactions.

From Table 19.2, it's clear that the number of frauds and the amounts involved in them have also gone up over the years. In 2015–16, the total number of frauds had stood at 4,693. This had jumped to 6,801 by 2018–19. While the total number of frauds had jumped by around 45 per cent, the amount involved had jumped by around 283 per cent, from Rs 18,699 crore to Rs 71,543 crore. Hence, the average size of the fraud had jumped from Rs 3.98 crore in 2015–16 to Rs 10.52 crore in 2018–19.

Of course, it needs to be stated here that Nirav Modi's fraud would have had a disproportionate impact on the average fraud amount in 2017–18 and 2018–19. PNB wrote off the fraud between January and March 2018 and April and June 2018, thereby spreading it across two quarters and two financial years.

What the data clearly tells us is that fraudsters have become bolder over the years. The only possible explanation for this lies in the fact that they have seen others like them get away over the years. As Urjit Patel, who was the RBI governor between September 2016 and December 2018, said in a speech in March 2018: 'Indeed, RBI data on banking frauds suggests that only a handful of cases over the past five years have had closure, and cases of substantive economic significance remain open. As a result, the overall enforcement mechanism – at least until now – is not perceived to be a major deterrent to frauds relative to economic gains from fraud.'[219] And this is something that needs to be set right.

Every small individual fraud being taken to court will help; but what will really help in this case is if Nirav Modi and the other

absconders who have left the country are brought back to India
and face the consequences of defrauding PNB and other banks.

* * *

In a May 2016 interview to the *Financial Times*, a few months
after he had left India, the fugitive businessman Vijay Mallya said:
'I am a small fry ... But I'm the big fish that people want to catch –
that's the trouble.'[220]

Indeed, Mallya wasn't totally wrong about this. In a reply to a
question raised in the Rajya Sabha, the government had said that,
as of 31 December 2016, Mallya owed PSBs Rs 8,191 crore.[221]
Reports in the media constantly put the total amount of loans that
he had defaulted on at greater than Rs 9,000 crore.

When we look at some of the bigger defaulters like Bhushan
Steel, Essar Steel, Alok Industries or, for that matter, even Nirav
Modi's fraud, which cost PNB close to Rs 13,000 crore, Mallya
might seem like a small fry in the overall scheme of things.

Having said that a default of over Rs 9,000 crore isn't exactly
small change either. The question is, at the time of fleeing India on
1 March 2016, how did Mallya reach this stage? For a man who
often travelled light, usually without luggage, he left India, lock,
stock and barrel, carrying six bags.[222]

Vijay Mallya was born to Vittal Mallya and Lalitha Ramaiah.
His father, Vittal Mallya, was a frugal liquor baron and the
chairman of United Breweries Ltd. While Vittal was based out of
Bengaluru, Mallya was raised by his mother in Kolkata. In one of
his early interviews that I remember watching, Mallya nostalgically
talked about travelling on the crowded trams of Kolkata.

Vittal died at the age of fifty-nine in 1983, and a very young
Mallya took over his business interests. The liberalization of 1991
allowed him to rapidly expand his liquor business. By 2001, his
company was selling 26 million cases a year. When he had taken
over from his father, the company used to sell 2.5 million cases
a year.[223] In fact, as the story goes, Mallya even launched the

Kingfisher brand, a defunct colonial-era brand, whose label was buried in the archives of United Breweries.[224]

Vittal Mallya, unlike his very flamboyant son, was a low-key businessman who had bought United Breweries cheaply just after World War II. He gradually expanded his business after Independence by buying out rival breweries.

Vijay Mallya showed a flair for promotion that is father lacked. Ultimately, he became a brand ambassador for his company, with the media following his parties, his holidays, his friends and the very famous Kingfisher calendars, which were shot every year with models wearing bikinis. This sort of made sense given that advertising alcohol is banned in India. Mallya even admitted in later years: 'I did what [Richard] Branson does ... I lived the brand.'[225]

In 2002, Mallya was elected to the Rajya Sabha, after being on friendly terms with Karnataka politician Ramakrishna Hegde. Except for a gap between April 2009 and July 2010, Mallya continued to be a member of the Upper House of Indian parliament until 2 May 2016, when he resigned. This was a day before the Rajya Sabha Ethics Panel was to meet and recommend his expulsion.[226]

Mallya, unlike many other star MPs, did not sleep through his years in parliament. It's said this was the time he built personal contacts across party lines, which helped him expand his businesses over the years.

In 2005, Mallya was ready for bigger challenges and he was also well-connected with India's politicians by then. The alcoholic beverage market in India was doing well, with the sales of whisky and beer expanding by 50 per cent and 49 per cent respectively between 2001 and 2006. Mallya's United Breweries, thanks to the Kingfisher brand, sold more than half of the beer consumed in India. Thanks to the acquisition of Shaw Wallace, his company now had control over half of India's whisky and rum market as well.[227] Of course, as we have seen earlier in the book, there was a general sense of the Indian economy doing very well in those years.

The feeling was that the good times were here to stay. And Mallya was feeling the same way as other industrialists at that time. The media even called him the king of good times.

In the middle of all this, Mallya launched Kingfisher Airlines in May 2005. The Indian aviation sector was just about to take off after being under the clutches of the government for many years. Mallya, unlike the other low-cost operators in the business, wanted to provide people with a five-star experience up in the sky. The travellers (including me) loved the experience. It was a genuinely good airline, which sold tickets at reasonable prices. In fact, by 2008, Kingfisher was carrying around one-fourth of India's domestic flyers.

The trouble was that airlines were, and continue to be, an expensive business. As a line often attributed to Richard Branson, a British businessman, goes: 'If you want to be a millionaire, start with a billion dollars and launch a new airline.' This line actually played out in Mallya's life.

While, Mallya's airline was doing very well domestically, he wanted it to fly abroad. The trouble was that the government had a certain requirement in place to let private airlines fly abroad. It has been often suggested that this requirement was put in place to help Jet Airways, which had started to fly internationally in 2005. As per this requirement, a private airline had to be flying for five years and have a fleet of twenty airplanes in order to be allowed to fly internationally.

If Mallya were to follow this rule, he would have to wait until May 2010 to fulfil the criteria of his airline having been in operation for five years. But he was a man in a hurry. In fact, as early as 2005, just having launched Kingfisher Airlines for domestic operations, he had his international plans in place. At the Paris air show that year, Mallya spent $3 billon buying twelve new Airbus planes, including five giant A380s. This was a clear signal that Mallya wanted Kingfisher to fly internationally.[228]

In 2007, Mallya ordered another fifty Airbus planes, including five A340s, which are economical to fly only over a long distance.[229]

As any Indian businessman who has been in business for a while will tell you, *jugaad** plays a huge role in ensuring that a business grows and continues to be in operation. Mallya also had a *jugaad* in place for going international. In June 2007, United Breweries Holding Ltd bought a 26 per cent stake in Deccan Aviation, which ran India's biggest low-cost airline at that point of time, Air Deccan. Air Deccan had started to fly in 2003 and was just a year away from being able to fly internationally.

In early September 2008, Kingfisher launched a Bengaluru–London direct flight. This was just around the time when the global financial crisis was starting. Air travel took a significant beating in the aftermath of the crisis. In October 2008, just about a month later, Kingfisher decided to stop expanding global operations. It even sold three of its five Airbus A340 planes it had bought for overseas flying to Nigeria's Arik Air.[230]

Airlines were not the only business that Mallya was expanding in. Over the years he had also acquired a whole host of different sports teams. He had bought a 50 per cent stake in the old Kolkata football clubs of Mohun Bagan and East Bengal. He had bought the Dutch Formula One Team, Spyker, spending $110 million to buy it. The team was renamed Force India. He had also bought a cricket team in the newly launched Indian Premier League (IPL) for $111 million and named it the Royal Challengers Bangalore. Along with these sports teams, he had also bought Whyte & Mackay, the world's fourth-largest producer of Scotch, spending $595 million on the transaction.[231]

The point is that Mallya, the king of good times, like many other industrialists around him, genuinely believed that the good times would continue forever. Given this, he expanded like never before. All this expansion needed a lot of money, which he was borrowing from banks; in particular, from PSBs.

The financial crisis broke Mallya's international flying plans. What did not help was that global oil prices started to rise late

---

*   An innovative fix or a simple workaround.

2009 onwards. This hurt the domestic airline business. In 2010, the banks who had lent to Mallya's companies helped him by restructuring the loans. He gave them a personal guarantee on these loans. In 2013, he claimed that the personal guarantee he gave on the loans in 2010, when they were being restructured, was extracted under duress.[232]

Meanwhile, Kingfisher Airlines continued to lose money – battered by the cheap fares offered by competitors along with the high oil prices. Kingfisher Airlines had to finally suspend operations in October 2012. It never made any money from its operations. Also, buying Air Deccan, which was a low-cost airline, led to confused positioning, which did not help the business. The international flying plans turned out to be too ambitious. More than anything, Mallya, like many other industrialists in that era, became a victim of overconfidence and over-optimism.

All this essentially brings us to the question: why is Mallya seen as a villain of the piece, more than perhaps any other industrialist? He got loans like a lot of other industrialists. He also got help from the banks in the form of restructured loans, like a lot of other industrialists did. And he defaulted on the loans, like a lot of other industrialists did. But, to give him credit, Mallya tried to rescue Kingfisher by selling his 30 per cent stake in United Breweries to international investors.

Many other industrialists had defaulted on significantly higher amount of loans than Mallya and continued to live a normal life, without the government going after them. But things clearly did not work out that way for him.

His sixtieth birthday celebrations, at the Kingfisher Villa located in Candolim, Goa, were not very lavish in comparison to his past celebrations, but they did not go unnoticed. The Spanish singer Enrique Iglesias had been flown in especially for the occasion, with the celebrations lasting for two days. His fiftieth birthday celebrations, on the other hand, at the same location, had gone on for four days. This did not go down well with the media and the people at large.

Raghuram Rajan, the then RBI governor, without naming Mallya, said in January 2016: 'If you flaunt your yacht, massive birthday bashes, etc., even while owing the system a lot of money ... it seems to suggest that you don't care.'[233]

At the same time, allegations were made that Mallya had diverted Rs 1,221 crore from his companies to private accounts abroad.[234] The law enforcement agencies were also investigating him. His political connections came to his help and he was tipped off that he could be arrested. Mallya put his diplomatic passport to use and left India on 2 March 2016, along with his girlfriend. What helped was the fact that a look-out notice for him had been downgraded just a month ago.[235]

Since then, Mallya has been living in London over the weekdays and apparently drives down to Ladwalk, a country estate around an hour away from London, which he reportedly bought for £11 million, on weekends.[236]

His extradition case is currently on. Mallya has since offered to repay the principal amount he owes to banks. But given how his default has panned out, no bank will take up this offer. Of course, this leads to the question that if he had money, why didn't he repay it earlier? The answer, like is the case with Ruias of Essar Steel (as we shall see later) and many other industrialists, was that he *probably* thought that he could get away with it.

Mallya is not any more guilty than the other industrialists, when it comes to defaulting on bank loans. As mentioned earlier, there are many others who have defaulted on far bigger amounts and continue to live happily ever after. But that isn't what happened with Mallya. It's just that his brashness, his over-the-top lifestyle – *supposedly* to build the Kingfisher brand – and the love that the media had for him combined to bring him down in the end. Of course, he also gave a personal guarantee on the loans taken by his company.

The media followed him closely in the good times to build up his image as a hero. And they followed him closely during the bad times, to build him up as a villain, and that is one of the reasons that brought him down. Most industrialists who defaulted on bank loans merely ended up as a statistic. Mallya became the poster – boy of this entire era, with his business and personal brashness getting mixed-up in the end, leading to the conclusion that what is good for the good times, can be bad for the bad times.

* * *

If you were to ask the man on the street who are the culprits behind the bad loan crisis in India, the most likely answer that you are to get are the names of Vijay Mallya, Nirav Modi and Naresh Goyal (of Jet Airways). While these individuals were responsible for bad loans, there are bigger defaulters who people have never heard of.

The biggest defaulter among all companies was Bhushan Steel.[237] The chairman of the company was Brij Bhushan Singal. Almost no one outside the business and banking community has ever heard of him. The other interesting thing is that the media has had a field day printing pictures and running stories around Vijay Mallya and Nirav Modi; the same was not true for Singal or the Ruia brothers (Shashi and Ravi), who ran Esssar Steel, the second-biggest defaulters after Bhushan Steel.

This is not to say that Vijay Mallya and Nirav Modi didn't do anything wrong, but there were bigger defaulters out there who people did not know about at all. In fact, if you were to go to Google images and search for a picture of Singal, you will only get a few pictures that have appeared in the niche business press and nothing beyond.

Of course, the story of a defaulter who dealt in diamonds and a defaulter who ran an airline, a liquor company, owned a cricket team and, more famously, was closely associated with the Kingfisher calendar is bound to be more interesting for the common man. More importantly, both partied and moved with celebrities. But even after taking this into account, the lack of coverage around Singal and the Ruia brothers is simply not justified.

In August 2018, the Serious Fraud Investigation Office (SFIO), the investigative arm of the ministry of corporate affairs, arrested

Neeraj Singal (son of Brij Bhushan), and a former promoter and managing director of Bhushan Steel. The SFIO charged Singal with siphoning off the company's bank loans of more than Rs 2,000 crore. This was done through eighty different companies which were used to rotate funds through bogus loans, advances and investments.[238] Neeraj was later released on bail.

In early May 2019, the SFIO arrested Nikhil Johri, the former chief financial officer of Bhushan Steel. The investigative body found Johri's direct involvement in inflating the inventories of the company. The inflated inventories were then used to avail enhanced working capital limits from banks.[239]

The question is how did the company reach this stage? In 2003, the company decided to build an integrated steel plant in Odisha. Its construction started in 2005 and the first phase was completed by 2009–10. As of March 2010, the company had a debt of Rs 11,404 crore.[240] With the banks more than happy to lend, the company's borrowing spree continued. First, this was to finance the next phase of construction, but as we shall see things changed after a point of time.

The problem was that by late 2012, the steel cycle had taken a turn for the worse. Steel prices fell to $300 per tonne by December 2012, from a peak of $1,265 per tonne in 2008.[241] Of course, Chinese steel being dumped into India did not help either.

The funny thing was that even with the steel cycle taking a turn and prices crashing, the banks continued to lend to the company. Bhushan Steel's debt rose from Rs 11,400 crore in March 2010 to Rs 17,900 crore in March 2012, and all the way to Rs 48,000 crore in March 2017.

It has been suggested in the media that the company was close to many bankers and got loans easily in the process. Take the case of the year ended March 2014 – the company had paid Rs 1,700 crore as interest on its loans and made a meagre profit of Rs 62 crore. It had still managed to get fresh loans of a whopping Rs 18,000 crore during the course of the year.[242] The company's annual report for the year had said: 'Despite these challenges, your company's bankers have demonstrated continued confidence on the company.'[243]

One school of thought suggests that there came a stage where the company was borrowing from one bank to pay off another, which is why its debt ballooned so fast. Another school of thought suggests that banks were just doubling down in the hope that the steel cycle would turn (which it eventually did, but not before the company had defaulted on the loans) and that Bhushan Steel would be able to come out of it.[244]

With the benefit of hindsight, it's clear that banks should have stopped lending to the company by 2014, but they didn't. It needs to be said here that the company had a state-of-the-art plant (one major reason why Tata Steel eventually picked it up), with a capacity of 5.6 million tonnes, and was producing steel and had some of the biggest automobile companies as its customers.[245] Of course, along the way, it seems that the promoters were helping themselves to some of the money taken as bank loans.

As we have seen earlier in the book, senior RBI officials and even public sector bankers, over the years, have been very open about corporate promoters siphoning off bank loans given for specific projects. In this scenario, it makes sense for the SFIO to look into the books of the large defaulters carefully. While they may have been unlucky with the economic cycle turning and the assumptions on which they had built the expansion going all wrong, that in no way justifies the siphoning off of funds.

A serious exercise by the SFIO will help in multiple ways. First, it will send a strong message for the future, where corporate promoters trying to siphon money off will always have the fear of getting caught at the back of their mind. Over and above this, if the SFIO is able to recover some money, that will help both the banks and the government.

20

Was the RBI Caught Napping?

The role of the RBI in the entire crisis also needs to be explored. In fact, it's safe to say that up until 2015, the central bank did not realize the gravity of the crisis. As Arvind Subramanian puts it in *Of Counsel*: 'For years, the RBI was unable to grasp the seriousness of the loan repayment problems or identify the prolonged frauds of Nirav Modi.'[246] Despite credible warnings being made as far back as 2011, it took the RBI a while to get its head around to recognizing the bad loans problem.[247]

The RBI releases the Financial Stability Report twice a year, once in June and once in December. Anyone who has followed these reports seriously over the years would know that the RBI failed on two fronts. One was the fact that for many years, the RBI failed to recognize the magnitude of the bad loans problem. Second, even when it did recognize it, mid-2015 onwards, when it forced banks to carry out an Asset Quality Review, it failed to recognize the scale of the problem.

In every Financial Stability Report released in June, the RBI estimates what is the bad loans rate of PSBs going to be next March under different situations, including a severe stress situation, where all hell is possibly breaking loose. So the Financial Stability Report released in June 2018 contained a prediction of the bad loans rate of PSBs under a severe stress scenario in March 2019. Figure 20.1 also plots the actual bad loans rate of PSBs over the years along with the RBI predictions.

Figure 20.1

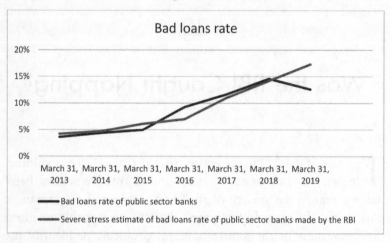

Source: RBI Financial Stability Reports.[*]

Figure 20.1 makes for a very interesting reading. What it tells us is that since March 2016, the actual bad loans rate of PSBs has turned out to be slightly higher than the bad loans rate under severe stress as forecast by the RBI. Let's take the case of March 2018. In June 2017, the RBI in its Financial Stability Report forecast that the bad loans rate of PSBs under a severe stress scenario would reach 14.2 per cent. It actually turned out to be 14.6 per cent. Given that both the curves in the graph almost overlap each other, it's safe to say that the actual bad loans rate has turned out to be slightly higher to the one predicted by the RBI. The only thing is that the broader economy itself hasn't seen anything like severe stress.

What this tells us is that the RBI has terribly underestimated the scale of the problem. Let's take a look at this issue from another angle. As Subramanian writes: 'In March 2015, the RBI was forecasting that even under a "severe stress" scenario—

---

[*]   The idea for this figure came from a chart in Arvind Subramanian's book *Of Counsel*.

where to put it colourfully, all hell breaks loose, with growth collapsing and interest rates shooting up—NPAs [bad loans] would at most reach about Rs 4.5 lakh crore.'[248] By March 2018, the total NPAs of banks had stood at Rs 10,36,187 crore. The PSBs accounted for around 86.5 per cent, or Rs 8,95,601 crore, of these bad loans.

The point being that the RBI was way off target when it came to estimating the total bad loans in the system. In fact, as late as June 2012, the RBI said: 'The position is not alarming at the current juncture.'[249]

One possible reason can be offered in the RBI's defence. Let's assume that the central bank in March 2015 had some inkling of the bad loans of banks ending up at around Rs 10 lakh crore. Would it have made sense for it, as the country's banking regulator, to put out such a huge number? Putting out numbers like that could have spooked the banking system in the country. It could even have possibly led to bank runs, something that the RBI wouldn't want. In this scenario, it perhaps made sense for the regulator to gradually up the bad loans rate prediction as the situation worsened, than predict it in just one go. Of course, I have no insider information on this and am offering this logic just to give the country's banking regulator the benefit of doubt.

The big question now is, are banks done declaring their bad loans or is there more to come? There are two sectors which are staring at bad loans. These are telecom and real estate. The overall telecom sector has been in a mess since the launch of Reliance Jio, which has dramatically cut both calling and internet rates in order to capture the market. This forced other players in the market to cut rates as well. In the process, their financials came under pressure and have made it difficult for these companies to continue repaying loans. Some companies like the Anil Ambani owned RCom, have even shut down in the process.

Other than increased competition, what has hit the sector is the issue of adjusted gross revenue – in layman's terms this means that a certain proportion of revenues earned by telecom companies needs to be shared with the government's department of telecom. The telecom companies and the government have been disagreeing on the definition of adjusted gross revenue since 2005. The companies only wanted revenue from their telecom business to be calculated for this figure, but the government wanted a much wider definition, including non-telecom revenue like sale of assets and interest earned on deposits.

In October 2019, the Supreme Court agreed with the government's definition of adjusted gross revenue and asked the telecom companies to pay the Rs 92,000 crore which they owed to the government. This has pushed the telecom sector further against the wall.

The other big problem looming is in the real estate sector. Over the years, the attention in this sector has been on the builders, who have taken money from prospective buyers and have not delivered the flats. This has basically broken the business model of real estate in India, with prospective buyers no longer ready to finance builders by buying under-construction properties.

But as far as the overall economy goes the bigger problem is the large inventory of unsold homes, which builders have built but are unable to find buyers for. The unsold inventory in the top eight cities of the country as of June 2019 has risen to 10 lakh units. The value of the inventory is Rs 8 lakh crore and equals what builders are likely to sell over four years.[250]

Builders have taken on loans to build these homes. Unless they are able to sell these homes, they won't be able to repay them. In the past, the major part of the funding to builders was provided by banks. Over the last few years, NBFCs have provided a greater part of the funding. As of March 2019, the real estate sector had a total outstanding loans of around Rs 5.4 lakh crore. The NBFCs accounted for around half of these loans. The total loans to the sector as of March 2015 had stood at around Rs 2.8 lakh crore. This has more or less doubled over a period of four years, with NBFCs accounting for a greater share of these loans.[251]

Of course, these loans had been provided on the premise that the builders will be able to sell their inventory of unsold homes and repay bank loans. But that has become increasingly difficult as buyers have stayed away from buying these unsold homes.[252]

Here is the irony; while the unsold homes of builders continue to grow, so do home loans of banks. As of October 2019, the total outstanding home loans of banks stood at Rs 12.7 lakh crore, having grown by around 19.4 per cent since October 2018. In October 2018, the home loans outstanding had stood at Rs 10.6 lakh crore, having grown by 15.7 per cent. These are just home loans provided by banks. Over and above this, there are home loans provided by housing finance companies. If home loans are growing that obviously means that people are buying homes. If people are buying homes, it is well worth asking, why the number of unsold homes has not come down? Between 2003 and 2012, investors went overboard while buying real estate. All these homes which have been locked up for years are now being sold. This is one possible explanation.

People are buying homes from individuals rather than builders. The builders are not in a mood to cut prices which the investors possibly are.

The main reason why homes are not selling are high prices. Builders could have cut prices and cleared their inventory. But they haven't. The trouble is that any cut in home prices would lower the notional value of the collateral (the unsold homes) against which builders have taken on loans.

This is a problem that is not going to go anywhere soon. Also, as mentioned earlier, there are ten lakh unsold homes with a total value of Rs 8 lakh crore. This basically means that the average price of an unsold home is Rs 80 lakh. Of course, this is in the top eight Indian cities. But even in the top eight Indian cities, how many people can afford to buy a house priced at Rs 80 lakh?

Also, given the high price, this inventory will take more than a few years to clear, assuming no more homes are built. All in all, this is not going to end well.

In fact, this can be concluded by looking at the number of real estate companies under the corporate insolvency resolution process more commonly known as the bankruptcy process. As of September 2018, the total number of companies under the real estate, renting and business activities sector had stood at 209. By September 2019, this had jumped to 500, showing the increased stress in the sector. Banks have direct as well as indirect lending exposure to the sector. The indirect lending has been carried out by lending to NBFCs, which have in turn lent to the real estate sector. In that sense, it is going to be a double whammy for banks as repayment for these loans starts to come up.

What hasn't helped is that many PSBs have been under-reporting their bad loans. The State Bank of India under-reported bad loans worth Rs 11,932 crore in 2018–19. The Bank of Baroda and Punjab National Bank under-reported bad loans worth Rs 5,250 crore and Rs 2,617 crore, respectively. This again adds to the doubt whether the PSBs have more skeletons in their closets, which are yet to tumble out. What further adds to the problem is the fact that economic growth during the first six months of 2019–20 has collapsed to less than 5 per cent. The slow growth is bound to create problems for many companies, making it difficult for them to keep repaying their loans on time. In fact, this is reflected in the fact that SMA-2 loans of large borrowers increased by about 143 per cent between March 2019 and September 2019. A loan account is categorised as SMA-2 loan if interest or principal on it is due for a period of 61-90 days. This is just before a loan becomes a bad loan. Also, a large borrower is any borrower with an exposure of Rs 5 crore or more to a bank.

The RBI in its Financial Stability Report released in December 2019 expects things to get worse. It expects the bad loans rate of PSBs to rise and touch 13.2 per cent in September 2020, in case of the baseline scenario. In case of the medium stress and severe stress scenario, the bad loans rate is expected to be at 13.4 per cent and 13.5 per cent, respectively. As we have seen in the past, RBI's forecasts for the severe stress scenario have turned out to be true, without the economy itself getting into that scenario.

There is another factor that needs to be taken into account here. As Subramanian writes: 'There is what I self-referentially call the Subramanian Iron Law of Non-Recognition: despite the progress, we know in our bones that the amount of stressed assets is always and everywhere at least 20–25 per cent more than what people believe and what the RBI claims.'[253]

He goes on to offer the example of Infrastructure Leasing & Financial Services (IL&FS). In October 2018, the government superseded the board of the company, which was believed to be in a financial mess. By the time, IL&FS and its subsidiaries started to default, its problems were not on the radar of the banks which had lent money to it. The entire IL&FS group had a debt to equity ratio of close to 17:1 and a total debt of a little over Rs 91,000 crore as on 31 March 2018. In a report, the RBI found that IL&FS had not declared bad loans in a period of four years up to 31 March 2018. The report also found that as of the same date, the bad loans made up 70 per cent of the total loans of IL&FS.

Over and above this, a problem with non-banking financial companies (NBFCs) seems to be brewing. Over the years, banks have gone slow on lending to corporates. Nevertheless, they needed to lend money to someone. Banks have lent a lot of money to NBFCs over the last few years. The lending between December 2016, in the aftermath of demonetization, and March 2019 went up by a whopping 99.1 per cent – from Rs 3,22,105 crore to Rs 6,41,208 crore. Non-food credit during the same period went up by 31.2 per cent. Banks in India lend extensively to the Food Corporation of India and other state procurement agencies to help them buy rice and wheat, directly from farmers. Once this lending is subtracted from overall lending of banks what remains is non-food credit.

Banks made up for a part of the slowdown in industrial lending and inflow of excessive deposits in the aftermath of demonetization, by lending to NBFCs. Over the past few years, many NBFCs in India have been very aggressive on the retail lending front. The trouble is that most of these NBFCs are not allowed to raise deposits directly from the public. In this scenario, they are dependent on raising money directly from banks or mutual funds (basically money invested in debt mutual funds finds its way into NBFCs).

Typically, money is borrowed for the short term and lent for the long term. The asset–liability mismatch is even graver for NBFCs. In June 2019, one housing finance NBFC, Dewan Housing, was in major trouble. It had defaulted on its maturing debt. In September 2019, Altico Capital, an NBFC focused on lending to real estate companies defaulted on its loans. Banks have an exposure of close to Rs 4,000 crore to the NBFC. The trouble is that the banks treat the exposure to such institutions as an exposure to an NBFC, but the actual exposure is to the real estate sector.[254] Whether this is a problem across other NBFCs or an issue with only a few NBFCs remains to be seen.

The representatives of the NBFC system in particular and the financial system in general want us, the general public, to believe that this is a one-off problem. But, as we have seen in case of bad loans, the financial system is very good at hiding its problems for a reasonably long period of time. In this scenario, one cannot say with surety that there will be no further problems with Indian NBFCs. Banks have lent more than Rs 6 lakh crore to NBFCs. Whether proper due diligence was done while giving out loans or have the loans been given out as freely as they were to corporates earlier? That only time will tell.

In fact, the only way to tackle this scenario is to carry out a second Asset Qualtiy Review. This needs to be a comprehensive review of the Indian financial system, which includes not just NBFCs, but also mutual funds which heavily buy financial securities issued by NBFCs and banks which lend to them.

'India must come clean on the entire financial system,' as Arvind Subramanian and Josh Feldman put it, in their working paper titled 'India's Great Slowdown: What Happened? What's the Way Out?'

What happens if the second round of the Asset Quality Review unearths more problems in the financial system? Well, it is better for the world to come to know of it through a proper review carried out by the RBI than suddenly one fine day, as was the case with the troubles of IL&FS and Dewan Housing.

21

What Did the RBI Do, Once It Woke Up?

D. Subbarao was the RBI governor between 2008 and 2013. After his retirement he wrote a wonderful book, *Who Moved My Interest Rate?* The book, other than detailing Subbarao's years at the RBI, also explains in very simple English what does a central bank of a country actually do.

But one thing that is totally missing in the book is any talk about the bad loans of the PSBs in India. This is kind of surprising because from 2011, credible warnings about the burgeoning bad loans in PSBs were already being made.

Whether the central bank was internally discussing the issue or not is something one can only speculate about. It was only after Raghuram Rajan became the RBI governor in September 2013 that the RBI started talking about the bad loans of PSBs. In fact, in the speeches that Rajan made during his tenure of three years, he was critical about regulatory forbearance as an idea. Here are some of the points that he made.

In a November 2014 speech, Rajan said: 'Regulatory forbearance … a euphemism for regulators collaborating with banks to hide problems and push them into the future, is a bad idea.'[255]

When the banks look the other way and kick the can down the road, they do not provision adequately for bad loans. After some point, the banks reach a stage wherein they can't continue to hide their bad loans and have to reveal them. At this stage, the hit on the bank's balance sheet as well as its income is larger than it would have been if regulatory forbearance wouldn't have been the norm and banks had recognized bad loans for what they were on time.

In the same speech, Rajan added: 'Put differently, forbearance is ostrich-like behaviour, hoping the problem will go away. It's not realism but naiveté, for the lesson from across the world is that problems only get worse as one buries one's head in the sand.' This ostrich-like behaviour became the norm for the RBI and the PSBs for a while. Of course, the market is not dumb and it figured out the real state of the PSBs, thanks to people like Ashish Gupta at Credit Suisse.

This led to a situation where the market considered both bad loans as well as restructured loans to be the same, and together termed them to be stressed loans. As Rajan put it, 'Mutilating Shakespeare, an NPA by any other name smells as bad!'[256]

In another speech in June 2016, a few months before his tenure ended, Rajan said: 'Forbearance may be a reasonable but risky regulatory strategy when there is some hope that growth will pick up soon and the system will recover on its own. Everyone – banker, promoter, investors, and government officials – often urge such a strategy because it *kicks the problem down the road* [emphasis added], hopefully for someone else to deal with. The downside is that when growth does not pick up, the bad loan problem is bigger, and dealing with it is more difficult.'[257]

The public sector banker, who, at best, has a few years at the top, is extremely interested in pushing the problem down the road, for his successor to deal with. In this scenario, the role of the regulator becomes very important. The regulator needs to ensure that banks recognize their bad loans in a timely manner and, at the same time, provision adequately for it. By doing so, the regulator is making its future work easier. But the RBI practised forbearance for quite a while and did not force banks to recognize their bad loans. Given this, it ended up creating a bigger problem for itself as well as the Indian banking system. As Rajan put it: 'It's when the bad loan problem is allowed to accumulate through forbearance or non-recognition that regulators have the difficult task of bringing the system back on track. That is the problem we have had to deal with at the RBI.'[258] This is the closest he ever got to – as the RBI governor – saying that the central bank took it easy for a while and, in the process, *screwed up*.

Having said that, once Rajan was at the helm of things, the RBI started to get its act right. It set up the Central Repository of Information on Large Credits (CRILC). CRILC is a database in which banks report information regarding all loans over Rs 5 crore. This information is then made available across all banks. The primary aim of the database is to make sure that every bank knows who has lent to whom.

The database also includes the status of loans, whether a particular loan is a performing loan, a bad loan or is heading towards becoming a bad loan. This allowed banks to identify in advance if a borrower was heading towards distress.[259] CRILC was started from the period of three months ending in June 2014.

CRILC tried to fill in a credit-data gap. Given the absence of detailed data of corporate borrowers and large borrowers (basically everyone who has an exposure of Rs 5 crore or more), banks were really not in a position to distinguish between the good borrowers and the bad borrowers.[260] In some cases, where the banks were more agile, or had hired better lawyers, the promoter continued to repay the loan to these banks, while defaulting on loans they had taken from other banks.[261]

The large borrowers played one bank against another, by threatening to pay off only the favoured bank. Over and above this, when banks had come together to lend to a large borrower, and the borrower seemed to be moving towards distress 'private banks were sometimes more agile in securing their positions with additional collateral from the promoter, or getting repaid, even while PSBs continued supporting projects with fresh loans'.[262]

In order to get over these coordination problems, on 14 February 2014, the RBI issued guidelines on the formation of a Joint Lenders' Forum (JLF) among banks. The idea behind CRILC was to develop an early warning system. The signals generated by this early warning system were to be used by the JLF to do something about the situation, which was worsening. Let's look at the JLF guidelines briefly.

Before a loan turned into a bad loan, banks were required to identify stress under three sub-categories of Special Mention Account (SMA). These were: 1) SMA 0: In this case, both interest and principal had been overdue for not more than thirty days. 2) SMA 1: In this case, both interest and principal had been overdue between thirty-one and sixty days. 3) SMA 2: In this case, both interest and principal had been overdue between sixty-one and ninety days.

The idea of categorizing loans which hadn't turned into bad loans as SMAs was to be proactive and do something about the loan, and prevent the situation from deteriorating further.

As soon as a loan of greater than Rs 100 crore was marked as SMA 2, the banks which had given out the loan needed to come together and form a JLF. In case the loan was lower than Rs 100 crore and was reported as SMA 0 or 1, lenders had an option of forming a JLF.

After a JLF was formed, the banks needed to come up with a corrective action plan within thirty days of one of the bank's marking the loan as SMA 2. In fact, a corrective action plan agreed upon by a minimum of 75 per cent of the creditors by value and 60 per cent of creditors by number was considered as the basis for proceeding.

There were other steps that the RBI took to stop banks from kicking the bad loans can down the road. One way the banks had been avoiding recognizing bad loans as bad loans was by restructuring them. From April 2015 onwards, the RBI ended the ability of banks to restructure projects without calling it a bad loan.

Along with the Securities and Exchange Board of India (SEBI), the RBI launched the Strategic Debt Restructuring (SDR) scheme in June 2015. The SDR scheme allowed banks to take over companies which had defaulted on loans by converting their debts into equity. The idea was to displace weak promoters who had defaulted on loans and sell the company to a new promoter.

The trouble was that every promoter wasn't a weak promoter. Some of them were just caught in a bad economic environment and were competent, even though highly indebted. To deal with this situation, the RBI introduced a Scheme for Sustainable Structuring of Stressed Assets (S4A) in June 2016. Under this scheme, the banks could provide corporate borrowers debt reductions of up to 50 per cent in order to restore the financial viability of the company. The extent of the debt reduction was to be converted into equity, which banks would hold in the firm.

The idea was to provide the promoter some incentive to perform in order to turn around the firm. If that happened, the share price of the firm would recover, banks could then sell their stake in the firm and make good part of the loan that they had given to the company.

Over and above this, the RBI also encouraged the establishment of private Asset Reconstruction Companies (ARCs). The idea was that ARCs would end up buying the bad loans of banks at a discount, and then work towards recovering the defaulted loans. This would let the banks concentrate on their bread-and-butter business of raising deposits and giving them out as loans, after proper due diligence. Of course, the ARCs would specialize in loan recovery. It's worth remembering here that at this point of time India did not have an effective corporate bankruptcy system. In the absence of one, the RBI was 'trying to create an entirely new bad loan resolution process'.[263] This also explains why the central bank introduced so many schemes and kept tinkering with them all the time.

It wasn't just the RBI introducing one scheme after another to tackle the bad loans problem. The government, as the owner of PSBs, also had a role to play. After the RBI initiated the Asset Quality Review in mid-2015, the government came up with the

Indradhanush reforms. The important features of the plan were as follows:

1) The post of the chairman and managing director of a PSB was split. In the days to come, one individual would be appointed as MD and CEO of a bank and another as its non-executive chairman. This move was in line with the best global practises. Furthermore, individuals from the private sector were also allowed to apply for the posts of MD and CEO of PSBs.

2) A Banks Board Bureau (BBB) was set up. The BBB, it was said, would be a body of eminent professionals. The former Comptroller and Auditor General Vinod Rai was appointed as its first head. Its job is to appoint the full-time directors as well as the non-executive chairmen of PSBs. The BBB was also expected to 'constantly engage with the Board of Directors of all the PSBs to formulate appropriate strategies for their growth and development'.[264] The BBB started to function from 1 April 2016.

3) The government also planned to infuse more capital into the PSBs (as we have seen on page 112).

4) The Indradhanush reforms also talked about taking several steps to de-stress PSBs from the bad loans that they were carrying, particularly those of infrastructure companies. One of the points suggested was that 'promoters be asked to bring in additional equity in an attempt to address the worsening leverage ratio of these projects'. If the promoters were unable to bring in fresh capital to bring down the leverage, then the PSBs 'would consider viable options for substitution or taking over management control'.[265]

   This was pretty much the language that the RBI was also using. This was a message to all erring promoters that the RBI and the government were on the same page.

5) The government also decided to set up six new Debt Recovery Tribunals (DRTs) for the faster recovery of bad loans. This was an important move, as the DRTs were dealing with a huge

backlog of cases. In 2013–14, the amount recovered from cases decided by the DRTs had stood at Rs 32,000 crore. The debt that was sought to be recovered had stood at Rs 2,63,021 crore. Hence, the recovery rate was a measly 12.1 per cent.

Also, the law indicates that cases brought to the DRT should be decided upon within six months. Nevertheless, at that point of time, only one in four cases pending before the DRT at the beginning of any year was decided upon during the course of that year. This suggested that it could take four years to clear all the cases, if the DRTs just concentrated on old cases alone. In fact, in 2013–14, the number of cases filed during the course of the year was one-and-a-half times the number of cases decided upon during the course of the year.[266]

* * *

Let's now take a look at the bouquet of schemes launched by the RBI to help the banks with their bad loans and how they performed. The main idea behind the JLF was to resolve the coordination issues between banks. But the coordination problems, in fact, continued. Banks which had given out the greater portion of the loan were reluctant to accept losses.[267]

At a simpler level, the banks which were part of a JLF never reached a consensus. As the Economic Survey of 2016–17 pointed out: 'In some cases, the firm's losses [weren't] even known, for they depend on the extent of government compensation for its own implementation shortfalls, such as delays in acquiring land or adjusting electricity tariffs.' In the process, the entire idea of a JLF to speed up things went for a toss.

Above all, the banks were not forming JLFs as mandated. This led to the RBI coming up with a notification according to which the bank which had the largest exposure in the loan given to the corporate would face a penalty if the JLF wasn't formed within fifteen days of a loan being categorized as SMA 2 (i.e., a loan not having been repaid for seventy-five days).[268]

Between April 2014 and February 2015, banks had formed 355 JLFs. Of these, PSBs formed 254 JLFs. Interestingly, only thirty-three of the 254 cases were referred for debt restructuring.[269]

While, JLF at least saw some activity, the same cannot be said for SDR and S4A. Twenty-four firms entered into negotiations under SDR. Nevertheless, as of December 2016, only two cases were concluded. The performance of S4A was even worse, as only two cases were resolved. A major reason for the S4A scheme not taking off lay in the fact that the banks had to grant large debt reductions to corporates. They were unwilling to do so for a few reasons. A major reason was the fact that write-downs of a large amount of debt would exhaust the capital of the bank very quickly.[270] It's worth remembering here that over the last decade a bulk of the recapitalization carried out by the government of the PSBs happened in 2017–18 and 2018–19, when the government invested Rs 1,96,000 crore in these banks. Before this as we have seen earlier, the government was investing a few thousand crore every year, which was clearly not enough if banks had to grant large debt reductions to corporates.

Also, more importantly, no public sector banker, in the few years he spent at the top, was willing to grant large debt reductions to corporates and in the process attract the attention of investigative agencies. It's also the 4Cs (the courts, the Central Bureau of Investigation, the Central Vigilance Commission and the Comptroller and Auditor General) which hold the PSBs back in granting debt reductions. Hence, bankers had a huge incentive to restructure loans and postpone the recognition of bad loans.

As of March 2016, sixteen asset reconstruction companies had bought bad loans worth Rs 72,626 crore from banks. The asset reconstruction companies, the first of which had been in business since 2013, found it difficult to recover these bad loans. This led to asset reconstruction companies wanting to buy loans only on lower prices from banks. Not surprisingly, banks were reluctant to sell the loans at lower prices. Also, the asset reconstruction companies as a whole did not attract enough capital to get their business going on a large scale. This was primarily because affluent investors who were interested in this kind of business were wary of the prevailing judicial and administrative environment in the country. There was also an accounting issue. If the bank carried out any settlement with a defaulting borrower, it could immediately book the money coming in as profit. But when it sold loans to an asset reconstruction company, the money had to be set aside for future provisioning.[271]

As far as the Indradhanush reforms were concerned, it was more a case of the government doing something for the sake of being seen as doing something. While the Indradhanush reforms were better than the government doing nothing at all, they did not tackle the basic issues at the heart of the problem of bad loans.

The Indradhanush reforms had nothing to say about the evergreening of balance sheets carried out by banks, which were not recognizing bad loans. As the owner of these banks, the government should have had something to say. It should have at least come up with a framework for tackling bad loans. Other than allocating Rs 70,000 crore for the recapitalization of banks, no major reforms were carried out. This was like throwing money at a problem and hoping that the problem would solve itself.

The question is, what kind of reform could have been carried out. A big problem for the PSBs is that a variety of authorities – everyone from the parliament to the Department of Financial Services to the board of the bank to the vigilance authorities to the RBI – monitor their performance. With too many bosses to please, the public sector banks' top management are perpetually caught between the devil and the deep sea. As Rajan put it in a speech: 'With so many overlapping constituencies to satisfy, it's a wonder that bank management has time to devote to the management of the bank.'[272]

All said and done, the Indradhanush reforms were an exercise to recapitalize banks. This was necessary as the RBI was running its Asset Quality Review and pushing banks to declare their bad loans.

The burgeoning amount of bad loans obviously led to a situation where the total amount of provisioning that the banks needed to do against these loans would go up. The provisions would first be made against profits and then against capital. Hence, the total capital of the banks would come down in the process. This meant that the government had to compulsorily recapitalize these banks.

The government invested Rs 25,000 crore in 2015–16 into PSBs. This was as per plan. The next year, in 2016–17, it invested Rs 24,997 crore, which was more or less as per plan too.

In the years 2017–18 and 2018–19, the plan was to invest Rs 10,000 crore each into the PSBs. Nevertheless, the government ended up investing Rs 90,000 crore and Rs 1,06,000 crore respectively. This was much more than what it had originally envisaged. Clearly, the PSBs ended up declaring a higher amount of bad loans than the government had originally expected. At the same time, the rate of recovery of bad loans had also come down.

One school of thought here is that the government should substantially recapitalize the PSBs at one go, instead of doing it in bits and pieces. In his book *Of Counsel*, Arvind Subramanian estimates that the recapitalization will cost 2–3 per cent of the GDP, in the worst-case scenario. As of March 2019, the total bad loans of PSBs amounted to Rs 7,89,569 crore. The worst-case scenario would be banks not being able to recover any of these bad loans and having to bear all the losses. Let's say the government decides to recapitalize banks to the tune of Rs 8 lakh crore to overcome these losses. The GDP (at current prices) forecast for 2019–20 stands at Rs 204 lakh crore. Hence, Rs 8 lakh crore of Rs 204 lakh crore works out to 3.9 per cent of the GDP.

Of course, the assumption that the banks will not be able to recover a single rupee of bad loans is a stretch of the imagination. So let's relax this assumption and assume that banks are able to recover one-fourth of the bad loans, which is much more than they have managed to recover over the last few years.

Let's say the government now decides to recapitalize these banks to the extent of Rs 6 lakh crore. This works out to 2.9 per cent of the GDP and is more along the lines of what Subramanian suggests.

In simple terms, 2.9 per cent of the GDP does not sound very big. But that is the case with any number when represented as a proportion of the GDP. Hence, that doesn't really mean anything. The question is where the government is going to get that Rs 6 lakh crore in a single go.

The budget of 2020–21 puts the total government expenditure for 2019–20 at Rs 26.99 lakh crore. In this case, Rs 6 lakh crore works out to 22.2 per cent of the expenditure. When we look at the number from this angle, it doesn't sound small any more.

22

The PARAchute That Did Not Open

In the Economic Survey of 2016–17, the then chief economic adviser Arvind Subramanian and his team came up with another suggestion to clean up the bad loans of PSBs. It was very euphemistically called the Public Sector Asset Rehabilitation Agency (PARA). PARA was basically a bad bank. As Subramanian recalls: 'I was a strong advocate for creating a "bad bank" ... I was told that I should not actually use that term because it had some bad connotations in political circles.'[273] Given this, Subramanian and his team ended up naming what was in reality a bad bank as PARA.

The idea was to move bad loans to PARA, which would concentrate on recovering them. After this had been done, the government would recapitalize PSBs to the extent required. The banks could then go back to raising deposits and lending money, in particular to industry. This would revive corporate investment and the country would go back to the rapid growth path. Q.E.D.

Many of the reasons offered in favour of PARA revolved around the other plans to clean up the bad loans of PSBs, for those had not worked the way they were supposed to.

Let's look at how PARA was supposed to work.

The bad loans were concentrated in large companies. As we have seen earlier, many companies which owed money to banks had an interest coverage ratio of less than one. Of these companies with an interest coverage ratio of less than one, fifty companies accounted for 71 per cent of the debt. On an average, these companies owed the banks Rs 20,000 crore each. Of these, there were ten companies which owed more than Rs 40,000 crore apiece.[274] The point being made by the PARA advocates was that the problem of bad loans was concentrated. It was these companies that were holding the banks and the economy back.

The Economic Survey further pointed out that based on the data for a period of twelve months ending September 2016, thirty-three of the top 100 stressed debtors would need a debt reduction of less than 50 per cent. Ten stressed debtors would need reductions of 51–75 per cent and the remaining fifty-seven would need reductions of 75 per cent or more. After these debt reductions, the stressed companies would then be in a position to pay the interest on the loans they had taken on, for their interest obligations would be at their current cash-flow levels.

While this sounded extreme, the Economic Survey said that there was no other way out of this. The twin balance sheet problem (where both the balance sheets of the banks as well as the companies they had lent to were under stress) had materialized nearly eight years ago (around 2008). Since then, the financial positions of the stressed companies which owed large amounts of money to banks only deteriorated. The ultimate cost of this was rising and was being borne by the government and the society – in terms of foregone economic growth as well as risks to future growth. Hence, it was not a morality problem but an economic one.

In this scenario, it made sense for the government to start a bad bank. PARA would buy the bad loans (for example, loans given to highly indebted steel and infrastructure firms) from banks at a reduced price, or so was the thinking offered in the survey. It would then work with the stressed companies. Depending on whichever strategy was value maximizing, PARA would either grant debt reductions or convert a portion of debt to equity. After it had bought the bad loans from the banks, these loans would no longer be on the books of the banks. The government could then recapitalize these banks by investing money in them. With bad loans off their books, the banks would be able to concentrate on their core business of raising deposits and lending them out, but after proper due diligence. At the same time, once the firms were granted debt reductions or a portion of their debt had been converted into equity, they would become financially viable again and concentrate on their operations, rather than their finances.[275]

Over and above this, PARA would have no coordination problems that the banks were facing in recovering their loans. In this case, a single agency, i.e., PARA, would be dealing with the problem, and unlike JLF, coordinating between different parties would be easier.[276]

Given that the idea was to buy loans from banks, establishing PARA would need a lot of money. It was proposed that the money could come from the government issuing financial securities to finance the agency. Over and above this, the agency could seek funding from the financial market as well.

On the face of it, it seemed like Arvind Subramanian and his team had laid out a well-thought out plan. Nevertheless, a few basic problems with the proposed scheme remained.

Subramanian said that PARA and what it proposed to do was an economic play and not a morality play. His logic was that, yes, some industrialists had diverted bank loans to other projects and the crony capitalists had played a role to play in the bad loans accumulating at PSBs. Nevertheless, the entire problem couldn't just be looked at through the crony-capitalism lens. At the same time, many companies had ended up defaulting because of the economic slowdown more than anything else.

While that may have been true from the point of view of an economist, the common man and politicians wouldn't look at the issue only through the economic lens. If an individual defaults on a home loan, he feels the entire weight of the bank system unleashed on him. The small and medium enterprises which had defaulted on loans were also facing the heat.

In this scenario, we had the chief economic adviser of the finance ministry of the country proposing that a major part of the loans to large, stressed companies be written off, because they had overborrowed and weren't in a position to repay these loans.

No politician worth his salt would risk this. And this is precisely what happened. As Subramanian writes: 'There was just no appetite amongst the government or any government agency for taking responsibility for the inevitable debt write-offs that would have to be made in favour of large companies.'

One mistake that Subramanian and his team made was that they didn't realize that the overall system, which would have to make PARA work, was still the same. At the heart of PARA was the idea of PSBs selling bad loans at a discount. As we have seen earlier in the book, public sector bankers have been reluctant to write down the value of the loans. PARA would face the same problem then. No public sector banker in his right mind would want to sell bad loans at a discounted price to PARA, and then risk inviting the wrath of investigative agencies.

Rajan summarized this situation best in a June 2016 speech: '[The bankers] accuse the vigilance authorities of excessive zeal when loans go bad, of immediately suspecting bankers of malfeasance when the bad loan could be an unintended consequence of sensible risk taking. Unfortunately, all too often, such investigations also uncover sloppy due diligence or loan monitoring by bankers. After the fact, it's hard to distinguish sensible risk taking from carelessness or from corruption.'[277]

Also, the model that Subramanian and his team were proposing was similar to the asset reconstruction company model. The main difference between the two was that there would be only one PARA against multiple asset reconstruction companies. But otherwise the idea at the heart of the model of buying bad loans from PSBs at a discount was the same.

As we have seen earlier, the asset reconstruction companies did not take off simply because of the reluctance of banks to sell loans to them at a discounted price. PARA would face the same problem as well.

If PARA was a public sector entity, then the bad loans would shift from one public sector entity to another and the reluctance of PSBs to act on the bad loans front would simply shift to PARA. If PARA was a private sector entity, then PSBs would be reluctant to sell loans to a private entity at a discount.[278]

Also, it made more sense for the government to invest money directly in PSBs, than raise money by issuing financial securities in order to get PARA going.[279] Given all these difficulties, this PARAchute never really opened.

23

No Borrowing, No Lending, No Problem

When an individual falls ill, the doctor sometimes asks them to rest; to take a break from their normal routine. This helps them recuperate and get back on their feet. The RBI did something similar with PSBs through the Prompt Corrective Action (PCA) framework.

At a very simplistic level, the PCA framework essentially restricts the ability of a bank to go about its normal business in case it doesn't meet certain performance parameters. The idea is to ensure that banks do not get into a further mess and are able to protect their capital.

The original PCA framework for banks in trouble was initiated in December 2002. The framework was revised in April 2017. Let's try and understand the basic idea behind putting a bank under the PCA framework through a small example.[280]

Let's consider a bank which has Rs 100 in assets, financed through insured deposits and capital. The banking regulator expects the bank to maintain a minimum capital of 6 per cent, or Rs 6. Let's say the bank maintains this capital of Rs 6.

Now let's say that, at some point of time, the bank has to write off a loan of Rs 2 against the capital of Rs 6. The remaining capital of the bank is now just Rs 4. There are two ways the bank can get back to the minimum capital level of 6 per cent. One is obviously by adding Rs 2 of capital. The other way it has in front of it is to shrink the total assets by a third, to Rs 66.67.

Then, the capital ratio of the bank equals 6 per cent (Rs 4 of Rs 66.67 expressed as a percentage). Of course, the corollary to this is that the absolute capital level of the bank (which has fallen to Rs 4) does not deteriorate even further. Hence, restrictions are put on the activities that a bank can then carry out, depending on several parameters.

Under the original PCA framework, when the capital, asset quality and profitability of a bank fell to a certain level, the bank was put under the framework and certain restrictions were imposed on its banking activities. Under the revised framework of April 2017, leverage was introduced to the list of parameters.

There are three risk thresholds under the PCA framework. If a bank has a capital to risk-weighted assets ratio of greater than or equal to 7.75 per cent and less than 10.25 per cent, along with a net non-performing assets ratio of greater than or equal to 6 per cent and less than 9 per cent, negative returns on assets for two years as well as leverage which is more than twenty-five times the Tier-I capital of the bank, it will then be deemed to be in Risk Threshold 1.

Banks need to set aside capital against different kinds of loans that they give out. Different kinds of loans have different kinds of risk weights attached to them. The higher the risk weight on a loan, the higher the capital the bank has to hold against it – which is why the ratio is referred to as the capital to risk-weighted assets ratio.

Throughout the book we have referred to gross non-performing assets (NPAs) as bad loans of banks. Against the gross NPAs, the banks set aside a sum of money referred to as provisions. Once these provisions are subtracted from the gross NPAs what remains are net NPAs. Tier I capital of a bank is its core capital, which consists of its equity capital along with its accumulated reserves.

In case a bank is placed in Risk Threshold 1, restrictions are placed on dividend distribution. The idea behind this is simple. Dividends are distributed from profit. If dividends are distributed, the amount of retained profit of a bank goes down. The retained profit is added to the Tier-1 capital of a bank. Hence, dividend distribution means that the Tier-1 capital does not go up. This does not matter in good times, when banks should be sharing its profit with its shareholders. But in bad times, when banks are barely making any money, dividend distribution is a bad idea.

Along similar lines, there are conditions for Risk Threshold 2. If a bank has a capital to risk-weighted assets ratio of greater than equal to 6.25 per cent and less than 7.75 per cent, along with a net non-performing assets ratio of greater than or equal to 9 per cent and less than 12 per cent, negative return on assets for three years as well as leverage which is more than 28.6 times the Tier-I capital of the bank, it will be deemed to be in Risk Threshold 2.

When a bank comes under Risk Threshold 2, restrictions are put on the opening of branches. Over and above this, higher provisions need to be made.

As far as Risk Threshold 3 is concerned, the bank needs to have an even worse capital to risk-weighted assets ratio than threshold 2. As far as the net non-performing assets ratio is concerned, it needs to be greater than or equal to 12 per cent. Further, the bank needs to have a negative return on assets for four years. Other than the restrictions put in hold because of thresholds 1 and 2, the bank needed to put a restriction on management compensation and directors' fees as well. These are the mandatory actions that banks need to take once they have been brought under the PCA framework.

Over and above this, there are actions related to strategy, human resources, governance, capital, credit risk, market risk, etc., that a bank under the PCA framework has to take. Some of the actions are listed below:

1. A special audit of the bank.
2. A detailed review of the business model in terms of sustainability of the bank.
3. Active engagement of the RBI with the bank's board on various aspects, as considered appropriate.

4. Reduction in exposure to high-risk sectors to conserve capital.
5. Preparation of a time-bound plan and commitment for reduction of stock of NPAs.
6. Preparation of and commitment to plan for containing generation of fresh NPAs.
7. Strengthening of the loan review mechanism.
8. Restriction of staff expansion.
9. Restrictions on entering into new lines of business.
10. Restrictions on accessing/renewing wholesale deposits/costly deposits/certificates of deposits.
11. Reduction in loan concentration in identified sectors, industries or borrowers.

Basically, the PCA framework puts a limit on what a bank can do. A few days after the RBI put out the revised PCA framework, Viral Acharya, who was a deputy governor of the RBI at that point of time, did some plain-speaking in a speech where he explained the true objective of the PCA: 'Undercapitalized banks could be shown some tough love and be subjected to corrective action ... Such action should entail no further growth in deposit base and lending for the worst-capitalized banks. *This will ensure a gradual "runoff" of such banks, and encourage deposit migration away from the weakest PSBs to healthier PSBs and private sector banks* [emphasis added].'[281]

The idea behind the PCA framework was to drive new business away from the weak banks, give them time to heal and recover, and at the same time ensure they don't make newer mistakes.

Eleven PSBs were put under the PCA framework. These were Allahabad Bank, United Bank of India, Corporation Bank, IDBI Bank, UCO Bank, Bank of India, Central Bank of India, Indian Overseas Bank, Oriental Bank of Commerce, Dena Bank and Bank of Maharashtra.

Let's see how these banks performed between March 2017 and March 2019.

The overall loans or advances of these banks shrunk by 9.1 per cent between 31 March 2017 and 31 March 2019. The overall advances of eight banks fell. The advances of Central Bank of India, Oriental Bank of Commerce and United Bank of India went up marginally.

The overall deposits of these banks shrunk by just 2.5 per cent over a two-year period. This shows the faith that people have in PSBs in India. Despite many of them being in grave trouble, their deposit base, on the whole, has held up. The deposit base of five of the banks shrank marginally.

Most importantly, the credit–deposit ratio of these banks shrunk from 64.6 per cent to 60.2 per cent. This meant that a lower proportion of their deposits were given out as loans.

As explained earlier, one of the main ideas behind putting banks under the PCA framework was to discourage a growth in lending carried out by the weaker banks and encourage deposit migration to other banks. While lending growth of these banks did come down over a two-year period, a similar deposit migration did not happen. The good part was that overall deposits with these banks did not grow. Hence, it's safe to say that newer deposits went to the healthier public sector and private banks.

How did these banks do on the net NPAs front? Take a look at Table 23.1.

Table 23.1: Net NPAs.

(In %)	31 March 2017	31 March 2018	31 March 2019
Allahabad Bank	8.91	8.04	5.22
Bank of India	6.90	8.26	5.61
Bank of Maharashtra	11.76	11.24	5.52
Central Bank of India	10.20	11.10	7.73
Corporation Bank	8.33	11.74	5.71
Dena Bank	10.66	11.95	8.02

(In %)	31 March 2017	31 March 2018	31 March 2019
IDBI Bank	13.21	16.69	10.11
Indian Overseas Bank	13.99	15.33	10.84
Oriental Bank of Commerce	8.95	10.47	5.93
UCO Bank	8.94	13.10	9.72
United Bank of India	9.97	16.51	8.64

Source: Indian Banks' Association.

Except UCO Bank, the net NPAs of all banks have come down over the two-year period. This is the healing touch provided by time. Being under the PCA framework ensures that banks do not pile up more bad loans than they have before. Along with that, as time goes by, the overall bad loans or gross NPAs also come down as loans get written off. Once bad loans are down and provisions are adjusted against what is remaining, the net NPAs also come down. Of course, this is also accompanied by the government having to pump in more money to these banks.

How did these banks do on the capital front? Let's take a look at Table 23.2, which lists out the capital to risk weighted assets ratio (CRAR) of these banks.

Table 23.2: Capital to Risk Weighted Assets Ratio.

CRAR (In %)	31 March 2017	31 March 2018	31 March 2019
Allahabad Bank	11.45	8.69	12.51
Bank of India	12.14	12.94	14.19
Bank of Maharashtra	11.18	11	11.86
Central Bank of India	10.95	9.04	9.61
Corporation Bank	11.32	9.23	12.30

CRAR (In %)	31 March 2017	31 March 2018	31 March 2019
Dena Bank	11.39	11.09	2
IDBI Bank	10.70	10.41	11.58
Indian Overseas Bank	10.50	9.25	10.21
Oriental Bank of Commerce	11.32	10.50	12.73
UCO Bank	10.93	10.94	10.70
United Bank of India	11.14	12.62	13

Source: Indian Banks' Association.

The CRAR has improved in most cases and that is primarily because of the government pumping money into these banks over the years. Between 2014–15 and 2018–19, the government has invested close to Rs 2.53 lakh crore in the PSBs. Of this, around Rs 1.55 lakh crore (or Rs 1,54,851 crore to be very precise) has been invested in banks which were categorized as PCA banks. A bulk of this money has been invested in 2017–18 and 2018–19.

But a few banks, like the Central Bank of India, Dena Bank, Indian Overseas Bank and UCO Bank, saw their CRAR fall over a two-year period. Dena Bank does not matter because its troubles have been merged away with the Bank of Baroda. But the other three banks need more capital to continue to be in operation.

Another parameter that we need to take a look at is the return on assets of the PCA banks. Take a look at Table 23.3, which lists that out.

Table 23.3: Return On Assets of PCA Banks.

Return on assets (In %)	31 March 2017	31 March 2018	31 March 2019
Allahabad Bank	(0.13)	(1.96)	(3.48)
Bank of India	(0.24)	(0.91)	(0.84)
Bank of Maharashtra	(0.86)	(0.73)	(3.01)

Return on assets (In %)	31 March 2017	31 March 2018	31 March 2019
Central Bank of India	(0.80)	(1.61)	(1.70)
Corporation Bank	0.23	(1.67)	(3.14)
Dena Bank	(0.67)	(1.59)	(5.49)
IDBI Bank	(1.38)	(2.46)	(1.53)
Indian Overseas Bank	(1.21)	(2.33)	(1.35)
Oriental Bank of Commerce	(0.46)	(2.31)	0.02
UCO Bank	(0.75)	(1.88)	(1.84)
United Bank of India	(0.16)	(1.04)	(1.60)

Source: Indian Banks' Association. *Brackets signify a negative figure.*

Table 23.3 makes for a very interesting reading. Only Oriental Bank of Commerce has improved when it comes to the return on assets and is barely in positive territory. What does this tell us? It tells us that all the banks under the PCA framework are continuing to lose money. They are not making a profit.

How can PSBs rebuild their capital bases without the government continuing to invest money in them? One way is to sell shares to outside investors (assuming they are interested). Between 2014–15 and 2018–19, the PSBs on the whole (and not just the PCA banks) raised around Rs 66,000 crore on their own. One problem here is the lack of investor interest in buying the shares of these banks. Over and above that, the government wants to maintain a majority control in these banks and, hence, these banks cannot sell fresh shares to raise capital beyond a point.

The second way to improve their capital bases is to turn profitable. The profit after tax and paying dividends becomes a part of the capital of the bank. This is something that isn't happening for PCA banks. In 2016–17, before most of these banks became a part of the PCA, the total losses of these banks stood at

Rs 17,286 crore. In 2017–18, the losses were at Rs 49,246 crore, and by 2018–19, the losses had increased to Rs 62,414 crore.

So, how has the PCA framework eventually turned out to be? It's safe to say that it has ensured that there has been some improvement on the bad loans front. But the PCA banks are still not out of the woods totally.

* * *

As I have been saying throughout this book, there is no free lunch in economics. There was a cost of banks being put under PCA, which the general public who chose to borrow money had to bear. Take a look at Figure 23.1, which basically plots the difference in the weighted average lending rate on outstanding loans of private sector banks and PSBs (in basis points).

Figure 23.1

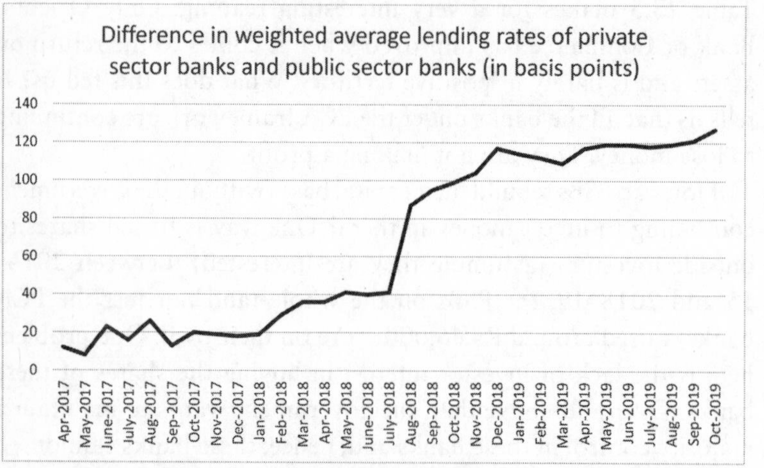

Difference in weighted average lending rates of private sector banks and public sector banks (in basis points)

Source: Author calculations based on RBI data.

Many PSBs were put under PCA. In April 2017, the difference between the weighted average lending rate oxn outstanding loans of private sector banks and PSBs was 11 basis points. By October 2019, this had jumped to 127 basis points. What this tells us is that with many PSBs being under PCA, the competition in the banking space came down. This allowed private sector banks to charge a higher rate of interest on their loans than they would have been able to charge, if the PSBs were in a better state and wouldn't have had to be put under PCA. This, as we shall see in Chapter 30, is another reason why the overall interest rates did not fall in 2019, despite the RBI cutting the repo rate significantly.

24

Merger Blues

By now, it's safe to say that the government really hasn't had much of a strategy in place on how to run PSBs. There is one exception to this, however. The government believes in the mergers of PSBs, so that they attain a certain size and are able to compete internationally. Or at least, as the former finance minister Arun Jaitley put it, 'India needs fewer and mega banks',[282] which are strong in every sense of the word.

The first thing that needs to be mentioned here is that most mergers fail. As a *Harvard Business Review* article, titled 'The Big Idea: The New M&A Playbook', points out: 'Study after study puts the failure rate of mergers and acquisitions somewhere between 70 per cent and 90 per cent.'[283]

What has the history of bank mergers in India been like? There have been two kinds seen in the country. The first kind is when a bank which is about to fail is merged with a stronger bank. Section 45 of the Banking Regulation Act 1949 empowers the RBI to 'make a scheme of amalgamation of a bank with another bank if it's in the depositors' interest or in the interest of overall banking system.' Hence, if a bank is in bad shape and there is a risk of the depositors losing their money, the RBI has the power to merge this bank with another in the interest of the overall banking system.

The merger of Global Trust Bank (GTB) with Oriental Bank of Commerce (OBC) in July 2004 is a good example of this. GTB was a private bank which found itself in trouble and was merged with OBC in the interest of the depositors.

When it comes to PSBs, an example of a forced merger was that of New Bank of India with PNB in 1993. The RBI had forced this merger under Section 45, because the New Bank of India had reached a precarious state of liquidity.[284] Simply put, this means that the bank did not have enough money to pay out its depositors. The after effects of the merger weren't good for the PNB. It ended up with losses of Rs 96 crore in 1996, after an uninterrupted record of profits. It had to face litigation relating to absorbing the employees of the New Bank of India. It took PNB five years and more to get over the negative effects of this forced merger.[285]

Since the onset of the economic reforms in India in 1991, there have been thirty-two voluntary mergers among private banks in India. As far as voluntary mergers go, a good example is the merger of ING Vysya Bank with Kotak Mahindra Bank. This merger had the so-called *synergy* necessary for a merger to take place.

As R. Gandhi, who was a deputy governor of the RBI, said in an April 2016 speech: 'ING Vysya Bank had a stronger presence in south India while Kotak had an extended franchise in west and north India. The merger created a large financial institution with a pan-Indian presence.'[286]

There have been other such mergers as well. The merger of Bank of Madura and Sangli Bank with ICICI Bank in 2001 and 2007, and the merger of Centurion Bank of Punjab with HDFC Bank in 2008 are other good examples of synergy-based mergers.

In 2008, the State Bank of Saurashtra was merged with the SBI. This was followed by the State Bank of Indore being merged with the SBI. In June 2016, the government issued a directive to merge the remaining five associate banks (State Bank of Bikaner and Jaipur, State Bank of Hyderabad, State Bank of Travancore, State Bank of Patiala and State Bank of Mysore), with the SBI. Along with these banks, the Bhartiya Mahila Bank, a very small bank, was also to merge with the SBI. The merger had to be completed by March 2017.

Let's take a look at Table 24.1. It plots the total advances and total bad loans of the SBI and the six banks before the merger happened. The merger happened starting 1 April 2017.

Table 24.1: Bad Loans, Before the Merger.

(as of 31 March 2017)	Total advances (in Rs crore)	Total bad loans (in Rs crore)	Bad loans rate (in %)
State Bank of India	15,71,078	1,12,343	7.2
State Bank of Bikaner & Jaipur	64,830	10,677	16.5
State Bank of Hyderabad	79,376	18,212	22.9
State Bank of Mysore	34,475	9,915	28.8
State Bank of Patiala	70,019	17,847	25.5
State Bank of Travancore	48,618	8,817	18.1
Bhartiya Mahila Bank	576	55	9.5

Source: Indian Banks' Association, as on 31 March 2017.

What does Table 24.1 tell us? It tells us that a bank which had a reasonably good bad loans rate of 7.2 per cent was forced to merge with banks which had very high bad loans rates, ranging between 9.5 per cent and 28.8 per cent. On their own, the six banks which were merged into the SBI had a bad loans rate of 22 per cent.

Of course, this meant that the bad loans rate of the SBI, after the merger, deteriorated, as the bad loans rate of the associate banks was very high. The bad loans rate of the SBI, as of 30 June 2017, had jumped to 10 per cent, up 280 basis points, from before the merger. The bad loans rate shot up to 10.9 per cent as of 31 March 2018 and then came down to 7.5 per cent as of 31 March 2019. Two years later, at 7.5 per cent, the bad loans rate was higher than where it was before the merger. In that sense, this merger was an effort to sweep the bad loans of the associate banks under the carpet.

This, despite the fact that the SBI and the associate banks had a lot going for them when it came to the merger.* In fact, the associate banks had shared SBI's logo for a while and had the same brand recall in the minds of the customer. So, from the brand point of view, this made immense sense.[287]

There were several operational factors as well, which went in favour of the merger. The chairman of the SBI presided over the boards of the associate banks. The associate banks were run by top executives of the SBI, who moved to these banks on deputation. Due to this, the norms of business, the operational systems and procedures, as well as the products offered by the associate banks, were the same as that of the SBI.[288]

Also, most importantly, in 2002, the SBI had engaged Tata Consultancy Services to roll out a core banking solution. This was supposed to cover the entire group, including the associate banks. Hence, the associate banks were operating on the same technology platform as the SBI. This was a major point in favour of the merger. Over and above this, the treasury operations of the associate banks had been integrated with that of the SBI for several years before the merger. Finally, the major lending decisions of the associate banks were vetted by the SBI.[289]

Despite so many things going for the merger, the accumulated bad loans of the associate banks pulled down the combined entity for a period of at least two years. Also, at the time of writing this, the challenges associated with the merger were still not over.

The merger had added 70,000 employees to the overall employee count of India's largest bank. This is, and will continue to remain, a major human resource challenge. The bank will have to figure out how to deploy this huge number of people productively.

---

*   In the overall scheme of things, the size of the Bhartiya Mahila Bank, at Rs 576 crore of advances, is too small and can be ignored.

The idea behind any merger is sold on one word and that is 'synergy'. What does the word really mean? One of my former professors used to say: 'Since we are all born on this Mother Earth, there is some sort of synergy between us.' That was his way of saying that synergy is basically bullshit. Once a merger has been decided on, people go looking for reasons to justify it; that is synergy. While that may be a very cynical way of looking at things, there is some truth in it.

Author John Lanchester defines synergy in his book *How to Speak Money* as, 'Synergy: Mainly BULLSHIT, but when it does mean anything it means merging two companies together and taking the opportunity to sack people.'[290] He then goes on to explain the concept through an example.

He writes: 'If two companies that make similar products merge, they will have a similar warehouse and delivery operations, so one of the two sets of employees will lose their jobs. The idea is that this will cut COSTS and increase profits ... When two companies merge, the first thing that ANALYSTS look at when evaluating the deal is how many jobs have been lost: the higher the number, the better. That's synergy.'[291]

How does this work in the case of mergers of PSBs as and when they happen?

If PSBs are merged, there are bound to be situations where both the banks have a presence in a given area. Synergy will demand that one of the branches be shut down. Interestingly, this is something that is happening. A Right to Information query revealed that over 3,400 branches of PSBs have either been closed or merged between 2014–15 and 2018–19. The State Bank of India merged or closed 2568 branches during this period. A bulk of the branches were merged or closed in 2017–18 and 2018–19, with the numbers being 2083 branches and 875 branches, respectively.[292]

While, the right thing has been done on the branches front, the same cannot be said about employees. When banks merge there will be multiple people with the same skills at the corporate level. Will this duplication of roles end with people being fired?

The answer is highly unlikely. In fact, Arun Jaitley, while he was finance minister, had clarified that there would be no loss of jobs due to the merger of PSBs.

Hence, the merger will only give us a bigger and a more inefficient bank. Take the case of the merger of Bank of Baroda, Vijaya Bank and Dena Bank – the other big merger announced by the government – in September 2018. The merger came into effect from 1 April 2019.

Take a look at Table 24.2 It lists out the total advances, bad loans and bad loans rate of Bank of Baroda, Vijaya Bank and Dena bank. The data used is as of 30 June 2018, the latest data available at the time of the announcement of the merger.

Table 24.2: Bad Loans, Same Story Again.

Name of the bank (as on 30 June 2018)	Total advances (in Rs crore)	Bad loans (in Rs crore)	Bad loans rate (in %)
Bank of Baroda	4,48,327	55,875	12.5
Vijaya Bank	1,22,348	7,579	6.2
Dena Bank	69,917	15,866	22.7
Total Bank	6,40,592	79,320	12.4

Source: Analyst/Investor presentations of the banks.

What does Table 24.2 tell us? Dena Bank was the worst bank of the lot. It had a bad loans rate of 22.7 per cent. Bank of Baroda was in a slightly better state with a bad loans rate of 12.5 per cent.

Vijaya Bank was by far the best of the lot with a bad loans rate of 6.2 per cent. In fact, among all the PSBs, this bank had the lowest bad loans rate. The bad loans rate of Vijaya Bank was even better than that of large private sector banks, like ICICI Bank and Axis Bank, at that point of time.

The merged entity would have a bad loans rate of 12.4 per cent – not very different from the bad loans rate of Bank of

Baroda, which as per advances made, would form 70 per cent of the new bank.

Again, the logic behind the merger is that of size. The combined entity of Bank of Baroda, Vijaya Bank and Dena Bank would be the second-largest PSB. The only trouble with this logic is that with the rise of information technology, alternatives to brick-and-mortar branch banking are now available.[293]

First and foremost, it makes sense to merge banks with common cultural identities, which these three banks clearly don't have. Also, unlike the merger of the associate banks with the SBI, there is no uniformity in the information technology architecture of these PSBs. In fact, each PSB has used several IT vendors to develop its information technology system. Just getting this part of the business right will be a challenge, which is likely to go on for a long time.[294]

It makes sense to merge banks with some sort of common cultural identity. Take the case of merging Punjab & Sind Bank with the much bigger PNB. Or take the case of merging Vijaya Bank with the much bigger Canara Bank. In both the cases, there is some common cultural identity, which can get the merger going.[295]

Also, mergers won't work unless the government decides to rationalize the workforce of the merged bank and shut down branches which are operating in the same catchment area. Without this being done, a merger will just turn out to be an exercise in ensuring that the severe bad loan problems of smaller banks are swept under the larger bank. This is precisely what has happened with the merger of Dena Bank, Vijaya Bank and Bank of Baroda. The problems of Dena Bank have been swept under the merged entity. Also, it has nipped the emergence of Vijaya Bank as a well-performing PSB from which other banks could learn a thing or two.

It makes sense for the smaller PSBs to have limited ambitions in terms of national presence as well as the areas that they operate in. Take the case of Dena Bank. For many years it was a profitable bank focussed on trade financing. It would have made more sense to get the bank to focus exclusively on small and medium enterprises and traders.[296] But that was not to be.

Gandhi summarizes the situation: 'Merger of a weak bank with a strong bank may make combined entity weak if the merger process is not handled properly. The problems of capital shortages and higher NPAs may get transmitted to stronger bank due to [an] unduly hasty or a mechanical merger process.'[297]

But then the government isn't really bothered about this. Like the banks that it owns, it also simply wants to kick the can down the road.

***

In late August 2019, more PSB mergers were announced. The Indian Bank and Allahabad Bank will merge. So, will Canara Bank and Syndicate Bank. The Union Bank, Andhra Bank and Corporation Bank will merge. The biggest merger will be that of Punjab National Bank, Oriental Bank of Commerce and United Bank. The merged entity will become the second largest PSB in India. The number of PSBs after the mergers will be reduced to twelve from the earlier eighteen.

25

What the Government Wanted to Do with Our Money but Didn't

In August 2017, a rather innocuous-sounding Financial Resolution and Deposit Insurance (FRDI) Bill was introduced in the Lok Sabha. After the Bill was introduced it was referred to a Joint Committee of members belonging to the Lok Sabha as well as the Rajya Sabha.

The major objective of the Bill was to provide a framework which went beyond just the failure of banks and look for a resolution for the bad loans plaguing financial institutions. This included NBFCs, insurance companies, regional or cooperative banks, mutual or pension funds, a payment system operator and a securities firm.[298]

The basic idea behind the Bill was to establish an all-encompassing Resolution Corporation. In case a financial service provider was staring at failure, the Resolution Corporation had the power to liquidate the firm or acquire and transfer its assets to another healthy firm, and thus carry out a merger.[299]

The different segments of India's financial sector were overseen by different regulators. Each of these regulators was set up by a different Act. The intention of the FRDI Bill was to amend around twenty such laws and bring the resolution function – when a financial service provider was staring at failure – under one umbrella of the Resolution Corporation.[300]

Within months of the Bill being presented in parliament, WhatsApp forwards highlighting what the Bill could do to deposits in banks started to do the rounds.

I came to realize the gravity of the situation only when I started getting questions from my family and friends, who normally never asked me anything, either on money in particular or economics in general. And they were asking me whether the WhatsApp forwards going around happened to be true.

There was one clause in the Bill which really spooked people in general. Clause 52 of the FRDI Bill used the term 'bail-in'. This clause essentially empowered the Resolution Corporation 'in consultation with the appropriate regulator, if it's satisfied that it was necessary to bail-in a specified service provider to absorb the losses incurred, or reasonably expected to be incurred, by the specified service provider.'

What does bail-in actually mean? It means that financial firms or a bank on the verge of failure can be rescued through a bail-in. Typically, the word bailout is used, and refers to a situation where money is brought in from the outside to rescue a bank or financial firm. In the Indian context, the government constantly recapitalizing PSBs over the last decade is a very good example of a bailout. But what is a bail-in? At a very simple level, in the case of a bail-in, the rescue is carried out internally by restructuring the liabilities of the bank.

Given that banks pay an interest on their deposits, a deposit is a liability for any bank. Clause 52 of FRDI essentially allowed the Resolution Corporation to cancel a liability owed by a specified service provider or to modify or change the form of a liability owed by a specified service provider.

Hence, Clause 52 allowed the Resolution Corporation to cancel the repayment of various kinds of deposits. It also allowed it to convert deposits into long-term bonds or equity for that matter. Haircuts could also be imposed on firms to which the bank owed money. A haircut refers to a situation where the borrower negotiates a fresh deal and does not repay the entire amount it owes to the lender.

Nevertheless, there were conditions to this. The bail-in would not impact any liability owed by a specified service provider to the depositors to the extent such deposits are covered by deposit insurance. This meant that the bail-in would impact only the amount of deposits above the insured amount. At that point of time, deposits of up to Rs 1 lakh were insured by the Deposit Insurance and Credit Guarantee Corporation (DICGC). This amount hadn't been revised since 1993.

Typically, anyone who has deposits in a bank tends to assume that they are 100 per cent guaranteed to get their money back. But that is clearly not the case. Over the years, the government has prevented depositors from taking any hit by merging banks which are in trouble with another bigger bank.

So, to that extent, the situation, if the FRDI Bill had been passed, wouldn't have been very different from the one that *already* prevailed. The trouble, as always, nuance and learnings from the WhatsApp University rarely go together. This time was no different.

Not surprisingly, one year after it was introduced, the Bill was quietly dropped in August 2018. It seems that the then finance minister, Piyush Goyal, told the parliamentary committee constituted to look into the Bill that the government had decided to drop it due to apprehensions that had developed among people around the 'bail-in' clause. The clause was perceived to be against the interest of depositors, Goyal informed the committee.[301]

In early 2020, it was reported that the FRDI Bill was making a quiet comeback under the new name of Financial Sector Development and Regulation (Resolution) (FSDR) Bill, 2019.

26

The Insolvency and the Bankruptcy Code

India did not have an effective corporate bankruptcy system and, therefore, the RBI tried to patch together a new bad loan resolution process, which resembled corporate bankruptcy.

In fact, Arun Jaitley, who was the finance minister through much of Narendra Modi's first term as prime minister between 2014 and 2019, admitted to the lack of a corporate bankruptcy process in the budget speech he made in February 2016: 'A systemic vacuum exists with regard to bankruptcy situations in financial firms.' In the same speech, he talked about the enactment of an insolvency and bankruptcy code.

The Insolvency and Bankruptcy Code, 2016 (IBC), received presidential assent on 28 May 2016, after the Lok Sabha and Rajya Sabha had passed it earlier in the month. It took a few months to get the system in place. The entire ecosystem of corporate insolvency was in place by the end of 2016.[302]

Of course, the main aim of having an insolvency and bankruptcy system in place was to help expeditiously solve the problem of PSBs' bad loans. Let's take a look at Figure 26.1, which plots the number of years it took to resolve insolvency across different countries in 2015.

Figure 26.1

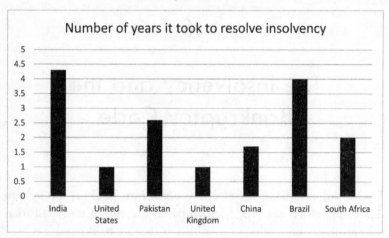

Number of years it took to resolve insolvency

Source: Time to Resolve Insolvency, World Bank. https://data.worldbank.org/indicator/IC.ISV.DURS.

Figure 26.1 tells us that India took a long time to resolve insolvency. This was primarily on account of the lack of a proper insolvency and bankruptcy framework. The IBC 2016 tried to address this. Let's take a look at how it sought to do so.[303]

Unlike the earlier patchwork of laws, the IBC provides for a time-bound process for the resolution of an insolvent company, which has defaulted on repaying a bank loan. In case a corporate defaults on the repayment of a loan, the IBC allows the lenders to take control of the company. They must then make decisions to resolve the insolvency within the next 180 days. During these 180 days, the borrower who has defaulted is provided immunity from the resolution claims of the lenders. The National Companies Law Tribunal (NCLT) adjudicates the proceedings of the resolution process.

When a corporate default occurs, the lenders (such as banks) or the company defaulting can initiate the resolution process. An insolvency professional is appointed to manage the entire process.

It's his job to provide the financial information of the defaulter to the lenders and, at the same time, manage the assets of the defaulter.

The existing board of the company is suspended. The insolvency professional then forms a committee of lenders who have loaned money to the defaulting company. This committee is called the committee of creditors. This committee decides a resolution plan for the future of the debt that is owed to them. More than 66 per cent of the committee needs to approve the plan; earlier this was placed at 75 per cent.

A resolution plan can typically entail the following things: a) a change in the management, product portfolio or technology of the defaulting company; b) the acquisition or disposal of assets, businesses or undertakings; c) a restructuring of the organization, business model, ownership, balance sheet; d) put in place a strategy of turnaround, buy-out, merger, acquisition, take over; and so on.[304] Over and above this, the committee of creditors can also decide on changing the repayment schedule of the loan which has been defaulted on.

While this sounds like quite a lot of options, from the resolution plans which have been executed up until now we can clearly see that the committee of creditors prefers to sell the defaulting company to another entity and recover whatever portion of the defaulted loan it can.

Whatever the committee of creditors decides on, it needs to do so in 180 days. Initially, when the IBC was put in place, this could be extended up to 270 days. In July 2019, this was increased to 330 days, including the period of litigation that might follow the resolution plan. If a resolution plan is not in place by then, the assets of the company go for liquidation, which is administered by the insolvency professional.

This is the process that has to be followed to resolve the insolvency and ensure that some recovery of bad loans happens for banks. Interestingly, the IBC empowers the operational creditors (trade suppliers, employees, workmen, etc.) of the corporate defaulter to initiate the insolvency process as well.

But before we go any further, it's important to understand why IBC is necessary.

As per the Global Competitiveness Report of the World Economic Forum, there are three broad sources of growth in a country: a) basic requirements, such as institutions and resources; b) competition; and c) innovation. Both competition and innovation are very important for a country looking to grow fast. Competition keeps current firms on their toes, ensuring that the consumers get a good deal on what they pay for, and, at the same time, helps efficient firms drive inefficient firms out of the market. Innovation, on the other hand, helps newer firms enter the market and, if they are good, drive out the older, more established firms.[305]

This means that in an economic system that allows competition and innovation to thrive, firms – both old and new – will keep failing all the time. In fact, in the United States, the chances of a small business surviving for a period of five years is around 35 per cent.[306]

Competition and innovation are both required for faster economic growth, and so it's important to deal with the frequent failure of companies smartly. The process of creative destruction should drive out unviable and failed companies from the market, and this should happen on a continuous basis.[307] The resources of these companies – physical, human and financial – should be freed up to be deployed elsewhere. This is even more important in a capital-deficient country like India. That's how IBC is supposed to work, at least in theory.

But it remains to be seen how well the IBC fulfils what has been explained above. This will only become clear to us over a period of time, once IBC has been around for a sufficient period of time – let's say at least a decade.

Over and above the IBC, the government also amended the Banking Regulation Act of 1949, and introduced a new Section

35(AA), which stated: 'The Central Government may, by order, authorise the Reserve Bank to issue directions to any banking company or banking companies to initiate insolvency resolution process in respect of a default, under the provisions of the Insolvency and Bankruptcy Code, 2016.'[308]

The RBI made use of this new section and on 13 June 2017, recommended that '12 accounts totalling about 25 per cent of the current gross NPAs [bad loans] of the banking system would qualify for immediate reference under IBC.'[309] These twelve companies which had defaulted on a huge amount of banks loans were Essar Steel, Monnet Ispat and Energy, Bhushan Steel, Bhushan Power and Steel, Era Infra Engineering, ABG Shipyard, Jaypee Infratech, Amtek Auto, Alok Industries, Jyoti Structures, Lanco Infratech and Electrosteel Steels.

With a default of over Rs 56,000 crore, Bhushan Steel was the biggest defaulter of them all. Essar Steel, with a default of over Rs 49,000 crore, came in second. These companies had to be put through the IBC and a resolution plan had to be put in place.

As on 31 March 2017, the total bad loans of banks stood at Rs 7,91,995 crore. One-fourth of that amounts to Rs 1,97,999 crore. Roughly, Rs 2,00,000 crore was at stake.

The insolvency process actually started working in mid-2017, despite coming into force in December 2016. How has the performance been since then?

Between December 2016, when it came into force, and September 2019, a total of 2542 defaulting companies have been admitted into the corporate insolvency resolution process (CIRP) adjudicated by the NCLT. Of this, a resolution plan has been approved in 156 cases. Given that 1045 cases have been closed, in nearly 15 per cent of the cases a resolution plan has been approved.

The total claim of the lenders stood at Rs 3,32,087 crore. Of this, Rs 1,37,919 crore, or around 41.5 per cent, has been recovered. This is clearly better than the recovery which was happening in the pre-IBC era. Also, if these firms were to be liquidated, the liquidation value would have come to Rs 74,997 crore. So, clearly, the recovery through CIRP looks much better.

Of course, politicians and bureaucrats have patted themselves on their backs on the basis of this data. But there is a little more to this. The biggest default on bank loans was carried out by Bhushan Steel. The claim admitted in this case was Rs 56,022 crore. As a part of the resolution plan, the banks decided on selling the company to Tata Steel,* which paid Rs 35,571 crore for it. This meant that the rate of recovery was 63.5 per cent of the loans defaulted by Bhushan Steel, with a haircut of 36.5 per cent.

The total amount of recovery that happened in the case of Bhushan Steel forms around 25.8 per cent of the overall recovery. Hence, this one result alone has had a disproportionate influence on the overall data and the overall recovery rate. How do things look if we ignore this case? The rate of recovery falls from 41.5 per cent to 37.1 per cent then. After taking this into account, things don't look as good as they did earlier.

What about the time taken to resolve those cases where a resolution plan has been approved? The average time taken to resolve the 156 cases has been 374 days, which is more than the stipulated period of 270 days (180 days + 90 days) first and 330 days later, but lesser than the 4.3 years it took in the pre-IBC era. Clearly, the resolution has been faster under IBC, at least up until now. In July 2019, the government increased the deadline to resolve the CIRP to 330 days. Interestingly, the 270-day deadline had applied only to the committee of creditors approving the resolution plan. It did not apply to the litigation that followed.

---

* Tata Steel acquired Bhushan Steel through its wholly owned subsidiary, Bamnipal Steel, and later renamed it Tata Steel BSL. The banks also got a 12.27 per cent stake in Bhushan Steel as a part of the resolution plan.

Now the 330-day limit applies to the judges handling the litigation as well.[310]

* * *

Let's take a look at the twelve big IBC cases the RBI asked the banks to take through CIRP. How has the rate of recovery been here? Take a look at Table 26.1, which lists the details.

Table 26.1: The Loan Recovery.

Name of the corporate defaulter	Amount admitted (in Rs crore)	Amount realized (in Rs crore)
Electroseel Steels Ltd.	13,175	5,320
Bhushan Steel	56,022	35,571
Monnet Ispat and Energy	11,015	2,892
Essar Steel India	49,473	42,000
Alok Industries	29,532	5,052
Jyoti Structures	7,365	3,684

Source: IBBI Quarterly Newsletter (July to September 2019).

Essar Steel India was sold to ArcelorMittal India as part of the resolution plan, but the deal was stuck primarily because the payment to be made to the operational creditors of the company was under dispute. In fact, in July 2019, the government made the necessary amendments to the IBC to make sure that the secured creditors, who have lent money to a company against a collateral, get priority on the pay-outs from the sale or the liquidation of insolvent companies.[311]

In November 2019, the Supreme Court cleared the way for ArcelorMittal India to take over Essar Steel by upholding the primacy of the financial creditors in the CIRP. All the data in Table 26.1 is as of 30 September 2019, except for Essar Steel, where the data is as of mid-December 2019, after ArcelorMittal India had initiated the payment of Rs 42,000 crore to banks.

How good has the rate of recovery been in the case of the six of the big twelve companies? Of the total amount of Rs 1,66,582 crore that the financial creditors of these firms had filed for, they have managed to recover Rs 94,519 crore, which works out to 56.7 per cent. As is clear from Table 26.1, the good recovery in case of Bhushan Steel and Essar Steel has made the overall numbers look good.

If we ignore these two companies and look at the recovery that has happened in case of the other 154 companies which have gone through resolution plans, how do things look?

The rate of recovery in other cases falls to 31.9 per cent, showing again that the good recoveries in the case of Bhushan Steel and Esssar Steel, the biggest defaulters, has had a major influence on the overall data.

We have seen that since it started 2,542 companies have been put through CIRP. Of this, in 156 cases a resolution plan has been approved. The liquidation of another 587 companies has been started. Of this, around 427 companies were already in BIFR (Bureau of Industrial and Financial Reconstruction). The economic value of most of these defaulters had already been destroyed before they had been admitted into the CIRP.

There has barely been any recovery in this case.

In fact, even though liquidation of 578 companies has been started, as of September 2019, the liquidation of only twenty-four companies has been completed. This shows us the negative side of IBC. Take a look at Table 26.2, which lists out the details of the companies in which case the liquidation had been completed, up until March 2019.

Table 26.2: Liquidation, Nothing Comes Back.

Name of the corporate defaulter	Date of order of liquidation	Amount of admitted claims (in Rs crore)	Liquidation value (in Rs crore)	Sales proceeds (in Rs crore)
Abhayam Trading	17/11/17	11.14	0.85	0.85
Dev Blessing Traders	26/10/18	5.81	0	NA*
Ghotaringa Minerals	31/08/18	4662.89	0	NA
Zeel Global Projects	07/05/18	1.28	0	NA
DDS Steel Rolling Mills	18/07/18	NA	0	NA
SDS Steels Private	30/07/18	NA	0	NA

Source: IBBI Quarterly Newsletter (January–March 2019).
*NA means not realisable/saleable or no asset left for liquidation.

What does the data in Table 26.2 tell us? This data and a look at the other data for companies being liquidated makes it clear that if a company goes for liquidation, the chances of any *significant* recovery happening are rather non-existent. One reason for this perhaps lies in the fact that India does not have an active organized market for used industrial assets. And unless this happens, the redeployment of these assets will be limited and won't ensure better recovery for banks.[312] Also, this doesn't allow the process of creative destruction to work.

What about the cases where the CIRP is still on? The number of ongoing CIRPs, as of 30 September 2019, stands at 1,497. Take a look at Table 26.3, which lists the timeline.

Table 26.3: Timeline of CIRPs.

Ongoing CIRPs	
>270 days	535
>180 days <= 270 days	324
>90 days <=180 days	276
<=90 days	362

Source: IBBI Quarterly Newsletter (July to September 2019).

The IBC basically says that the resolution plan should be in place within 180 days. As of March 2019, it allowed a maximum of 270 days, which was extended to 330 days in July 2019. Nevertheless, as we see in Table 26.3, 535 of the 1,497 CIRPs, which were in progress as of 30 September 2019, had been going on for more than 270 days. This includes some of the big twelve corporate defaulters that the RBI placed under the CIRP. Indeed, this is worrying. Every day of delay leads to a loss of interest income for banks. Take the case of Bhushan Power and Steel, one of the twelve big defaulters. The company defaulted on a total of Rs 47,158 crore. The company was all set to be acquired by JSW Steel for Rs 19,350 crore, as a part of its resolution plan. This was set aside because of an on-going investigation into money laundering and fraud being carried out against the former owners of the company.

A single day of delay in this case leads to a notional loss of interest of Rs 4.2 crore. In case of Essar Steel, which was also stuck in litigation, it led to a loss of Rs 10 crore per day, which is not a small amount of money.[313]

Over and above this, when bankers recover a portion of their bad loans, they are able to strengthen the overall capital they have. This means the government needs lesser money to recapitalize these banks. Hence, delays in recovery hurt in various ways.

One reason for this lies in the fact that the number of CIRPs being brought to NCLTs has been going up over the years. Take a look at Figure 26.2, which plots this.

Figure 26.2

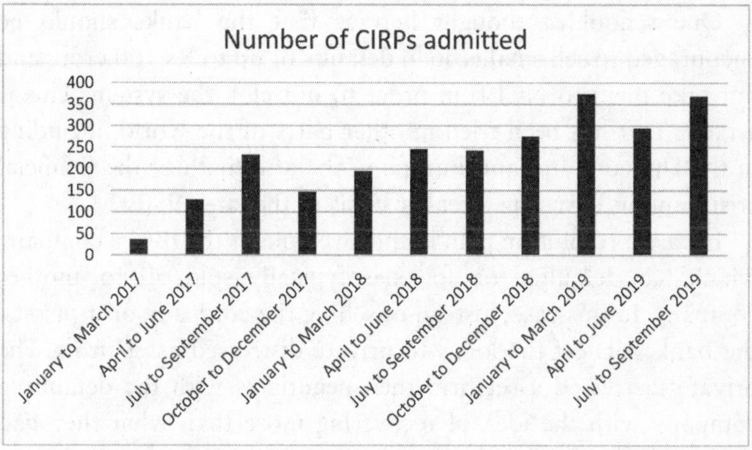

Source: IBBI Quarterly Newsletter (July–September 2019).

As can be seen from Figure 26.2, the number of CIRPs being taken to NCLTs has risen majorly since January to March 2017. As the number of CIRPs still in process stands at 1,497, what it tells us that CIRPs are accumulating at NCLTs faster than it can dispose them of. This is the problem that Debt Recovery Tribunals used to face earlier.

Also, at the current rate of disposal of cases by NCLT, it could take nearly five to six years for the most important cases to be settled. There is also a serious risk that the new system is getting overloaded with too many corporate defaults being brought under the CIRP.[314]

The NCLT has twelve benches operating currently. Given the pile-up of CIRPs, clearly more benches are needed. The ministry of corporate affairs is contemplating doubling the benches, which is also something that is badly required as of now.[315]

What more can be done about it? The IBC allows a creditor to take a defaulter to NCLT, even if there is a delay of just one day and the amounted defaulted on is more than Rs 1 lakh. In this scenario, it's not surprising that the number of CIRPs stood at 1,497, as on 30 September 2019. Clearly, the NCLT is overloaded.

One school of thought here is that the banks should be encouraged to sell smaller loan defaults of up to Rs 100 crore and not take them to NCLT, in order to not clog the system. This is a tactic that has been tried in other parts of the world, including in the United States and Europe in the aftermath of the financial crisis, and in East Asia after the crisis of the late 1990s.[316]

In case a resolution plan is approved under the IBC, a company which has defaulted on loans is typically sold off to another company. In this case, instead of selling the company or its assets, the bank sells off the loans to private distressed asset firms. The private distressed asset firm then negotiates with the defaulting company with the idea of recovering more than what they had paid to the bank while buying the loan. This difference makes up their profit. World over this strategy has made sense primarily because distressed asset firms have the required experience and the specialized skills to carry out the recovery and are generally in a better position than banks. Over and above this, in the Indian case, the distressed asset firms are not limited by the guidelines that PSBs need to follow. Also, they don't have to fear the vigilance agencies.[317]

India has had asset reconstruction companies, a form of a distressed asset firm, working for a while now. But their recoveries have been below par. One reason for this lies in litigation delays. Also, banks, while selling their loans, tend to insist on all-cash deals, which asset reconstruction companies find difficult to fulfil.[318]

Banks also find it convenient to recognize a loan as a bad loan and keep it on their books, rather than sell it to an asset reconstruction company. If a bad loan is sold to an asset reconstruction company, the bank needs to recognize the loss immediately.[319] On the flip side, if a bad loan continues to be a bad loan on the books of the bank, it's provisioned for over a period of four years. In that sense, losses can then be spread over four years, which is not the case if a bank decides to sell a bad loan to an asset reconstruction company. Hence, the incentive is so structured that it doesn't make much sense for a bank to sell a bad loan to an asset reconstruction company.

If banks decide to sell off loans of smaller defaulters, it will ease pressure on the NCLT. This means the chances of the bigger corporate defaults getting resolved more quickly will get better. Of course, for all this to happen, there needs to be enough distressed asset firms going around and banks need the right incentives to sell to them. Currently, only asset reconstruction firms are allowed in the distressed asset space. The RBI needs to open up this market for private equity funds, and even high net worth individuals, for that matter.[320] A wider pool of prospective buyers in any market always makes the market function better.

And finally, any new system takes time to evolve and mature. As the years go by and the IBC system matures and becomes more predictable, more buyers are likely to become a part of the process. This will also work towards attracting more foreign buyers and foreign money into the process.[321]

* * *

Quite a few changes have been made to the IBC since its introduction. This isn't surprising as it takes any code some time to mature and take the workings of the system into account. The US Bankruptcy Code has seen 237 amendments since its inception. Any law which aims to implement a new system is bound to get amended as it matures. The IBC is no different on this front. On 18 January 2018, Section 29A was inserted into the IBC. This section bars defaulting promoters and related persons from presenting a resolution plan and bidding for an insolvent company. Before this section was introduced, promoters preferred their companies going into liquidation so that they could buy back the assets of the company (which essentially means the company itself) without any debt.[322] By doing this, they could gain control of the company again and, at the same time, manage to reduce its debt.

The idea of promoters presenting a resolution plan for what used to be their company and then managing to buy it back at a steep discount, benefiting themselves at the cost of lenders, is morally questionable. One school of thought suggests that the entire moral argument around promoters buying back their insolvent company cheaply does not work if they are ready to repay the entire amount owed to financial and operational creditors. Shouldn't we then be looking at the situation differently, as this would maximize recovery of defaulted loans as well as what is owed to operational creditors? Also, if the company which defaulted on its debt is sold back to its promoter, the requirement of any due diligence and any fact-finding can be done away with.[323]

Let's take the example of Essar Steel. The company and its promoters (the Ruia brothers) defaulted on bank loans of Rs 49,473 crore, the second-largest default after Bhushan Steel. The committee of creditors decided to sell the company to ArcelorMittal at Rs 42,000 crore. This worked out to a recovery rate of 85 per cent, which was excellent to say the least. Essar Steel Asia Holdings (another company of the Ruia family) was ready to pay Rs 54,000 crore, but this was not taken up by the committee of creditors (i.e., the banks whose loans Essar Steel had originally defaulted on). Other than repaying the financial creditors, the operational creditors would also be paid. Of course, Essar Steel Asia Holdings' offer was better than that of ArcelorMittal, so should that have been taken on?

The trouble is that if a defaulting promoter is allowed to present a resolution plan, there will be no fear of losing the company for him. And this fear is at the heart of the IBC.

How does this fear work? In the pre-admission stage, 4,452 cases of default were disposed. What does this mean? These 4,452 companies had defaulted on bank loans and were to be put through the CIRP, but then decided to settle with the banks. The amount settled was around Rs 2.02 lakh crore.[324]

The fear of losing their companies made all these promoters settle with the banks before going through the CIRP. This fear will go away if promoters are allowed to buy back their insolvent companies. If this means that banks lose out on some recovery in case of companies going through the CIRP, then so be it.

In their book *In Service of the Republic – The Art and Science of Economic Policy*, Vijay Kelkar and Ajay Shah say that public policy work is a test match and not an IPL. What they mean here is that any change in the system because of the IBC will take time. As they write: 'When the Insolvency and the Bankruptcy Code was enacted in 2016, this had no immediate impact on the ground, as the state and private insitutions that were required to implement the law did not exist. A multi-year process began, which included building the National Company Law Tribunal and the Insolvency and Bankruptcy Board of India. On the private side individuals started specializing in the field of bankruptcy.'[325]

The bulk of the gains from the bankruptcy reform will come from the change in behaviour of the borrowers. And this will take time. As Kelkar and Shah point out: 'At first, the threat of the law has to change. In time, this will induce changes in culture, in the ways in which contracting and negotiation take place. The full impact takes time.'[326]

Another factor which has hurt the functioning of the IBC is the fact that it was rushed through for a quick launch, without adequate processes, systems or for that matter, even people being in place. As Kelkar and Shah point out: 'Many corners were cut in getting to a quick launch ... Would it have made sense to lay the groundwork from May 2016 to May 2018, and only then declare IBC open for business? We suspect that things would have looked better by early 2019, if that slow path had been taken.'[327]

Getting back to Section 29A, it also came in for good use in the case of Sterling Biotech, whose promoters, Nitin Jayantilal Sandesara, Chetan Jayantilal Sandesara, Dipti Chetan Sandesara and Hiteshkumar Patel, are absconding after defaulting on loans worth Rs 7,500 crore. The absconding promoters offered the banks, led by Andhra Bank, a one-time settlement of Rs 3,100 crore. On 7 March 2019, the committee of creditors used Section 12(A) of the IBC to withdraw the insolvency proceedings against Sterling Biotech, and go for a one-time settlement with them.[328] Thankfully, the NCLT questioned the motive of the lenders to withdraw the bankruptcy petition and go for a one-time settlement instead. This is another example which shows why Section 29A is a necessary part of IBC.

***

There has been a demand for companies which have defaulted on bank loans and which operate in the steel sector. The same cannot be said about other sectors, like textiles and power. Given this, the extent of recovery that the creditors will manage to carry out under the IBC at any point of time will also depend on the sectors that are doing well at that point of time. Currently, the steel sector is doing well and it has been relatively easier for creditors to sell steel companies as a part of a resolution plan, compared to other companies. As we have seen earlier, the rate of recovery in case of Bhushan Steel was 63.5 per cent and 84.9 per cent in case of Essar Steel. Other than the fact that the steel sector had been in an upcycle over the last couple of years, Bhushan Steel offered a large established capacity as well. Since mid-2019 the steel cycle has started to reverse and by the time ArcelorMittal's acquisition of Essar Steel will be completed, the company may have ended up overpaying.

One sector which has been down in the dumps has been the textile sector. Let's consider the example of the textile company Alok Industries, which had defaulted on bank loans of Rs 29,523 crore, and was among the twelve big defaulters that the RBI asked banks to take through the CIRP. There was only one bidder for the company, a consortium of Reliance Industries Ltd (RIL) and JM Financial Asset Reconstruction Co. (JMFARC). They offered

Rs 5052 crore for the company. This meant that lenders (which included nine PSBs, LIC and Axis Bank) would recover only 17.1 per cent of the total loans which the company had defaulted on. This would mean a massive haircut of around 83 per cent.[329]

In fact, the committee of creditors did not get the required 75 per cent vote to pass the resolution plan. It got only 70 per cent of the votes. An ordinance, which reduced the minimum vote required to pass a resolution plan to 66 per cent, was introduced by the government. The voting was carried out again and after this, the company was sold off.[330]

Of course, this risk of an out-of-favour sector not being sold at a good price is one which will always remain. There seems to be no way out of this. Another sector which is not in favour right now, and has been causing huge problems for banks, is the power sector, and which is where we will turn our attention next.

27

The Power Trap

In 2007, the private sector contributed just 13 per cent of the total power production in India. A decade later, in 2017, it made up for 44 per cent of the production. This was primarily on account of the fast addition of power capacity between 2012 and 2017. The cumulative addition during the period stood at 99,209 MW against a target of 88,537 MW.[331] The private sector added a bulk of this capacity.

This fast growth in the power sector capacity came with its own set of problems. When it came to its inability to repay loans, the Department of Financial Services identified thirty-four stressed thermal power plants. The list included power plants which had stopped repaying loans and, hence, the loans they had taken had become bad loans. Along with this, it also included loans of those power plants which had the potential to become bad loans.

These plants had a total production capacity of 40,130 MW. Of this, the commissioned capacity was 24,405 MW. The remaining 15,725 MW was under construction.[332] The cost of these power projects was expected to be Rs 2,90,028 crore. The power companies had taken on loans worth Rs 1,76,130 crore to fund these projects. The promoters of these companies had invested Rs 60,177 crore.[333]

What went wrong with these projects? Let's take a look.

The overall debt to equity ratio of the stressed power plants works out to 2.9:1. This is on the higher side and reflects the era of easy lending during which these loans were given out. In fact, eight out of the thirty-four power plants had a debt to equity ratio of greater than 4:1. The basic structure of these loans with the promoter taking little risk and the bank taking on a higher risk was wrong.

In 2014, in an effort to clean up the Coalgate scam, the Supreme court cancelled the licences of 204 coal mines, which had been given out by the government. A thermal power plant needs coal as fuel. With coal mining licences cancelled, many power projects became stranded without adequate arrangements of fuel supply. Over and above this, some power plants were set up without firm coal linkages from Coal India Ltd (which produces a bulk of coal in India) in place. This resulted in a high cost of generation.[334]

Also, the private sector very quickly added a lot of power generation capacity. Coal India's production increases couldn't keep pace with this. This led to a reduction in supplies from Coal India, which was needed to maintain a plant load factor of 80 per cent (basically a situation where the power plants produce 80 per cent of the power they can actually produce at full capacity). This led to low plant load factors and, in the process, reduced the ability of power firms to earn enough to repay their loans. Further, other than not increasing production adequately, a shortage of railway rakes came in the way of the transportation of coal.[335]

The power plants were not compensated for the short supply of coal due to the fault of Coal India or, for that matter, the Indian Railways, which moves the coal.[336]

The reason for the short supply of coal by Coal India is simple enough. It just doesn't produce enough to meet the demands of the country. The government-owned Coal India and Singareni Collieries produce more than 90 per cent of the coal produced in the country. The rest is produced by those companies which have coal mines for captive consumption.

Let's take a look at Table 27.1, which lists the details of the total coal produced by Coal India and the target that had been set

Table 27.1: Coal India.

	Total production (in million tonnes)	Target (in million tonnes)
2016–17	554.1	598.6
2017–18	567.4	600
2018–19	606.9	610

Source: Lok Sabha Unstarred Question No. 699, answered on 26 June 2019.

It's clear that over a three-year period between 2016 and 2019, Coal India did not meet its production targets, though the difference in 2018–19 was very low. In this scenario, it's not surprising that power plants sometimes did not get an adequate supply of coal from the company. Now, take a look at Table 27.2, which plots coal production, coal imports and coal demand, over a longer period.

Table 27.2: Everything About Coal.

Year	2013–14	2014–15	2015–16	2016–17	2017–18
Total demand (in million tonnes)*	769.7	787	822.4	884.9	908.4
Total domestic production (in million tonnes)	565.8	609.2	639.2	657.9	676.5
Total import (in million tonnes)	166.9	217.8	204	191	208.3

Year	2013–14	2014–15	2015–16	2016–17	2017–18
Value of imports (in Rs crore)	92,329	1,04,507	86,034	1,00,231	1,38,477
Price of imported coal per million tonne (in Rs crore)**	553.2	479.8	421.7	524.8	664.8

Source: Rajya Sabha Unstarred Question No. 2614, answered on 4 January 2019.

* All-India demand estimated by NITI Aayog.

** Author calculations.

It's clear from Table 27.2 that India does not produce enough coal to meet its overall requirements. The basic problem is that the rate of increase in coal production is very low. Between 2013–14 and 2017–18, coal production increased at the rate of 4.6 per cent per year, which is simply not enough to meet the increasing demand. It's not that India does not have enough coal reserves. The total proven coal reserve in the country stands at 148.8 billion tonnes. Despite these huge reserves, India still needs to import coal.

The only way to extract more coal is to dig more mines, which is not happening at the pace required. This is primarily because of 'reasons like problems in land acquisition owing to unclear land records, physical possession of land, rehabilitation and resettlement issues, evacuation and logistics constraints and law and order problem in coalfield areas'.[337]

Over and above this, a major reason for the slow increase in the total production lies in the low per-employee productivity of Coal India employees. Coal India produces around 1,100 tonnes of coal per employee in a year. Now compare this with the 36,700 tonnes per employee produced by Peabody Energy, based in the United States. The Chinese Shenhua Energy produces 12,700 tonnes per employee.[338]

To correct this, that is, to increase the coal production at a faster rate and import lesser coal, the government allowed commercial mining in coal in February 2018. The aim of this policy 'is to create a marketplace for coal with multiple producers to drive competition.'[339]

The logic is plain and simple. As Partha Bhattacharya, a former chairman of Coal India, pointed out, there was a great need to create competition in the sector: 'Multiple players that have both bandwidth and competence … [will turn] the current situation of acute coal shortage into one of abundance.'[340]

Nevertheless, this is not going to produce results overnight. It will take a few years for the coal blocks to be auctioned to private parties for commercial mining and then for them to start producing a significant amount of coal, which will help bring down imports.

The bigger point here is that the lack of reforms can hurt in ways one can't even imagine beforehand. It's obvious that if the major coal producer in the country is not able to increase production at a significant rate every year, then coal consumers would have to resort to imports beyond a point. And this is something that has been well known for a while now.

The lack of coal for producing electricity has forced power plants to opt for the expensive e-auction route as well as coal imports.[341] In the normal scheme of things, if an input into something becomes more expensive, the producer can increase the price of the final product and then more than make up for it. In India, it's not that simple as the electricity sector is government regulated and private power producers *typically* need to sell the power that they produce to the electricity distribution companies, or Discoms, owned by the state governments. And this is where things get trickier.

When a company enters a power purchase agreement, the tariff at which it will supply electricity to the Discom is already decided. Meanwhile, what happens when the price of imported coal, the most important input into producing thermal power, goes up? Take a look at Table 27.2 once again. The price of imported coal in 2015–16 was Rs 421.7 crore per million tonnes on an average. It jumped to Rs 664.8 crore per million tonnes on an average in 2017–18. The price per unit of power should have gone up because of this increase. But the power sector is regulated in India and therefore that can't possibly happen. In this scenario, it became very difficult for power companies to continue repaying the debt they had taken on.

There are projects which haven't been able to put in place power purchase agreements, especially long-term agreements with Discoms. Without a medium- or a long-term power purchase agreement in place, coal linkages aren't possible. A coal linkage is permitted only if a long- or medium-term power purchase agreement with an electricity distribution company is in place.

The Discoms are not in the mood to sign long-term or medium-term power purchase agreements. The reason for this lies in the fact that many Discoms are in a huge amount of debt themselves. One of the first things that the Narendra Modi led government had tried to do when it was elected in May 2014 was to clean up the huge debt that Discoms had accumulated over the years.

As of September 2015, the Discoms had an accumulated debt of around Rs 2.75 lakh crore.[342] On this, the Discoms were paying an interest of 14–15 per cent. After paying the interest, very little money was left for anything else.

The Ujwal DISCOM Assurance Yojana, or Uday as it was more popularly known, basically proposed a debt transfer between the Discoms and their respective state governments. The scheme proposed that state governments take over 75 per cent of the debt of their respective Discoms. This swap would lower the interest load to 8–9 per cent per year, because governments can borrow at lower rates of interest.[343]

The Discoms that had signed on to Uday had to initiate structural reforms. They had to reduce their Aggregate Technical and Commercial (ATC) losses from the pre-Uday era by 900 basis points. They also needed to carry out regular tariff hikes of 5–6 per cent per year.

While the Discoms reaped the benefits of the debt swap, they have been slow on the structural reforms front. As of December 2018, the ATC losses had been reduced by 400 basis points from pre-UDAY levels, through 'operational efficiency improvements, like compulsory smart metering, upgradation of transformers, meters, etc'.[344]

At the same time, tariffs had been increased by 3 per cent per year against the proposed 5–6 per cent. The initial debt swap helped the Discoms bring down their debt and, by March 2017, the total debt of Discoms was down to Rs 1.56 lakh crore, from Rs 2.75 lakh crore in September 2015.[345]

Nevertheless, with the proposed structural reforms not coming through at the pace they were expected to, the debt started rising again. By March 2019, it was at Rs 2.28 lakh crore and by the end of March 2020 it's expected to touch Rs 2.64 lakh crore, almost back at the pre-UDAY level, at least in absolute terms.[346]

In this scenario, given that Discoms are in a financially fragile situation, they have not been interested in entering long- and medium-term power purchase agreements with private power companies. A clear impact of this was the significant under-utilization of the thermal power capacity. Take a look at Figure 27.1, which plots the average plant load factor of thermal power plants over the years.

Figure 27.1

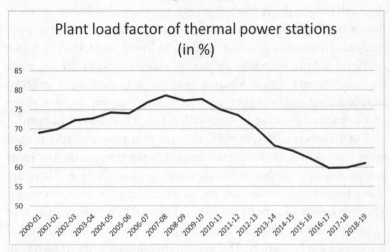

Plant load factor of thermal power stations (in %)

Source: Central Electricity Authority.

The plant load factor of thermal power plants in 2007–08 stood at 78.6 per cent, which meant that nearly four-fifths of the production capacity of thermal power plants was being used. By 2016–17, this had dropped to 59.8 per cent. This meant that only three-fifths of the production capacity was being used. Since then, it has improved marginally and in 2018–19, it stood at a little over 61 per cent.

When we look at the plant load factor of private power plants, it had stood at 84 per cent in 2009–10 and has since come down to 54 per cent in 2018–19.[347]

In fact, even Discoms, which have power purchase agreements in place, do not pay up on time. As of April 2019, Discoms owed Rs 21,198 crore to power companies.[348] These delayed payments leads to the exhaustion of working capital of the power companies.[349] What did not help was the fact that most PSBs were unwilling to give out working capital loans, as they were under the PCA framework and, at the same time, had vacancies at the top level, which hindered decision making.[350]

Over and above this, private plants added 53,661 MW to thermal power generation capacity between 2012 and 2017.[351] Basically, the power generation capacity rose at a faster pace compared to power demand, leading to lower plant load factors.

What did not help was the overall sluggishness of the economy on the industrial front. Many power projects (like steel projects) were planned and built on the anticipation of power demand rising on the back of growing industrial demand. That did not happen.[352]

On a slightly different note, the fact that power supply is now more than power demand has often led to the conclusion that India is now a power surplus country, which isn't really true. There are many households in the country which still do not have electricity. The per capita electricity consumption is still nowhere near that of the level of developed nations.[353] It's also lower than the global per capita consumption. The per capita consumption of power in India stood at 1,122 units in 2016–17 against the global per capita consumption of 3,110 units.[354]

The financially stressed Discoms do not buy as much power as the area they supply to needs, and they under-supply power by resorting to power outages, or what in Indian parlance is referred to as load-shedding.[355]

Also, interest rates on the loans went up over a period of time. When the race to build power plants started sometime in 2007–08, bank loans were given at an interest of around 11 per cent per year. By 2011–12, the interest rates had risen to 14 per cent per year. This clearly played spoilsport with the assumptions on which the projects were based. Over and above this, during the initial phases of capacity addition, many private power producers quoted very low tariffs in order to sign up long-term power purchase agreements with Discoms.[356]

This helped in speeding up the entire process of building a power plant, as no bank would give a loan without a power purchase agreement in place. The problem was that many projects got delayed (due to delays in land acquisition, statutory clearances, etc.) and this pushed up costs. Interest rates also went up. This led to a situation where the tariffs where simply not sustainable in the long term. This led to the erosion of equity that the promoters had invested in the project. The promoters were then unable to bring in fresh equity.[357]

All these reasons have stalled many power projects and, at the same time, left many thermal power plants running with plant load factors of lower than 50 per cent. And at such low plant load factors, it has become difficult for these power companies to continue repaying the loans they had taken on to build these projects.

* * *

Power plants aren't exactly the most attractive assets going around at this point of time. Given this, doubts have been raised on whether there will be buyers for them when they are put through the CIRP.

Let's look at this in greater detail, pointwise:

1) There has been large addition to the power-production capacity over the last few years. This has led to a large amount of the capacity lying unutilized. At the same time, there are many old power plants which have outlived their utility. One estimate suggests that around 30,000 MW coal-based, power-producing capacities of the Central and state governments have surpassed an operational life of twenty-five years.[358] Other than being non-compliant with environmental norms, these plants also consume more coal than the more efficient, newer plants. Old and inefficient plants with a power-producing capacity of 7,149 MW have already been retired. Another 10,000 MW of capacity is expected to be retired over the next two to three years.[359] This will help the new power plants improve their plant load factors and, in the process, be able to repay the bank loans they have taken on.

2) One major reason for the power companies being in stress is the delayed payments from Discoms. This can be addressed in two ways. When a power company signs a power purchase

agreement with a Discom, it has the right to terminate the agreement in case the latter defaults on the payment. The problem is the coal linkage is connected to the long-term power purchase agreement that the company has with the Discom. If a power company terminates the agreement, it loses the coal linkage as well. And without coal, how do you produce power? Basically, the financial troubles of the Discoms get passed on to the power producer.

The High-Level Empowered Committee, which was set up to address the issues of stressed thermal power projects – and which submitted its report in November 2018 – had suggested that in case a power plant terminated its power purchase agreement with a Discom, it should be allowed to use the coal linkage for supply of power through short-term power purchase agreements for a period of two years (or until it finds another buyer of power under a long- or a medium-term power purchase agreement). In late June 2019, the Union cabinet allowed power plants which terminated the power purchase agreements due to Discoms defaulting on payments to retain their existing coal linkages.[360]

The committee also looked at the inability of Discoms to pay on time and how it hurt power producers. One suggestion made was that a public financial institution, like a Power Finance Corporation (PFC), should pay the dues of the power companies and later recover the money from Discoms. It also suggested that the PFC be allowed to charge an interest from Discoms for this.

There is an inherent problem at the heart of this suggestion. If Discoms have a financial problem paying power producers, they will also have a problem paying the PFC. In fact, this is precisely what the PFC told the committee: 'there was a risk that they may not be able to recover the dues from the DISCOMs.'[361] Hence, in case of a default, 'the RBI may recover the dues from the account of states and make payment to thePFIs (public financial institution, which PFC is)'.[362] As I have said throughout this book, there is no such thing as a free lunch in economics – someone's got to pick up the tab. And that someone in this case happens to be the government or, indirectly, we, the people of India, who pay different kinds of taxes collected by the government.

3) The power sector has wanted the government to help it come out of this mess. As we have seen, there are various ways in which the government has tried to help out the sector. One of the demands from the power sector stemmed from the fact that the public sector NTPC (formerly known as the National Thermal Power Corporation Limited) had many long-term power purchase agreements with Discoms. In fact, it even had power purchase agreements for projects which were yet to be commissioned or were still under construction.[363] Towards the end of June 2019, the Union cabinet allowed NTPC to buy power from stressed power companies and sell it to Discoms against these power purchase agreements.[364]

The government also launched the rather tackily named Shakti, or Scheme for Harnessing and Allocating Koyala (Coal) Transparently in India. The scheme was launched in May 2017. The initial aim of it was to provide coal linkages to power plants which already had a power purchase agreement in place. It did not do anything about power plants which did not have these agreements in place. In late June 2019, the Union cabinet allowed power plants to apply for coal linkages even if it didn't have the agreements in place.[365]

Before this, the plants were relying on high-priced coal bought from e-auctions or had to import coal.[366] Both these ways essentially pushed up the cost of power generation. This ensures that power companies have regular access to coal at the right price. Over and above this, the government is also buying 2,500 MW of power from stressed operators and selling it to state Discoms.

The point is that the government has actually done quite a few things to help out the power sector.

4) Doubts have been raised over whether the CIRP is the right
   process for the power sector too. Various reasons have been
   offered for the same. These are as follows: a) it's difficult to
   sell a power plant; b) it's difficult to liquidate a power plant
   if no buyers are found; c) running a power plant is a complex
   process and resolution professionals do not have the adequate
   expertise; d) also, in the event of a power plant being shut
   down, its value can erode drastically.[367]

Unlike the steel sector, where buyers have shown some interest,
the same has not been the case in the power sector. Investors have
been few and far between. Some players, like Tata Power, Adani
Power, JSW Energy and Vedanta, have shown interest, but the
same cannot be said about players such as Torrent Power and
CESC. The government undertaking NTPC has also not shown
any interest. Other than power companies, there are financial
investors, like the National Investment and Infrastructure Fund
(NIIF), as well. While such investors have the money to buy the
stressed power companies, they don't have the expertise and the
requisite technical partners to run them.[368]

Then there are issues which are peculiar to the power sector.
It's not easy for lenders to convert debt into equity for the simple
reason that the power purchase agreements have clauses stating
that the promoters (who have since defaulted on the debt) have a
minimum equity stake in the project. Over and above this, if the
power company is sold to another company without going through
a CIRP, the state regulators demand that the new company pass on
the benefit of the restructuring to consumers and renegotiate the
power purchase agreement. This creates another problem because
the prospective buyer had factored in a certain rate of return
assuming a certain tariff that it would be able to earn while selling
power to the Discom.[369]

Take the case of Resurgent Power (backed primarily by Tata
Power and ICICI Bank) buying a 1,980-MW power plant from
Jaiprakash Associates. The energy regulator of Uttar Pradesh,

where the power plant was located, asked the company to reduce power tariffs by 40 paisa per unit.[370] The Union cabinet needs to make a decision on this, in order to ensure that state electricity regulators do not change the rules of the game midway.*

The broader point is that the economic incentives here are misaligned. The prospective buyer is looking for a cheap asset and, therefore, wants the banks to take a haircut on the debt that has been defaulted on. The regulators, who are a part of the game through the Discom, are looking out for consumers and, hence, want to renegotiate the power purchase agreement. On the other hand, the lenders want the old management out and are looking for a one-time cash settlement, so that they can move on and concentrate on banking. Not every prospective buyer is in a position to offer a one-time cash settlement, as it's difficult to raise money for such projects.[371]

In this situation, some experts are of the view that power companies need to be treated differently.

Arvind Subramanian has an interesting suggestion to get around this problem. The suggestion is similar to the proposition for a bad bank, which we have seen earlier. He says that the stressed power assets should be taken off the books of banks, allowing them to concentrate on their core business. These power plants should then be warehoused. Then, he suggests, the government should purchase these assets and create a holding company to manage these plants and ultimately sell them off once they are able to find buyers. He also proposes that the prices paid to the power companies should be based on the recommendations of independent parties, such as investment banks, so that the entire process can be transparent.[372]

In the second half of 2018, there was a lot of chatter in the media about the government setting up a National Asset Management

---

*   In September 2019, in a case filed by Resurgent Power, the Appellate Tribunal for Electricity pronounced that the state regulators cannot change tariffs determined through competitive bidding.

Company for identified stressed assets in the power sector. The plan was that the company, with the help of the NTPC, Power Finance Corporation, REC Ltd. (formerly known as Rural Electrification Corporation) and the banks, will auction the stressed power plants or lease them out on a contract basis. This would be after the lenders took control of the power companies that have defaulted on loans.[373] Thankfully, nothing of this sort has materialized up until now.

If it isn't clear by now, let's state this directly: a large part of the power sector is in trouble because of too much government involvement. So, is more government involvement, as Subramanian suggests, really the solution? Also, the government will need money to buy these power companies. Once bought, there will always be pressure on the government to nationalize these companies. It won't be easy for it to sell them. Further, there is that perpetual question: where is the money to buy power companies going to come from?

More importantly, India is trying to build a process of corporate insolvency and bankruptcy, which works on its own. If the government keeps interfering in it, in its nascent stages, how is the process ever going to evolve?

There is another issue that we should consider here. The power sector is currently unattractive in the overall scheme of things. A few years down the line, some other sector may become unattractive for investors and that sector, like the power sector now, may also want special treatment. What will the government do in a situation like this, if a precedent with the soft treatment of the power sector is set?

Another point made for the soft treatment of the power sector is that resolution professionals, at the heart of the corporate insolvency and bankruptcy resolution process, do not have the expertise required to run a power plant, given its complexities.[374] This argument can also be made for the steel sector or any other complicated sector in manufacturing. Also, if we don't let the system evolve, how is any expertise going to get built?

And given all this, what is the way out? Power projects, which have no power purchase agreements or coal linkages in place can be better resolved by being put through a corporate insolvency process. Banks can recover some money through this, though the haircuts are expected to be in the range of 55–65 per cent. At the same time, it will offer an opportunity to the bigger players in the power sector (companies like NTPC, Adani Power, JSW Energy, Vedanta, etc.), to buy assets at a competitive price. The analysts expect average transactions in this case to be in the range of Rs 3–3.5 crore per MW. In contrast, if a company were to actually build a new power plant, it would have to spend around Rs 7.5 crore per MW. Also, buying a power plant doesn't come with the land acquisition issues which building a new power plant from scratch faces.[375]

This is another reason why the bigger power companies have a good opportunity to buy some cheap power assets. Around 20,000 MW of power capacity being built by NTPC and the government is at an initial stage, where an insignificant amount of investment has been made. The power industry has suggested to the government that it would make more sense for the NTPC to acquire ready-made power plants at a lower price than continue building the ones that it currently is.[376] Theoretically, this might sound like a good idea, but governments don't work like this. Once a project has been commissioned and work has started on it, it's difficult to stop and move resources to something else.

While a 55–65 per cent haircut sounds like quite a lot on the face of it, the thing to remember is that before the IBC came in, recoveries were next to nothing. Also, in the initial years, as the system matures and becomes robust, it will come with some cost attached with it. This is why it's important that the government lets the insolvency process do its work, even in the case of the power sector.

28

RBI's Final Countdown

One of the techniques that banks used not to recognize bad loans was to restructure them. But the restructuring failed in many cases. As N.S. Vishwanathan, a deputy governor of the RBI, said in an April 2018 speech: 'Prolonging the true asset quality recognition suited both the bankers and the borrowers. The former could make their books look cleaner than they actually were; the latter could avoid the defaulter tag even while, in fact defaulting.'[377]

Take a look at Figure 28.1. It plots the total corporate loans given by banks that were restructured over the years.

Figure 28.1

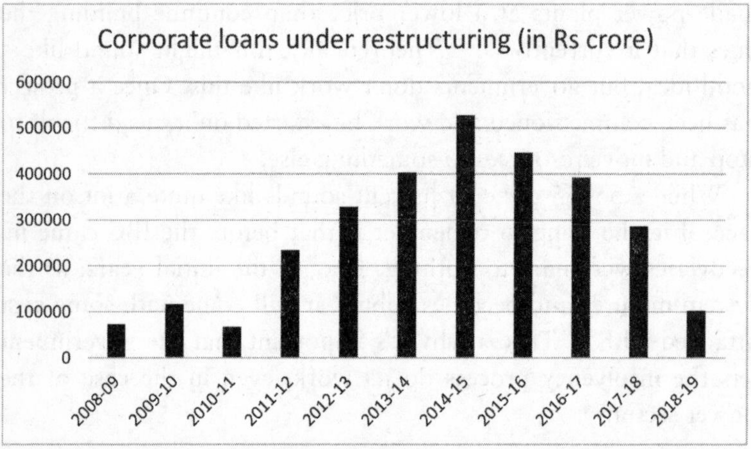

Corporate loans under restructuring (in Rs crore)

Source: Centre for Monitoring Indian Economy.

As can be seen from Figure 28.1, the restructured loans peaked in 2014–15 at Rs 5,28,538 crore, before the RBI initiated the Asset Quality Review.

After this was started, banks were forced to recognize their bad loans, and therefore, the numbers came down. Nevertheless, even as of 31 March 2017, the total restructured loans stood at Rs 2,87,362 crore, which is a fairly high number.

On 12 February 2018, the RBI came out with a notification, which made it almost impossible for banks to continue playing the restructuring game. By March 2019, the restructured loans stood at Rs 1,02,276 crore. This was the biggest fall in restructured assets ever seen.

As Ashwani Kumar, former chairman and managing director of Dena Bank, said regarding the 12 February notification: 'I was in the banking industry for thirty-six years ... I don't remember a single circular being as powerful.'[378]

So what were the key features of the circular? Let's take a look.

1) Before this, there were twenty-eight circulars on various forms of restructuring. All of them were scrapped.[379] Schemes like corporate debt restructuring (CDR), strategic debt restructuring (SDR), the scheme for sustainable structuring for stressed assets (S4A), etc., were withdrawn with immediate effect.

2) The RBI said that all these restructuring schemes were to be replaced by a single restructuring plan. As the notification said, 'as soon as there is a default in the borrower entity's account with any lender, all lenders – singly or jointly – shall initiate steps to cure the default' through a resolution plan. Basically, banks and other financial institutions had to start the resolution process as soon as the borrower defaulted. Before this notification, banks had up to sixty days after the date of default to initiate the resolution plan.[380]

3) Given that all other schemes of restructuring had been withdrawn with immediate effect, the RBI mandated that in

case of defaults of more than Rs 2,000 crore, a resolution plan would be implemented within 180 days from 1 March 2018, which meant by 31 August 2018. If that did not turn out to be the case, the lenders would have to file an insolvency petition under the IBC, within fifteen days of the expiry of the said timeline.

4) In case of a default of more than Rs 2,000 crore after 1 March 2018, the RBI mandated that banks and other financial institutions put a resolution plan in place within 180 days. If that did not happen, they had to file an insolvency petition. The expiry of timelines was basically the upper limit. The bankers could file insolvency petitions against the defaulting borrowers even before the expiry of the timelines or even without attempting a resolution plan.

The RBI was trying to align the banking regulations with the IBC. As Vishwanathan said: 'The restructuring schemes were required at a time when we did not have an effective bankruptcy law in place. The schemes essentially created a framework for resolution that should normally happen under the aegis of an insolvency and bankruptcy law.'[381]

At the same time, the notification also tried to reduce the arbitrage that the corporate borrowers had been enjoying until that point of time. Let's say a borrower had raised money from the financial markets by selling bonds. The company selling these bonds had to pay interest on them on certain specific dates.

Also, they had a certain maturity date on which the principal amount would be repaid to the investor. If the corporate issuing the bond delayed the payment of interest or repayment of principal even by a single day, the market would penalize it heavily. The rating of the bond would be downgraded. Many investors would sell out the bond, pushing its price down and yield up. This would mean that if the company wanted to raise more debt by selling bonds, it would have to pay a higher rate of interest.[382]

This sort of market discipline was missing when it came to lending carried out by PSBs to corporate borrowers. Only, when repayment was due for ninety days or more was a loan categorized as a bad loan. Corporates tried to avoid the bad loan tag on their loan by trying to get it restructured; the banks played along, leading to the debt contract losing its sanctity in a big way.[383]

The new RBI notification required the banks to report even a one-day default and draw up resolution plans thereafter. It also made the reporting of defaults mandatory on a weekly basis for borrowers having an exposure of Rs 5 crore or more with a bank (a large borrower basically). While it was mandatory to report defaults on a weekly basis, the loan became a bad loan only after ninety days had passed from the date of default. The definition of a bad loan did not change. What the notification tried to do was nudge the banks, which had given out loans to take timely corrective action and ensure that the loan did not deteriorate in quality.[384]

When the notification came out, there was some criticism around the fact that it expected lenders to put a resolution plan in place within 180 days of default, which was insufficient because multiple banks were involved. The RBI's contention was that a default in payment is a lagging and not a lead indicator of the financial situation of the borrower. If banks are proactive in monitoring the state of a loan and its borrower, they would know well in advance if a borrower is facing financial stress, without having to wait for the default to occur. Hence, an early identification of financial stress would give banks sufficient time to have a resolution plan in place.[385] This explanation made perfect sense.

In fact, thanks to the circular, another way of how corporates were gaming the banking system soon came to light. When term loans are given to corporates by banks, the repayment schedules are decided well in advance. This means that the corporates have enough time to arrange for the money, well before the payment is due. As per the 12 February notification, it was mandatory for

banks to report defaults on a weekly basis. When the data first
started to come in, it was observed that non-payment on the due
date was seen as the norm, not just by borrowers but by the banks
as well. Interestingly, some well-rated borrowers also failed to pay
on time. The only possible explanation for this was that they saw
better short-term investment opportunities elsewhere than repay a
term loan on time.[386]

In the past, they could do this because a default turned into a
bad loan only ninety days later. Also, a resolution plan had to be
put in place during a period of up to sixty days after the default, and
not immediately after it. In that way, this notification wasn't only
about solving the current bad loans problem, but it was also about
ensuring that the corporates paid on the days that their payments
were due. As Urjit Patel put it: 'This approach is a positive step
towards strengthening the credit culture in the economy'.[387] It
wasn't just about bad loans.

The other big change that the notification introduced was that
the resolution plans could be implemented individually or jointly
by banks, depending on what they were comfortable with. This
was a major change from the earlier Joint Lenders Forum (JLF),
where the decision made by the majority of the lenders was binding
on the minority (of course, the minority lenders had the option of
opting out of the JLF). As per the notification, the RBI withdrew
the instructions on the JLF, and gave complete flexibility and
discretion to banks to formulate their own policy while dealing
with defaulting borrowers. Under JLF, the resolution plan was
largely the same across banks. The new notification allowed each
bank to implement its own resolution plan the way it deemed fit.

The circular caught the PSBs unaware; that is for sure. Their
bad loans, which had amounted to Rs 7,77,279 crore as of
31 December 2017, jumped to Rs 8,95,601 crore by 31 March
2018, three months later. Basically, the RBI circular ensured that
the game that banks played of passing off bad loans as restructured
loans came to an end.

The net losses of PSBs in 2017–18 jumped to Rs 85,731 crore from Rs 11,388 crore a year earlier. This was primarily because their provisions and contingencies jumped from Rs 1,70,410 crore to Rs 2,41,061 crore. The PSBs had to properly provide for the bad loans being passed off as restructured loans.

On 2 April 2019, the Supreme Court struck down RBI's 12 February 2018 notification. The immediate default norm, where the resolution process had to be started as soon as the default happened, instead of the sixty-day limit that stood earlier, hadn't gone down well with the industry. Companies and industry associations (particularly in the power sector) had filed cases across different courts. In September 2018, the Supreme Court directed that all these cases be transferred to it.[388]

On 7 June 2019, the RBI came up with a new notification taking into account the Supreme Court's decision. Let's look at its salient points:

1) Once a borrower has defaulted on a loan, the banks and other financial lenders are supposed to 'undertake a prima facie review of the borrower's account within thirty days from such default'. During this period, the banks may put a resolution plan in place. They can also choose to initiate legal proceedings for insolvency.

2) If the banks and other lenders decide to implement the resolution plan, they need to enter into an inter-creditor agreement. Any decision agreed upon by 75 per cent of the lenders by value and 60 per cent of the lenders by numbers shall be binding upon all the lenders. This was a new clause which wasn't there in the 12 February notification. The 12 February notification had allowed different banks to pursue the same borrower in different ways.

3) For borrowers who default on more than Rs 2,000 crore, the resolution plan has to be implemented within 180 days from the end of the review period.

4) If the resolution plan is not implemented within 180 days of
   the end of the review period, the lender needs to undertake
   an additional provisioning of 20 per cent of the total loan
   outstanding. If the implementation is delayed by 365 days, the
   bank or the financial institution needs to make an additional
   provision of 15 per cent (i.e., a total provision of 35 per cent
   of the outstanding loan). This was a major change from the
   12 February notification.

As per the earlier notification, the bank had to compulsorily
start insolvency proceedings against the defaulter. As per the new
notification, that was left to the judgement of the lenders. This is
where the new notification was similar to the older one in letter,
but not in spirit.

Sunil Mehta, who was the chairman of the Indian Banks'
Association, at that point of time, welcomed the decision by
saying: 'The RBI circular ... has given more freedom to bankers to
bring their own resolve and instead of directions.'[389]

One would expect an industry lobby to welcome a decision
which made things easy for banks and bankers. On the flipside,
this decision allowed a way out for the defaulters, especially crony
capitalists. As we have seen earlier in the book, public sector bankers
are not in a position to take on crony capitalists. As Patel put it,
in reference to the 12 February notification: '[T]he Insolvency and
Bankruptcy Code along with RBI's revised framework will help
break the promoter–bank nexus which has led to crony capitalism
and attendant NPA/credit misallocation problem.' The new 7 June
2019, notification might lead to crony capitalists winning all over
again.

29

The Backlash Against Rajan

Meanwhile, a small industry had emerged in Delhi, which tried to put the blame of the Indian economy slowdown on the RBI in general and on Raghuram Rajan in particular.

By the time, the PCA framework was revised in April 2017, Rajan was already back to his academic job in Chicago. Earlier, he had served as the chairman of the Committee on Financial Sector Reforms, which had submitted its report in September 2008. 'A Hundred Small Steps', as the report was called, read: 'The system of prompt corrective action and resolution of weak banks should be strengthened and made more explicit ... It should be recognised that the continued existence of weak banks without resolution spreads weakness to the rest of the system [and] is a potential source of instability.'[390] Even though Rajan was no longer at the RBI, his thinking, reflected in the lines of the report quoted above, still was.

In September 2018, economist Rajiv Kumar, vice-chairman of the NITI Aayog, took a potshot at Rajan and blamed him and the policies he followed at the RBI for the overall slowdown in the Indian economy. Kumar said: 'Under the previous governor, Mr Raghuram Rajan, who revised the mechanisms, *the NPAs began to grow which is why the banking sector stopped giving credit to the industry* [emphasis added] ... This is the cause of the economic slowdown.'[391]

For the lack of a better word, this was a very *immature* statement made by the head of the government's main economic think tank. The RBI, or Rajan for that matter, was not responsible for the lending by PSBs, which created all the bad money in the financial system to begin with.

All that the RBI did was carry out an Asset Quality Review which forced the PSBs to recognize bad loans as bad loans. Until then, these banks had been happy pushing off the bad loans for someone else to deal with. Under, and after, Rajan, the RBI simply tried to put a stop to this.

As Rajan said in a Note to the Parliamentary Estimates Committee on Bank NPAs: 'Bankers, promoters, or their backers in government sometimes turn around and accuse regulators of creating the bad loan problem. The truth is bankers, promoters, and circumstances create the bad loan problem. The regulator cannot substitute for the banker's commercial decisions or micromanage them or even investigate them when they are being made. Instead, in most situations, the regulator can at best warn about poor lending practises when they are being undertaken, and demand banks hold adequate risk buffers. The RBI is primarily a referee, not a player in the process of commercial lending. Its nominees on bank boards have no commercial lending experience and can only try and make sure that processes are followed. They offer an illusion that the regulator is in control, which is why nearly every RBI Governor has asked the government for permission to withdraw them from bank boards.'[392]

One of the mechanisms that the RBI set up to tackle the bad loans problem of PSBs was the PCA framework. As we saw earlier, it slowed down the lending of PCA banks by around 7 per cent between 31 March 2017 and 31 March 2019. This did not mean that the overall credit given by the banking system slowed down as well.

The non-food credit of the banks as a whole went up by 10.3 per cent per year between March 2017 and March 2019. This was better than the growth seen between March 2014 and March 2017. In fact, if we look at the non-PCA PSBs, they grew by 10.9 per cent per year during the period. This growth happened despite the fact that banks under the PCA framework were contracting.

What did this mean? As Acharya said in an October 2018 speech: 'While it is true that PCA banks are experiencing lending contraction on average (in terms of their year on year growth in overall advances), the nominal non-food credit growth of scheduled commercial banks has been close to or above double-digit levels for the past several quarters ... This is because the reduction in lending at PCA banks is being more than offset by credit growth at healthier banks. This is indeed what one wants – *efficient reallocation of credit for the real economy with a financially stable distribution of risks across bank balance sheets* [emphasis added].'[393] So, to that extent, the PCA framework achieved what it set out to do.

Of course, the non-food credit growth is nowhere near where it was during the go–go years. But a major reason for that is also because many large corporates in India are currently over-leveraged and not in a position to borrow money. As Acharya put it: 'There is also a call for more lending by PCA banks to large industries where the overall credit growth remains muted. Note that many of these industries are heavily indebted to start with and are going through a deleveraging process.'[394]

But the government believed otherwise. Media reports suggested that Rajan's successor, Urjit Patel, got into a tussle with the government and the ministry of finance. The ministry wanted the RBI to go slow on pushing banks to recognize their NPAs. Patel put it in his papers on 10 December 2018, citing personal reasons. Acharya also followed suit a few months later.

Shaktikanta Das, a former finance secretary, who had managed the demonetization process for the government, and who happened to be a postgraduate in history, took charge of India's central bank. Das was more willing to listen to the finance ministry and the government than Patel. This changed the situation for the banks which had been placed under the PCA.

On 31 January 2019, three banks, Bank of India, Bank of Maharashtra and Oriental Bank of Commerce were all taken out of the PCA framework. On 26 February 2019, two more banks, Allahabad Bank and Corporation Bank, were taken out of the PCA framework.

As we have seen earlier, the books of banks are looking slightly better primarily because of the recapitalization carried out by the government and the time-healing factor. Also, as the PCA framework for banks points out,[395] 'a bank will be placed under PCA framework based on the audited Annual Financial Results.' If the entry of banks into PCA is based on annual financial results, it's logical to think that the exit too should work this way. But banks were pulled out of the PCA framework before their annual results came out.[396]

In early June 2019, the RBI relaxed the leverage ratio, the parameter that was added when it came up with the revised PCA framework in April 2017. This was again another step to dilute the framework and help banks exit the process.

The new dispensation at the RBI is gradually undoing the systems that had been put in place to help the PSBs gradually come out of their bad loans problems.

The thing is, PSBs are still not out of the woods. As of 31 March 2019, their bad loans stood at Rs 7,89,569 crore, down from Rs 8,95,601 lakh crore seen a year earlier. Take a look at Figure 29.1, which plots the bad loans of PSBs over the years.

Figure 29.1

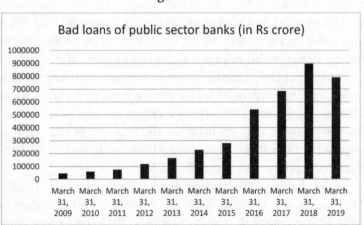

Source: Reserve Bank of India.

Figure 29.1 shows us that in 2018–19, the bad loans of PSBs fell for the first time in a decade. As pointed out earlier, the PSBs seriously started recognizing the bad loans after the RBI unleashed its inspectors on their books in mid-2015, through the Asset Quality Review. Nevertheless, even before that some recognition of bad loans had started to happen in 2013–14. These reasons explain why the bad loans of banks jumped so majorly from Rs 2,27,264 crore as of March 2014 to Rs 8,95,601 crore as of March 2018.

As we saw earlier in the book, loans which have been unpaid for four years can be dropped from the balance sheet of banks by way of a write-off.

Serious recognition of bad loans started in 2013–14. In 2018–19, many such bad loans had spent four years on the balance sheets of banks, and, hence, were written off as per the norms. Take a look at Figure 29.2, which plots the same.

Figure 29.2

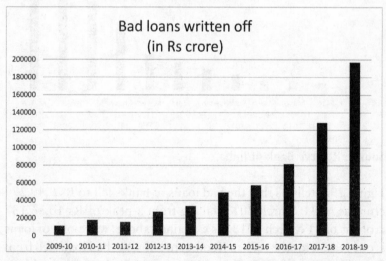

Source: Lok Sabha Unstarred Question No. 295, 24 June 2019.

The bad loans written off by PSBs have gone up over the years. This stems from the fact that a bad loan can be written off once its four years old. Given that the recognition of bad loans started only in 2013–14 and serious recognition started only post mid-2015 onwards, most of these bad loans are being written off only now. What this means is that up until 2022, many of these bad loans, which are not recovered, will continue to be written off, as they become more than four years old.

Most of the loans written off are technical write-offs and, therefore, efforts to recover them continue.

When it comes to bad loans, how do things look for commercial banks as a whole? Take a look at Figure 29.3.

Figure 29.3

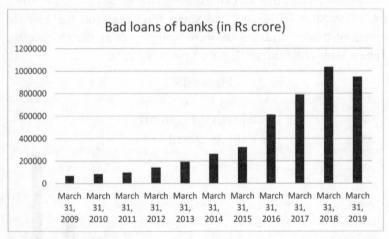

Source: Reserve Bank of India.

Figure 29.3 tells us that the bad loans of banks fell to Rs 9,49,279 crore as of 31 March 2019, falling from a peak of Rs 10,36,187 crore as of 31 March 2018. As explained above, write-offs of loans is one reason for this. When it comes to PSBs, the bad loans fell from Rs 8,95,601 crore to Rs 7,89,569 crore. As Dr K.C. Chakrabarty, a former deputy governor of the RBI, remarked in a newspaper interview: '… you write off big industrial loans and that's why NPA is less'.[397] Another reason lies in the fact that there has been a fall in the fresh recognition of bad loans. In 2018–19, this fell by 45 per cent. So, are banks in general and PSBs in particular done with recognizing bad loans? This is a tricky question to answer.

First and foremost, the power sector, the real estate sector and the telecom sector, all big borrowers, continue to remain precariously positioned. Over and above this, banks are perpetually trying to paint a rosy picture of the state of their loans. Take the case of IL&FS: until the NBFC started to default on its loans in September 2018, neither the RBI nor the banks seemed to have any idea the crisis brewing. The same stands true for Dewan Housing Finance Ltd., another NBFC, which has been having huge problems servicing its loans through 2019.

Hence, there is enough evidence which tells us that Indian banks aren't done dealing yet with their bad money problem.

30

Why Interest Rates Are Not Falling

The former RBI governor, Y.V. Reddy, recalls something his late mother told him regarding the interest on her bank deposits: 'Venu, why is it that the bank is giving me a lower interest rate than before on my deposit? They tell me it's because of the Reserve Bank'.[398]

There is a belief among people across different sections of society (and this includes politicians, businessmen and their lobbyists) that the RBI controls the interest rates that banks charge on their loans and on their deposits.

But as we saw in Chapter 2, the RBI can, at best, influence interest rates in the banking and the financial system through various tools it has at its disposal.

Over the last few years, there has been a great hue and cry about how the RBI needs to bring down interest rates, so that people can borrow and spend more, and businesses can borrow and expand.

This, as we have seen a little earlier, isn't exactly true. Retail lending of banks, including PSBs, remains quite strong. The problem is with lending to industry. Also, if high interest rates were a bother then private banks wouldn't have been doing so well at lending. The rate of interest they change on their loans are as high as those charged by PSBs, if not higher. As Reddy puts it in *Advice & Dissent: My Life in Public Service*: 'Credit is important for growth, but its availability is more important than its price'.[399] The price of credit or a loan is the interest the borrower pays on it.

In Chapter 2, we saw how the credit–deposit ratio of banks has an impact on interest rates. Hence, if the credit–deposit ratio is high, which means that banks are lending out all the deposits they manage to raise – after meeting regulatory requirements – the interest rates are likely to continue to be high, despite the RBI cutting the repo rate.

One reason lending interest rates haven't fallen as much as people think they should have is because PSBs have increased their interest margins over the last few years. An interest margin is the difference between the interest banks charge on their loans and the interest that they pay on their deposits.

Take a look at Figure 30.1. It plots the interest margin or the difference between the weighted average term deposit rates of PSBs (the interest rate at which banks borrow) and the weighted average lending rates of PSBs (the interest rate at which banks lend) from mid-2015 onwards. This was around the time that the RBI started the Asset Quality Review of PSBs. Term deposits are better known as fixed deposits.

Figure 30.1

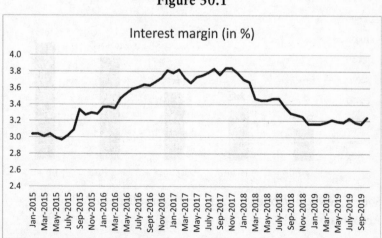

Source: Reserve Bank of India.

Figure 30.1 makes for a very interesting reading. In June 2015, the interest margin of PSBs was 2.97 per cent. This was the time when the RBI cracked the whip and forced these banks to start recognizing their bad loans. This led to banks gradually increasing their interest margin, which peaked at 3.84 per cent in October and November 2017. This again shows that there is no such thing as free lunch in economics. As the bad loans went up, the borrowers ended up paying a higher rate of interest than they actually would have had to otherwise.

Since the end of 2017, the recognition of bad loans by PSBs has stabilized and, hence, the interest margin of PSBs has come down. In October 2019, it had stood at 3.24 per cent – still higher than where it was before the serious recognition of bad loans started.

Along with this, the banks also compete for deposits with the small savings schemes from the post office. Take a look at Figure 30.2. This plots the collections under the different small savings schemes run by the post office, net of withdrawals.

Figure 30.2

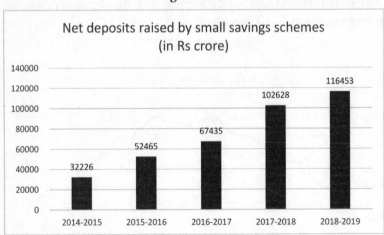

Source. www.indiabudget.gov.in and Controller General of Accounts.

It is clear from Figure 30.2 that the deposits raised through small savings schemes between 2014–15 and 2018–19 have gone up big time. In 2014–15, they were at Rs 32,226 crore. By 2018–19, they had jumped by 361 per cent to Rs 1,16,453 crore.

In 2014–15, the net deposits raised by small savings schemes formed just 4.3 per cent of the term deposits (or fixed deposits) raised by banks. By 2018–19, this had jumped to 11.6 per cent. Clearly, the competition for savings has increased majorly over the last five years. This further explains the reluctance of banks to cut interest rates on their deposit and, therefore, their lending rates.

The interest paid on many small savings schemes is around 8 per cent or more. Investment in some of these schemes even allows for a tax deduction. Interest rates on fixed deposits, as of now, typically range around 6–6.5 per cent.

The government can, of course, change the parameters on which interest rates on small savings schemes are decided and align them with the interest rates on bank deposits. Nevertheless, it is in the interest of the government to offer a higher rate of interest on the small savings schemes and get more money flowing into these schemes.

The money collected by the small saving schemes goes into the National Small Savings Fund (NSSF). Up until a few years back, NSSF money was invested in government securities. Now, a lot of it is lent out to public sector enterprises. Take the case of the Food Corporation of India (FCI). As of 1 April 2018, the FCI owed the NSSF Rs 1,21,000 crore and as of 1 April 2019, the FCI owed it Rs 94,000 crore. The NSSF lending money to the FCI is a recent phenomenon. It started only in 2016–17.

How does this help the government? The FCI primarily buys rice and wheat directly from farmers. It then sells the grains at a very low price through the public distribution system, or ration shops, as they are more popularly known as, to meet the needs of food security in the country. The government needs to compensate the FCI for this to ensure that the organization remains a going concern (i.e., it continues to exist).

It does so through the allocation for food security made in the Budget. Let's take the case of 2018–19. As per the revised estimate, an allocation of Rs 1,71,298 crore was made towards food subsidy, but with tax growth not happening as expected, an allocation of Rs 1,01,904 crore was finally made. A lower allocation towards food subsidies meant that the FCI wasn't adequately compensated. In the process, the government expenditure was kept under control. And once the expenditure was in control, the fiscal deficit could also be tamed.

The funny thing is that this has been happening for a while now. In 2018–19, the total food subsidy that FCI had to claim stood at Rs 2,61,020 crore. Given that the allocation towards food subsidy was only Rs 1,01,904 crore, the FCI is likely to end up getting less than Rs 1,00,000 crore of that. This means that the government would continue to owe the FCI more than Rs 1,60,000 crore. In order to continue to be in operation, the organization needs to borrow this money from somewhere. Of this, Rs 94,000 crore has been borrowed from the NSSF. The rest of the borrowing will happen from the normal banking system. All this borrowing should technically be on the books of the government, as it owes this money to the FCI. But it is on the books of the FCI instead.

Not just the FCI, the NSSF has lent money to other public sector enterprises as well. As of 1 April 2019, it had lent Rs 40,000 crore to National Highways Authority of India (up from Rs 20,000 crore as of 1 April 2018). It had lent Rs 17,500 crore to Indian Railway Finance Corporation (up from Rs 10,000 crore as of 1 April 2018). A total of Rs 12,500 crore had also been lent to the Power Finance Corporation (with it having bought the REC Ltd).

While these are at least investments, the same cannot be said about the excess rice and wheat bought by the FCI using the borrowings from the NSSF, much of which rots away.

A good inflow of money into small savings schemes (which goes into the NSSF) is necessary to keep this going and help the government show a lower fiscal deficit than is the reality. The borrowings from the NSSF play an important part in this. In 2019–20, the FCI expects to borrow Rs 1,10,000 crore from the NSSF.

And these borrowings can happen only because of the inflows into the NSSF, which depend on the investments made into small savings schemes. These investments benefit from the fact that they offer a higher rate of interest than fixed deposits. Hence, the higher rate of interest on small savings schemes benefits the government and helps them show a lower fiscal deficit. Given this, it is unlikely that the interest rates on these schemes will fall majorly, and, in turn, the banks can't reduce their interest rates either.

Another factor that needs to kept in mind is that the household savings of Indians have been falling over the years (which is also responsible for a slower deposit growth of banks). Falling household savings need to finance the deficits of the Central government, state governments as well as the borrowings by the public sector. This overall borrowing is referred to as the public sector borrowing requirement (PSBR). Taking into account the combined deficit of the Central government, the state government, the off balance sheet borrowing (the FCI, for instance) and borrowing by all Central public sector enterprises, the total public sector borrowing requirement works out to 8.5 per cent of the GDP in 2017–18 and 2018–19. This is much higher than the supposed fiscal deficit of 3.4 per cent of the GDP of the Central government in 2018–19.[400]

Take a look at Figure 30.3, which plots the PSBR.

Figure 30.3

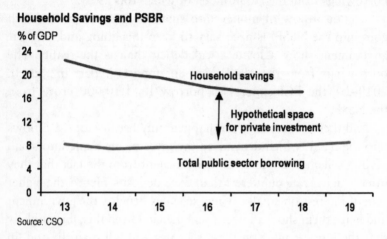

Household Savings and PSBR

Source: CSO

Figure 30.3 clearly tells us that while the total borrowings of the governments and its companies have gone up slightly over the years, the household savings needed to finance them have fallen dramatically. In this environment, expecting interest rates to fall majorly is equal to not knowing the basics of supply and demand.

Basically, with a public sector borrowing requirement of 8.5 per cent of the GDP, the government runs a huge borrowing programme. As Reddy writes: 'The huge borrowing programme of the government implies a large demand from it on resources, in a dominant and inflexible manner. Such a fiscal dominance does impede the operational effectiveness of monetary policy.'

What does this mean in simple English? It means that the government as a whole, and not just the Central government, borrows a lot of money to meet its expenditure. Hence, there is lesser money for everyone else to borrow from, as there are only so much savings going around in the financial system. Economists call this crowding out. The excessive demand of savings from the government crowds out others.

In this scenario, when demand for savings is high, as the law of demand suggests, the price of savings, that is the interest rate on deposits, has to be higher than what it would have been otherwise. When the price of savings is high, the price of loans will but naturally be high as well.

To cut a long story short, lower interest rates are not just about the RBI reducing the repo rate. There are many other factors involved here, with the bad loans of banks being one of them.

31

Personal Finance Lessons from the PMC Scam

On 23 September 2019, the RBI placed Punjab and Maharashtra Cooperative (PMC) Bank, an urban cooperative bank, under what it called Directions. As per these Directions, depositors of the bank were allowed to withdraw only up to Rs 1,000 from their bank accounts. The bank was also not allowed to grant any new loans or make a new investment. It couldn't seek fresh deposits or borrow funds. The Directionss were supposed to remain in force for a period of six months.

Rather ironically, despite having Punjab in its name, the bank did not have any branch in Punjab and was largely a Maharashtra based bank, though it did have branches in several other states like Delhi, Karnataka, Goa, Gujarat, Andhra Pradesh and Madhya Pradesh. The bank had 137 branches at the time the RBI placed it under Directions.

The bank catered extensively to Mumbai's Sikh community. Given that the bank had more than a few branches and depositors in Mumbai, the Rs 1,000 limit placed on deposit withdrawals immediately led to a lot of hue and cry. Giving in to the pressure, on 26 September, the RBI increased the withdrawal limit to Rs 10,000. It also said that that the Directions 'were necessitated on account of major financial irregularities, failure of internal control and systems of the bank and wrong/underreporting of its exposures'.[401] In simple English, PMC wasn't properly reporting the loans that it had given out.

Over a period of time, this deposit withdrawal limit was increased. On 3 October, it was increased to Rs 25,000. On 14 October, it was increased to Rs 40,000. It was further increased to Rs 50,000 on 5 November, which is where it was at the time of writing this towards the end of December 2019. At Rs 50,000 nearly 78 per cent of depositors could withdraw the entire balance they had with the bank.

In the bad loans accumulated by PSBs there has always been a lot of talk about the banker–corporate nexus. But that is what it has remained, just talk. In the case of PMC this nexus was clearly established. As of March 2019, the total deposits of the bank had stood at Rs 11,617 crore. The total loans of the bank had stood at Rs 8,383 crore. And the bank had made a profit of Rs 99.7 crore during 2018–19.

As things turned out, the profit was an illusion because the bank was misstating its accounts. In a letter, Joy Thomas, the managing director of the bank, later revealed that at least 21,049 dummy accounts had been used to hide loans of Rs 6,500 crore to the real estate company, Housing Development and Infrastructure Ltd (HDIL). The Rs 6,500 crore exposure to HDIL formed around 73 per cent of the bank's total loans as of 19 September 2019. As per regulations, the exposure of a bank to a single company cannot be more than 15 per cent of its capital.[402]

HDIL hadn't repaid these loans and thus the loans of PMC turned into bad loans. PMC had gone about hiding these bad loans from the auditors as well as the RBI, by creating dummy accounts. As Thomas said in the letter: 'As the outstandings (loans) were huge and if these were classified as NPA, it would have affected the bank's profitability and the bank would have faced regulatory action from RBI.'[403]

The problem was that HDIL itself was in a mess, and insolvency proceedings were ordered against the company in August 2019. It was primarily a Mumbai based real estate company which specialized in slum redevelopment. One of its large redevelopment projects was with the Mumbai International Airport Pvt. Ltd, for the redevelopment of slums around the Mumbai Airport. The Rs 6,500 crore project involved rehabilitating 80,000 families, but it got stuck midway and by that time the company had taken on too much debt to get it going. The prolonged slump in real estate did not help the company, either.[404]

Meanwhile, the Wadhawan family, which ran HDIL, had started using PMC as a personal ATM. Media reports suggest that the RBI found out about the scam on 19 September 2019. A few days later it issued Directions which limited the ability of depositors to withdraw money in the bank and the ability of the bank to lend money. This limit, even though it was increased to Rs 50,000 in a few weeks, created problems for depositors.

Andrew Lobo, a resident of Mumbai, died of a cardiac arrest because he couldn't pay for the oxygen machines he needed to breathe. The limit placed on withdrawals led to a situation where he couldn't break his fixed deposits to pay for the machines.[405]

Chirag Sanghani, another Mumbai resident, who happens to be a businessman, had all his savings in PMC. After the limits were placed on deposit withdrawal, his business came to a standstill and he had to survive on loans from friends and relatives.[406] In fact, around the time the scam broke out, several WhatsApp videos of PMC depositors who were negatively impacted by the limit placed on deposit withdrawal, started going around. The good money of these depositors had turned into bad money.

There were many such individuals who were badly affected due to the limit placed on deposit withdrawals from PMC. In fact, the experience of PMC depositors offers us a few basic lessons in personal finance all over again. These lessons are valid for every person who has a deposit in any bank. Let's look at them pointwise.

1) The oldest cliché in personal finance is diversification, or as financial planners like to put it: Don't put all your eggs in one basket. This applies within and across asset classes. Hence, it is important to divide the money you want to save in the form of deposits among accounts of different banks. In case one bank

falls in trouble, you would still have access to the money in other banks. This is as basic as it gets.

2) The moment people put their money in a bank, they assume it is safe, forgetting that, at the end of the day, banking is just another business. And businesses fail all the time. A bank borrows money at a certain rate of interest and lends it at a higher rate. If the money the bank lends is not repaid, then it may not be able to repay a part of the deposits.

However, it is rare for a bank to default on its deposits. That is simply because when a bank reaches that stage, the RBI typically merges it with another bank. In the past, the New Bank of India was merged with the Punjab National Bank while the Global Trust Bank was merged with the Oriental Bank of Commerce. The assumption that the central bank is going to intervene in such situations creates an illusion of safety around banks.

In case of PSBs the government keeps pouring money into them to ensure they are able to repay the deposits that mature regularly. Between 2017–18 and 2019–20, the government will have invested Rs 2.66 lakh crore in these banks to keep them going. This money saves PSBs from defaulting on their deposits even though as businesses they have been in a mess over the past few years.

Yet, most people are unaware of these aspects of banking. They deposit their money in a PSB without bothering about the safety aspects since they assume the government will come to their rescue in case things go south.

3) Several PSBs have a bad loans rate of over 10 per cent. This means that of every Rs 100 loaned by them, more than Rs 10 has not been repaid for ninety days or more. Some even have a bad loans rate of 20 per cent and above. But people continue to willingly bank with them. So, what is it these banks offer that keeps people hooked to such banks? Maybe an extra 0.5 per cent interest compared to another bank? Maybe the clerks are polite? Maybe they have a locker facility? Maybe the

branch manager is a nice chap? But is all of it really worth the risk? When a better PSB is available to deposit money, why go for a less healthy option? Laziness is the only plausible answer here. This is not to say the government will not rescue these banks if they falter. It will. But what if the RBI, while sorting out the mess, restricts access to deposits for a certain period as it has done in the case of the PMC Bank. While the safety of deposits is paramount, access to deposits is equally important. At the end of the day, what good is any money if it cannot be spent when required.

4) The attitude that just because money is in a bank it is safe really needs to be dispensed with. There is always a certain amount of risk attached to money that is invested. A prudent way of dealing with this is to stay away from banks which have a high rate of bad loans. Anything over 10 per cent is a no-no.

5) There is a lack of transparency around what most cooperative banks do with the money they take from depositors. Many of these banks are run by politicians and their cronies. This is not to say all cooperative banks are bad. But it is certainly difficult to figure out which are the good ones. Also, given their huge number and political connections, the ability of the RBI to regulate cooperative banks is rather limited. In such a situation, it makes sense to stay away from these banks, even if they offer higher interest rates on deposits than commercial banks.

*　*　*

PMC was also India's first crisis related to a bank which played out on social media. Within hours of the RBI limiting withdrawals, the news was all over mainstream and social media. One message that went viral on WhatsApp was that after the PMC Bank, the RBI and the government planned to shut down not one, not two, not three, but nine PSBs.

My first response to the message was, Why would anyone in their right mind believe it? Why would the government shut down nine PSBs at the same time and risk creating social tension in large parts of the country?

But such was the virality of the message, for lack of a better term, that even the RBI had to put out a press release on Twitter pointing out that no such plan was on the anvil.

Why did I feel the message was ridiculous and totally false? First, the RBI does not have the power to shut down a PSB. Of course, this is a technical point and not many people would know.

One bank on the list was Dena Bank, which had already been merged with the Bank of Baroda. Another bank on the list was Corporation Bank, which is being merged with the Union Bank of India. So, we had a bank which had ceased to exist and another that would cease to exist. How could these banks be shut down?

Soon, videos of bank depositors were going around on WhatsApp. One video that I remember well had a schoolteacher who had put her life savings in the PMC Bank and had no access to the money. Another news item that went viral was about a depositor who died of cardiac arrest.

All this has created a sense of panic among depositors across the country. WhatsApp and other social media platforms like Twitter and Facebook ended up creating a perception that bank deposits are unsafe. How did this happen? Let's look at it pointwise.

1) Producing fake news is cheap. All it requires is a literate person who is largely idle and has a mobile phone with an internet connection. The same is not true for news produced by the media, which at least up until a few years back used to cost a lot of money. As Abhijit Banerjee and Esther Duflo write in *Good Economics for Hard Times*: 'Circulation of news on social media is killing the production of reliable news and analysis. Producing fake news is of course very cheap and very rewarding economically since, unconstrained by reality, it is easy to serve to your readership exactly what they want to read. But if you don't want to make things up, you can also just

copy it from elsewhere. A study found that 55 per cent of the content diffused by news sites and media in France is almost entirely cut and pasted, but the source is only mentioned in less than five per cent of cases.'[407]

The larger point here, as Banerjee and Duflo put it, is 'the economic model that sustained journalism as a location for "public space" (and correct information) is collapsing'. In this scenario, 'without access to proper facts, it is easier to indulge in nonsense'.

The rise of Twitter and WhatsApp has come at the cost of people's belief going down in what used to be the conventional media. Of course, the rise of Twitter and Facebook isn't the only reason for this. Given that people don't trust the media much, they end up trusting *a lot of nonsense* that gets sent over on WhatsApp.

2) Let's go back to the example of the WhatsApp message that said the government and the RBI were planning to shut down nine PSBs. Why did people believe it, without even doing some basic fact-checking?

As Robert J. Shiller writes in *Narrative Economics*: 'The human mind seems to have a built-in interest in conspiracies, a tendency to form a personal identity and a loyalty to friends based on the desire to protect oneself from the perceived plots of others.'[408]

People had seen the state of the depositors of PMC Bank on social media. Hence, there was a desire to protect their deposits in PSBs, from a perceived plot by the RBI or the government, to shut down these banks. In this scenario, it didn't matter for most people whether the piece of news about the RBI shutting down banks was true or not.

Of course, this does not mean that everyone bought the fake news. There would definitely be people who realized it was fake news but still ended up forwarding the message. Why did this happen? As Shiller writes: 'People are more likely to share novel information. In other words, contagion reflects the urge to titillate and surprise others.'[409] Even if a news story is false, and the person forwarding it knows it's false, he or she might still forward it *just to surprise others*. One forward that I get every year from highly-educated relatives is about how fish are flying in the air in Mumbai.

This is something that happened in case of the PMC Bank as well. As Shiller writes: 'Fake news is not new. In fact, people have always liked amusing stories and they spread stories that they suspect are not true ... In other words, at some level, many people enjoy believing the story and do not care about its factuality'.[410] This just adds to the panic.

Even if a new story correcting the false story is published, as tends to be the case with so many fact-checking sites now in vogue, the new story may not be as contagious as the false story. This means there will be people out there who will continue to believe the false story, just because someone sent it to them on WhatsApp.

3) Social media has the capacity for *endless repetition* or what is known as an echo chamber. This is what political parties all over the world try to make use of, by feeding content that their supporters like to believe in and creating hatred towards a class or a community or a caste or a religion.

Nevertheless, this characteristic of the social media creates a problem in case of false forwards in the areas of economics and finance. As Banerjee and Duflo write: 'The problem with echo chambers is not just that we are only exposed to ideas we like; we are also exposed to them again and again and again, endlessly'.[411]

This is primarily what happened in case of the PMC Bank. I got the message regarding the RBI and the government planning to shut down PSBs, from many different people. I am slightly better informed about these things than an average Indian. But imagine what would be going on in the mind of a person who got this particular WhatsApp message over and over again. The fact that many different people sent the same false message to him might have led him to believe that the government actually had such a plan and the money in bank was actually unsafe.

4) Air travel is by far the safest mode of travel, though it may seem to be otherwise to many people. But why does travelling by air seem so unsafe? The answer lies in the fact that every air crash gets reported in the media. But all the safe landings that happen every day don't make it to the news at all.

As Hans Rosling, Ola Rosling and Anna Rosling Rönnlund, write in the *Factfulness*: 'In 2016, a total of 40 million commercial passenger flights landed safely at their destinations. Only ten ended in fatal accidents. Of course, those were the ones the journalists wrote about: 0.000025 per cent of the total. Safe flights are not newsworthy.'[412]

How is this linked to what I am trying to communicate? For every video you see of a PMC Bank depositor who does not have access to all his or her deposits, there are millions of other depositors who continue to have access to their deposits and they continue to withdraw them as and when they feel like. Nevertheless, they are not making any videos to say so. And that's because continuing to have access to deposits isn't considerend newsworthy. Not having access is.

5) The human mind needs simple information. As Sanjoy Chakrovorty writes in *The Truth About Us*: 'Simple information … makes it possible for experts and non-experts to make sense of the overwhelming quantity of data that has to be processed by the human senses. The human brain has limited data-processing capacity and works best when it does not have to process new or too much information all the time; that is, when it can slot all or most incoming data into pre-existing categories in the mind. The preference for simple information is universal.'[413]

Now how does this apply in the case of WhatsApp and the unsafeness of bank deposits? The deposit insurance available on bank deposits, at the time deposit withdrawals in PMC Bank were restricted, was Rs 1 lakh. This hadn't changed since

1993.* Quite a lot of people believe that all bank deposits are guaranteed by the government. They aren't. Still others believed that in case of a bank ending up in trouble, they will get back only Rs 1 lakh. Technically, that is true. But that is not going to happen. Typically, any bank in trouble is rescued and merged with a stronger bank.

Also, the government rescues PSBs every year, just that it doesn't say so. This is the reality of the situation, but it's a little more complicated than what people end up believing.

To conclude, if you are a depositor with a PSB or any other bank, it is worth remembering that it is your money in the bank at the end of the day, and if you don't care about it, no one else will.

---

* In the budget speech made on 1 February 2020, the finance minister, Nirmala Sitharaman said: 'The Deposit Insurance and Credit Guarantee Corporation (DICGC) has been permitted to increase deposit insurance coverage for a depositor, which is now Rs one lakh to Rs five lakh per depositor.'

32

A Good Crisis Gone Waste?

Rahm Emanuel, an American politician, who served as the Chief of Staff of President Barack Obama from 2009 to 2010 – and as the mayor of the city of Chicago between 2011 and 2019 – famously said: 'You never want a serious crisis to go to waste. And what I mean by that is an opportunity to do things you think you could not do before.'

What Emanuel means here is that any serious crisis gives a government an opportunity to push through unpopular reforms, which it wouldn't have been able to do in the normal scheme of things for it would disturb the status quo and, in the process, disturb the people who have an incentive in the status quo continuing. These people would then show their nuisance value.

An excellent example of a crisis not going waste in India are the economic reforms of 1991, which were pushed through after we almost ran out of foreign exchange and had to borrow money against gold.

The bad loan crisis in India never became a serious emergency (it came nowhere near how things were in 1991), simply because the government kept recapitalizing PSBs. Hence, at any given point of time, no bank came to a situation where it was unable to pay off the maturing deposits.

A serious crisis scenario was generated, at least briefly in the minds of people, sometime in late 2017 and early 2018, when the FRDI WhatsApp forwards were doing the rounds. This was also the time when Nirav Modi defrauded PNB and escaped from

266

the country. If the government wanted to, at that point of time, it could have pushed through some reforms of public sector banking in India. Of course, this is said with the benefit of hindsight.

While analysis always happens in hindsight, economic policy and reform have to be carried out in real time. I have no special information on this front, but one factor holding back the government at that point of time could have been the fact that the next Lok Sabha elections (which ultimately happened in April and May 2019) were a little over a year away. Given that, pushing for reforms in public sector banking then would not have made much political sense.

One reform that has been pushed through is the IBC. But the usefulness of the IBC comes in only once a firm has defaulted on the loan and not before it. The structure of public sector banking in India has more or less remained the same. In this scenario, the chances of another bad loan crisis might turn up at our doorstep in the years to come are very high. This can be prevented by implementing a series of reforms. Let's take a look at them.

* * *

PSBs needs to come under one regulator and that is the RBI. The meddling by the bureaucrats of the ministry of finance in the PSBs needs to stop.

The Committee to Review Governance of Boards of Banks in India (better known as the Nayak Committee, after its chairman, P.J. Nayak) which presented its report to the RBI in May 2014, had also proposed that when it comes to the PSBs, the government should follow the Axis Bank model – wherein the government is an investor, rather than the promoter of banks.

Axis Bank was originally called UTI Bank. It was set up in 1993. It was owned by the Unit Trust of India (UTI) and a clutch of PSBs. Even though ownership was 100 per cent in the public sector, the bank got a licence to operate only as a private sector bank. The bank was listed on the stock exchanges in 1998. Even at that point of time, the public sector shareholding continued to be the majority shareholding. In early 2000s, when the Unit Trust of India ran into trouble, the government broke it down into two parts. One part became the UTI Mutual Fund and the other was the Specified Undertaking of the Unit Trust of India (SUUTI).[414]

In February 2003, the shareholding of UTI in the bank was transferred to SUUTI. UTI Bank was later renamed Axis Bank.

As the Nayak Committee Report points out: 'Since then, the Government-as-Investor stance has characterised the control of the Bank, with SUUTI acting as a special purpose vehicle holding the investment on behalf of the Government. The CEO is appointed by the bank's board, and because the bank was licensed in the private sector, it sets its own employee compensation, ensures its own vigilance enforcement (rather than being under the jurisdiction of the Central Vigilance Commission), and is not subject to the Right to Information Act. SUUTI appoints the non-executive Chairman and up to two directors on the Board, and there is no direct intervention by the Finance Ministry'.[415]

This means that the bank has been run as a proper business, without much intervention from the government. Between March 2003 and March 2014, the share price of Axis Bank rose thirty-two times. In fact, in March 2014, the government, through SUUTI, sold a 9 per cent stake in the bank for Rs 5,500 crore. Over the years, the government has been able to sell its stake in the bank to raise a decent amount of money.

In fact, as of June 2019, the SUUTI's 5.4 per cent stake in the bank was worth close to Rs 11,353 crore. The point being that even though, as per its shareholding, Axis Bank 'was for many years a PSB', but 'fortuitously, the bank was licensed at the commencement of its business as a private sector bank'.[416] The Nayak Committee Report suggests that the government should look at PSBs as an investment and not as a business it has to run, and follow the Axis Bank model. This essentially means the government reducing the stake in PSBs to less than 50 per cent, and letting the bank's management and its board do their job, like in the case with private sector banks.

* * *

Any reform of PSBs needs to deal with the problem of these banks having dual regulators – the RBI as well as the ministry of finance. In fact, just between October 2012 and January 2014, the government issued eighty-two circulars to PSBs, leaving very little degree of autonomy to them.[417]

During the period, PSBs obviously had to deal with circulars being issued by the RBI too. The private sector banks, on the other hand, had to deal with circulars issued just by the RBI. This meant that they had eighty-two fewer circulars to deal with. Given this, it's not surprising that private banks are more competitive than their public-sector counterparts in India.

As the report submitted by the P.J. Nayak Committee pointed out: 'Governance difficulties in PSBs arise from several externally imposed constraints. These include dual regulation, by the Finance Ministry in addition to the RBI; board constitution, wherein it's difficult to categorise any director as independent; significant and widening compensation differences with private sector banks, leading to the erosion of specialist skills; external vigilance enforcement though the CVC (Central Vigilance Commission) and CBI (Central Bureau of Investigation); and limited applicability of the RTI Act. A more level playing field with private sector banks is desirable.'[418]

In fact, the PSBs are not required to comply with the Listing Obligations and Disclosure Requirements of the stock exchanges. As the Nayak Committee report points out: 'Private sector banks have a large proportion of independent directors in compliance with ... the stock exchange listing requirements, while in PSBs other than elected shareholder directors, all other directors are nominated by the Government (and one by RBI) and cannot be construed as independent. This is an egregious violation ... Sadly, even the elected shareholder directors generally owe their election to LIC, given LIC's dominance as a shareholder in most banks, and the perception is widespread that LIC's support is best "managed through the Government".' Also, 'unlike in private sector banks, the boards have no governance role or control over bringing in directors with special skills'.[419] This is something that needs to be corrected quickly.

The committee had also proposed a solution to these problems. It said: 'If the Government stake in these banks were to reduce to less than 50 per cent, together with certain other executive measures taken, all these external constraints would disappear. This would be a beneficial trade-off for the government, because it would continue to be the dominant shareholder and, without its control [on] banks diminishing, it would create the conditions for its banks to compete more successfully. *It's a fundamental irony that presently the Government disadvantages the very banks it has invested in* [emphasis added]'.[420]

The Nayak Committee had proposed that the government's stake in PSBs be moved to a Bank Investment Company, registered under the Companies Act. It had proposed that this company should bring down its stake in the PSBs to less than 50 per cent. In such a situation, the dual regulation of the PSBs would disappear, and the RBI would be the sole regulator of these banks. Further, this would ensure that the PSBs have the ability to offer a competitive compensation structure, in line with that of private banks. While the compensation structure of PSBs at lower levels is extremely competitive, the same cannot be said for the middle and upper levels, where private sector banks offer employee stock options.

There is a reason why the idea of a Bank Investment Company is so important. Even with a stake of lower than 50 per cent, the government can still act as a nuisance for the management of PSBs. The government did not stop fiddling around with the Industrial Finance Corporation of India, even after its stake went well below 51 per cent. It managed to frustrate T. Rowe Price, the foreign partner of UTI Mutual Fund, even with no direct stake in the mutual fund. Also, despite seeing the success of UTI Bank and having a minority indirect stake in the bank, it managed to irritate its CEO frequently.[421] In this scenario, the Bank Investment Company run by professionals will ensure that the government will stay away from running PSBs, and just look at them as investments from which they need to make money.

A government stake of below 50 per cent would also ensure that banks would be free from the external vigilance of the Central Vigilance Commission, as well as the RTI Act. The committee had also recommended that the government resist from issuing any instructions that are applicable only to PSBs.

It also proposed that both PSBs and the Bank Investment Company be incorporated under the Companies Act of 2013. As the report points out: 'With the enactment of the new Companies Act in 2013, India now has a modern and powerful legal governance mechanism for enforcing good standards for company behaviour, including in the governance of company boards. In contrast, the nationalised PSBs have anachronistic provisions, emanating from the Bank Nationalisation Act, which govern the functioning of boards as also powers given to the government as the principal shareholder'.[422]

For example, the Bank Nationalisation Act has nothing to say about the consequences of bad judgements and decision-making of bank boards. The criteria for membership to the board of banks is set in vague terms, such as special knowledge or practical experience in areas like operations, finance, small-scale industry, etc. Areas like financial literacy or expertise in information technology, for that matter, are not even listed. The Bank Nationalisation Act is more concerned with process issues of bank boards. In contrast, the Companies Act of 2013 is 'more concerned with outcomes and boards risk action if damaged outcomes are a consequence of poor governance'.[423]

The Nayak Committee has recommended that the CEO of the Bank Investment Company should be allowed to recruit his own team. It also recommended that the employees of the Bank Investment Company be incentivized on the basis of the financial returns that PSBs deliver. As the report points out: 'If such incentivisation requires the Government to hold less than 50 per cent of equity in Bank Investment Company, the Government should consider doing so, as it will be the prime financial beneficiary of Bank Investment Company's success.'[424]

The boards of public sector enterprises and PSBs in India are usually used to award retiring bureaucrats and people close to the party in power. This is something that needs to end if PSBs are to be professionally run. As Rajan writes in *I Do What I Do*: 'Unless PSBs are run like normal corporations, they will not be competitive in the medium term. I have a simple metric of progress here: We will have moved significantly towards limiting interference in PSBs when the Department of Financial Services (which oversees public sector financial firms) is finally closed down, and its banking functions taken over by bank boards and the Bank Board Bureau'.[425]

The government nominees on PSB boards exercise disproportionate power primarily because they represent both the shareholder (with the government being the major owner of PSBs) as well as the sovereign. Hence, it's important that they have some understanding of the functioning of banks in particular and the economy in general. As Reddy writes: 'We wanted the directors nominated by the government to the PSBs to satisfy the 'fit and proper' criteria on par with those prescribed by the RBI for private sector banks'.[426]

***

Non-retail and non-agriculture bank lending is largely of the following kinds: 1) PSBs lending to public sector corporations; 2) PSBs lending to private corporations; 3) private banks lending to private corporations; 4) private banks lending to public sector corporations.

Problems crop up only if a bad loan has arisen from a PSB lending to a private corporation. Any move to resolve the loan through debt reduction or any other kind of restructuring leads to the bank being seen as favouring a big businessman. There is also the possibility of attracting the attention of the courts, Central

Bureau of Investigation, Central Vigilance Commission and Comptroller and Auditor General.[427]

In this scenario, it makes sense for the government to keep reducing its stake in PSBs.

There is no point in the government continuing to own majority stakes in eighteen PSBs. (The number before 31 March 2019 was twenty. With the merger of Bank of Baroda, Dena Bank and Vijaya Bank, from 1 April 2019, the number has been reduced to eighteen.) There is nothing new about this proposal. The Committee on Banking Sector Reforms of 1998 (the Second Narasimham Committee) had also made a similar suggestion. The committee had clearly said that the minimum shareholding of the government in PSBs be brought down to 33 per cent. The government had accepted this proposal and the then finance minister, Yashwant Sinha, had talked about it in the Budget speech he made on 29 February 2000.

As Sinha had said: 'To enable the banks to expand their operations, PSBs will need more capital. With the government Budget under severe strain, such capital has to be raised from the public, which will result in a reduction in government shareholding. To facilitate this process, government [has] decided to accept the recommendations of the Narasimham Committee on Banking Sector Reforms for reducing the requirement of minimum shareholding by government in nationalized banks to 33 per cent. This will be done without changing the public sector character of banks and while ensuring that fresh issue of shares is widely held by the public.'[428]

Interestingly, Sinha, in his speech, had also talked about the importance of the boards of the PSBs being given sufficient autonomy to make decisions.

Two decades later, the solution to get PSBs going continues to remain the same. The answers to India's economic problems are all there in the reports of various committees, which have been formed over the years. Now all it needs is the political will to push through with the recommendations.

Back in 2000, the proposal to bring down the government stake in PSBs to 33 per cent was abandoned in the face of stiff political opposition. It's worth remembering here that the Atal Bihari Vajpayee government, which governed the country at that point of time was a coalition. The Modi government which governs the country in 2020 has a majority. And in this situation, if the government wants, it can push through the proposal of bringing down the government's stake in PSBs to 33 per cent.

After this is done and the banks are allowed to be professionally run with minimum interference, the residual stake of the government in the years to come shall be worth much more than the stake it holds now.

* * *

We saw in Chapter 18 that the banking sector is gradually getting privatized, despite the government continuing to own a bulk of the banks. One reason for this lies in the way the economic incentives are structured – private banks are naturally more aggressive than PSBs on the marketing and the selling front. But it isn't just about that.

When it comes to recruiting employees, at least those employees responsible for the retail part of the business of a bank, the private banks (in particular, new-generation private sector banks), follow the moneylender model of recruitment.

We are in 2019, but moneylenders still have a part to play in the Indian financial system. As per the All-India Rural Financial Inclusion Survey 2016–17, nearly 11 per cent of all households had borrowed money from a money lender between July 2015 and June 2016. The average amount borrowed was Rs 10,085.

One reason why moneylenders have survived all these years, despite the exorbitant rate of interest they charge, lies in the fact that they dare to go where banks and other financial institutions don't. Of course, their lending is light on documentation and is available at a drop of a hat.

But more than that, the reason moneylenders survive is because they lend in particular neighbourhoods and know their clientele very well. They know the borrower's sources of income and wealth, and the amount he or she is in a position to repay.[429] (Of course, they can also use rough methods to get a borrower to repay. This is something that banks can't do, at least not on paper or openly.)

The point is that the moneylender's local knowledge comes in handy while lending. Private banks, while expanding into areas where they are not present earlier, tend to recruit from the local population or at least people who have past experience of having worked locally. A good example of this is HDFC Bank and what it did in Kashmir. It recruited local youth, who knew the local people, could make a good assessment of who was creditworthy and, in the process, helped the bank expand its loan portfolio in the region.[430]

On the other hand, a PSB has a disadvantage on this front. A local branch is normally run by a branch manager, who is recruited through an all-India entrance exam, probably from another state. The problem is that, in many cases, the manager does not know the local language, culture and is not familiar with the people of that area.[431] This is not to say that the managers don't make an effort to familiarize themselves and became a part of the community. A lot of them do. But a lot of them don't. This is one reason why PSBs are losing out to private banks, which tend to recruit locally and, in the process, are much better at soliciting business.

In fact, in the recent past, PSBs have been a little more innovative and have gone beyond the all-India examinations to recruit lower-level management by visiting campuses of business schools. But in August 2014, the Department of Financial Services wrote to PSBs asking them to desist from recruiting officers straight out of campuses. This was because of court judgments not allowing the same.

In fact, as Rajan lamented in an August 2016 speech: 'One of the difficulties PSBs have is court judgments that prohibit hiring from specific campuses. This leads to anomalies like the PSB–supported National Institute of Bank Management sending most of its high-quality graduates to work for private sector banks.'[432]

Another advantage of recruiting locally will be that banks can pay salaries which are commensurate with the local labour market.[433]

While it may be easy to suggest here that PSBs should be allowed to recruit locally, in order to be able to take on private banks, it will never be that simple to implement anything like this. PSBs are owned by the Central government. In that sense, when PSBs recruit, they can't be seen to be recruiting only locally, from one part of the country. This will go against their very character. Also, it will tend to favour people living in the developed parts of the country. Take the example of the state of Jharkhand, where I come from. As of 31 December 2018, the state had 3,196 functioning offices of banks. On the other hand, the National Capital Territory of Delhi had 3,873 offices. Obviously, Delhi has a much smaller area than the entire state of Jharkhand, though it has a lot more money and is a lot more developed.

If banks opening in Delhi recruit only people who have lived and worked in Delhi, it will be held against people from other parts of the country, including Jharkhand. The people living in Jharkhand will not get a crack at PSB jobs, simply because very few branches are likely to open in the state in comparison with other more developed states.

* * *

As we have seen earlier, in Chapter 14, the American economist Thomas Sowell talks about the separation of knowledge and power, in the context of why central planning does not work. It was not possible for the higher officials who ran the centrally planned Soviet economy to be experts at everything. As Sowell writes in *Basic Economics: A Common Sense Guide to the Economy*: 'Those with the power in the central planning agencies were to some extent dependent on those with knowledge of their own particular industries and enterprises. This separation of power and knowledge was at the heart of the problem'.[434]

Let's try and understand this separation of power and knowledge through the example of glass production. In the Soviet Union, everything was owned by the government and, as with other things, the government produced glass.

The idea, of course, was to produce different types and enough quantity of glass to meet the needs of other industries. The trouble was that there was no pricing mechanism in place, which could inherently coordinate the demand and supply of the different kinds of glass. All that was in place were government diktats.

As Swaminathan Aiyar writes in *From Narasimha Rao to Narendra Modi: 25 Years of Swaminomics*: 'Soviet planners set physical targets of glass production in terms of weight, factory managers started producing the heaviest sorts of glasses to meet plan targets. This meant shortages in terms of square feet'.[435]

The planners then decided to shift the targets from tonnes to square feet in order to correct this. 'Alas, this induced factories to produce the thinnest glasses to meet targets, and much of it shattered,' writes Aiyar.[436]

In this case, those who worked at glass factories would, at any point of time, have had the right knowledge on what kind of glass was needed. But those individuals who had the knowledge did not have the power to make decisions. The power to decide what kind of glass to produce lay with officials in the central planning agencies.

Now what has all this got to do with the operation of PSBs in India? As we have seen earlier, when PSBs give out retail loans, they do a decent job of it. But the same cannot be said when they give out loans to industry.

When they give a retail loan, all the information they require is in place, as the prospective borrower submits all the documents that a banker needs to figure out whether he or she will be able to repay the loan or not.

When it comes to lending to corporates, there can be other factors at play. Crony capitalists close to politicians need to be entertained, irrespective of whether they have the capability to repay the loan or not. In this case, there is a clear separation of knowledge and power. Bank managers may have the knowledge – that giving a loan to a particular corporate may not be the best thing to do – but they may not have the power to deny the loan, simply because of some pressure from a politician or bureaucrat. This was one of the reasons behind the bad loans mess that prevails in PSBs, though not the only reason for it.

As long as PSBs remain public sector in character, politicians can influence loan-giving operations and, thus, the separation of power and knowledge will remain. Another problem that crops up because of politicians is that they expect PSBs to open branches in their constituencies, irrespective of whether it makes business sense or not.

* * *

The PSBs do not have significant in-house expertise when it comes to project evaluation. In the past, they have had to be dependent on investment banks and other consultants, who have had incentives to be biased. In this scenario, it's important that PSBs get around to building in-house expertise for project evaluation. This would mean understanding demand projections and a project's output, along with the competition the project is likely to face, how much expertise the promoter has in the area and how reliable he is. Over and above this, bankers will have to work towards developing domain knowledge in a few areas.[437]

In short, public sectors banks will have to develop an expertise towards lending to industry, which they currently lack. At the same time, they need follow up on loans adequately, with the post-loan monitoring having been lax in the past. In the past, collaterals that were offered by corporate borrowers were not perfected to make sure that no other lender had rights to the same collateral.

Over and above this, the personal guarantees of borrowers were not tracked.[438]

In such cases, even without a politician interfering, a banker has the power to give a loan, but he or she doesn't have the necessary knowledge. Hence, it's important to fill this gap.

Over the last few years, lending to industry has not been something that PSBs seem interested in. But this will change sooner rather than later, as money will be borrowed for the making of new roads, airports, railway lines, power plants and, hopefully, manufacturing plants. It's banks that will have to finance this simply because there are no other mechanisms in place.

When it comes to long-term lending, the corporate bond market in India continues to remain underdeveloped. In his book *Advice & Dissent*, Y.V. Reddy talks about a time when he was the RBI governor, between 2003 and 2008. He writes: 'Development of the corporate bond market was another area of priority for the government in the belief that financing of infrastructure would be enabled through the bond market. We [i.e., the RBI] were also keen to develop the corporate bond market'.[439] It has been more than a decade since Reddy retired from the RBI and not much has changed on this front. Hence, whenever the next round of industrial lending happens, the PSBs will be at the heart of it all over again. This is something that needs to be kept in mind.

The DFIs of yore are now dead and gone. In fact, in November 2019, ICICI bank shut down its project finance division, probably the last remnant of the erstwhile ICICI from which the bank sprung. Mutual funds are more interested in lending money for the short-term. That leaves just banks doing the long-term lending.

It's a fairly long shot for all PSBs to develop expertise in the area of corporate finance and industrial lending. What is the way around this? The Committee on the Financial System of 1991 (better known as the First Narasimham Committee) had recommended a three-tier banking structure in India: with three large banks with international presence, eight to ten national banks, and a large number of regional and local banks.[440]

Something along similar lines needs to be done with the structure of PSBs in India. Only the biggest five to six banks should be allowed to carry out lending to industry. This suggestion stands irrespective of whether the government reduces its stake in PSBs to 33 per cent or not.

In order to do this, the top banks allowed to carry out industrial lending need to be encouraged in different ways. Let's say a bank decides to finance a road project and decides to lend Rs 15,000 crore for it. Now, in order to fund this loan, the bank will have to raise much more than Rs 15,000 crore, simply because it needs to maintain a cash reserve ratio, a statutory liquidity ratio and carry out priority-sector lending. For long-term infrastructure projects of, let's say, five years or more, the banks can be exempted from such obligations. In fact, this will create a level playing field between banks and other financial institutions, like insurance companies carrying out long-term infrastructure funding.[441]

If the top PSBs concentrate on industrial lending, what happens to the other banks? The smaller banks should concentrate on retail lending and working capital finance. In this case, carrying out proper due diligence is easier. At the same time, even if a bank ends up with bad loans, they are easy to recover.

Also, it has been suggested that some of the weaker small banks concentrate on operating in one part of the country, instead of having national ambitions. An excellent example of this is the Bank of Maharashtra, which could become a bank focused in the state of Maharashtra, as it has detailed knowledge of the region. At the same time, it enjoys high brand equity in the local population.[442]

The middle-level management, which would do much of the due diligence on whether or not to give loans to industrial and infrastructure projects, has thinned out at PSBs. This has happened primarily because of retirements and the fact that for many years the process of recruitment had slowed down across public-sector enterprises. There is a need to recruit people to fill in these posts. These recruitments need to be done laterally, and banks need to hire experts in areas like project evaluation and management, risk management, information technology, etc.[443]

Of course, the question is why would anyone join a PSB at the middle management level, without an increase in remuneration? This is where the issuance of ESOPs (i.e., employee stock options) makes immense sense, especially once one takes into account the fact that the current prices of public sector banking stocks have been terribly beaten down.[444]

Other than hiring laterally, the banks also need to petition and request courts to let them hire some individuals directly from campuses. This will help them build long-term expertise in the above-mentioned areas.

Over and above this, the way lending is carried out needs to change. Currently, it is carried out through a committee-based approach. While a committee clearing lending decisions has its share of advantages, there is a huge disadvantage to it as well. When a committee lends, no one can be held responsible for a loan going bad.

What's the way out of this? While PSBs can still follow a committee-based approach towards lending, every loan proposal cleared needs to have a senior banker's name on it. Hence, when the lending turns out to be good, he or she should be rewarded in the form of a bonus as well as ESOPs. With a banker's name on the document, he or she will have an incentive to monitor the loan closely, which is something that doesn't happen right now.

There is another thing that this will achieve. With a banker's name on every loan document, it will be easy to figure out at the end of the year the performance of bankers in terms of the good loans and bad loans given out. On the basis of this, ESOPs and bonuses can be awarded. Of course, loans will go bad over a period of time and not as soon as they are awarded. If and when this happens, the clawback of ESOPs and bonuses can happen, to make sure that bankers are rewarded as per performance. Clawback is the act of retrieving the money that has already been paid.

* * *

All commercial banks in India are regulated by the RBI under the Banking Regulation Act of 1949. Over and above this, the PSBs are regulated by the Government of India under the following Acts: a) Banking Companies (Acquisition and Transfer of Undertakings) Act, 1970; b) Bank Nationalisation Act, 1980; c) SBI Act, 1955.

Interestingly, Section 51 of the Banking Regulation Act clearly states which portions apply to PSBs. Given this, there are certain things that the RBI can do when it comes to private banks but cannot do when it comes to PSBs.

These are listed as follows: a) it cannot remove either the directors or the management at PSBs. It can also not remove the chairman and managing director of a PSB; b) the RBI cannot suppress a PSB board because they are not banking companies listed under the Companies Act; c) the RBI cannot force the mergers of PSBs; d) It cannot revoke a banking licence of a PSB because their banking activity does not require a licence from the Central bank; e) the RBI cannot trigger the liquidation of a PSB.[445]

In a speech given in March 2018, Urjit Patel, the RBI governor at that point, offered the example of a managing director of a PSB, who also happened to be its chairman, and said: 'In some cases there is duality of Managing Director and the Chairman – they are the same – implying the MD is primarily answerable only to himself or herself'.[446]

This is primarily because PSBs have two regulators, the RBI and the Department of Financial Services in the ministry of finance. This anomaly needs to be corrected. As the Nayak Committee report pointed out: 'RBI should be the sole regulator for banks, with regulations continuing to be uniformly applicable to all commercial banks'. In fact, it even suggested that 'the Government should also cease to issue instructions to PSBs in pursuit of development objectives. Any such instructions should, after consultation with RBI, be issued by that regulator and be applicable to all banks.'[447] The idea here is to create a level playing field between the two kinds of banks.

Let's take the case of Jan Dhan accounts that the PSBs have a mandate to open. As on 12 June 2019, 35.86 crore Jan Dhan accounts had been opened in banks across India. The average deposit was Rs 2,762. India has around 25 crore households. When we take this fact into account, it seems that a decent number of Jan Dhan accounts have been opened by now. Many of these accounts are used to transfer money in lieu of government-provided direct benefits. In this scenario, it makes sense for the government to compensate banks (both PSBs as well as private banks) adequately for this. Even if this is moderately profitable for banks, they will have an incentive to provide some service as well as compete for the customer who happens to be poor.[448]

One of the most basic lessons that one can learn from economics is that the right incentives go a longer way in influencing the required behaviour than directives. I guess, it's time that the Government of India also learnt this lesson.

Getting back to a level playing field, it also means that the RBI be allowed to supersede boards, remove board members and convene a meeting of PSBs, like it can do in the case of private banks. Of course, just giving these powers to the RBI is not enough. The central bank should also be willing to exercise them.[449]

How will a level playing field between these banks help? Let's consider the case of a private bank which is not doing well and is put under the PCA framework. The CEO of this bank will be concerned about his post (as the RBI can fire him) and also about the fact that the bank be able to quickly come out of PCA and come back to normal business. If it continues to be in PCA, its stock price will be beaten down and it will be difficult for it to raise fresh capital when the need arises. So, the combination of regulatory (from the RBI) as well as market discipline (from the stock market) works well in the case of private sector banks.

The market discipline works less for PSBs, primarily because they are backed by the government. If the stock price is beaten down and these banks need fresh capital, the government will come in with the amount that is required. Given that market discipline is weak, it makes logical sense for the government to want stronger regulatory discipline when it comes to PSBs. As Urjit Patel put it in a speech: 'Since the original idea behind bank nationalisation was complete government control over credit allocation to the economy, the situation in India is exactly the reverse: RBI's regulatory powers over PSBs are *weaker* [emphasis in the original] than those over the private sector banks'.[450]

This explains why the MD and the CEO of PNB, who should have taken the blame for Nirav Modi's Rs 12,646 crore fraud, continued to be in office. In January 2019, two executive directors of the bank were fired.

Imagine if such a big fraud had happened at a private sector bank: heads would have rolled. Look at what happened to Chanda Kochhar, the former chief executive officer and managing director of ICICI Bank. The bank had provided a loan of Rs 3,250 crore to Videocon in 2012. Six months later, the Videocon promoter, Venugopal Dhoot, is said to have provided crores of rupees to NuPower Renewables Pvt. Ltd, a company he started with Kochhar's husband – Deepak – and two relatives. Dhoot transferred the ownership of the company to Deepak Kochhar for Rs 9 lakh.[451] In October 2018, Kochhar had to unceremoniously exit ICICI Bank.

Shikha Sharma, chief executive officer of Axis Bank, had to cut short her fourth three-year tenure after the RBI asked the bank's board to reconsider their decision to award her a fourth term. The bad loans of the bank had jumped from Rs 5,724 crore as of March 2015 to Rs 25,001 crore as of December 2017.[452]

In another case, RBI forcefully retired Rana Kapoor, one of the founders and the managing director and CEO of Yes Bank. In a stock exchange notification in September 2018, the bank said: 'RBI has intimated that Shri Rana Kapoor may continue as the MD & CEO till 31 January 2019'.[453]

The RBI had found that Yes Bank had underreported its bad loans by Rs 10,470 crore in 2015–16 and 2016–17. In October

2017, the RBI had fined the bank Rs 6 crore for breaching standards on bad loans recognition.[454]

And here we had a situation where India's second-largest PSB, at that point of time, suffered a Rs 12,646 crore loss, and nothing happened to the MD and CEO of the bank. This lack of market and regulatory discipline is also reflected in managing directors of PSBs under PCA telling the media that it was business as usual for them. Even if they did not meet the requirements stipulated under the PCA framework, the RBI couldn't do anything about it, as 'the ultimate authority over their tenure is with the government and not with the RBI'.[455]

In fact, replies to Right to Information applications pointed out that across PSBs most of those penalized for bad loans happened to be managers across different scales, with the highest being general manager and the lowest officer. In fact, no chairman, director, deputy director or a managing director of a PSB was penalized for bad loans, simply because these executives do not come under the purview of staff disliplinary rules.[456]

***

To conclude, it is important that these reforms be brought in sooner rather than later. As we have seen earlier in the book, the PSBs have rapidly lost market share to their private sector counterparts, over the last few years. This privatization by benign neglect is hurting them badly. If private banks continue to capture the market like they currently are, they will have a larger share of the market than PSBs in less than a decade's time. Maybe even a decade is a stretch here.

This means that many PSBs will continue to lose value and will rapidly go the down the route telecom and airline companies owned by the government have gone in the past. In this scenario, the government investment in PSBs will lose value and, over a period of time, be worth next to nothing.

If the government wants to prevent that from happening, and ensure that its jewels continue to be jewels, the only possible way out for it is to look at PSBs as investments and not as businesses which they have to run. It's basically as simple as that.

Conclusion: The Parent Will Keep Feeding Children Permanently

During the process of researching and writing my previous book, *India's Big Government*, I realized that, over the decades, countless government committees have been set up to look at and find solutions to India's social and economic problems.

Over and above this, there are economists and other domain experts, working for the government, who come up with regular recommendations in reports and other communication published by the government, which are rarely read by those who should be reading them (i.e., the politicians and bureaucrats running the country).

More often than not, these committees come up with the right recommendations and solutions, which have a shot at solving India's social and economic problems. The thing is, any solution disturbs the status quo and any disturbance of the status quo means that everything will not be hunky-dory, and the politicians will have a tough time handling the situation that arises.

Hence, the easy way out, at least according to them, is to ignore much of what these committees say and ensure that their reports are confined to the dustbins of history, only to be dug up and read by people like me.

The Second Narasimham Committee of 1998 suggested more than two decades ago that the government should dilute its stake in PSBs to 33 per cent. The P.J. Nayak Committee's basic suggestion of lesser government and more governance in PSBs by following the Axis Bank model is also along similar lines. Former RBI governors have also said more or less the same thing.

How will this help? In the case of a private bank, if the banker wants to do the right thing, his chances of doing so are considerably high. Take the case of Paresh Sukthankar, who was a deputy managing director at HDFC Bank, India's biggest bank when it comes to market capitalization. He refused a loan to Vijay Mallya. This was revealed by Aditya Puri, the managing director of the bank, at a public function in July 2019. He said: 'If you are a bad risk, you are a bad risk. You can be my good friend, I can give you coffee and send you away'.[457]

At the same time, even if a private banker gives into temptation and does something that he or she shouldn't be doing, then, if later discovered, the banker is more than likely to face punishment. Look at what happened to Chanda Kochhar at ICICI Bank and Rana Kapoor at Yes Bank. Now compare it to PNB. After the Nirav Modi fraud came to light, two executive directors were sacked, but the MD and the CEO went scot-free.

Also, the corruption charges against public sector bankers have rarely stuck because how do you differentiate corruption and a bad lending decision. Nevertheless, as P.J. Nayak puts it: 'There is corruption in the system and there is no point in pretending otherwise'.[458]

There is another point that needs to be made here. The government does not want to be the purveyor of bad news or, to put it more succinctly, it wants to avoid doing that as far as possible. Take the case of PSBs and the fact that their Asset Quality Review finally happened in mid-2015. By that time, the PSBs were already sitting on a pile of bad loans. The government, as the owner of these banks, could have easily pushed it through earlier, but it tried pushing it back as far as possible.

In fact, with a few NBFCs getting into trouble, there has been a demand for an Asset Quality Review of this sector as well. But, again, the government doesn't want to be the purveyor of bad news and, hence, this proposal has not been taken up. Of course, unlike banks, the government doesn't own NBFCs, but is still reluctant to ask them to review their assets.

At the end of the day, the people running the government – politicians and bureaucrats – have very little incentive in running PSBs like a proper business. If PSBs make wrong lending decisions, which then leads to bad loans, neither the bureaucrats nor the politicians have to pay for it from their own pockets. The taxpayers end up picking up the tab. The PSB employees also keep getting their salary. In the case of a private bank, a lot depends on the profitability of the bank. If the profitability goes down due to bad loans, bonuses and employee stock option plans go down with it as well. And more than anything else, people end up losing jobs.

Which is why, much to the annoyance of Raghuram Rajan, the Department of Financial Services will continue to be in operation and will continue to meddle with PSBs. The chances of Rajan winning the Nobel Prize in Economics are higher than the Department of Financial Services being shut down. This parent will keep feeding its many children permanently.

A columnist once remarked with regard to PSBs, 'they can't change a toilet without the approval of the finance ministry'.[459] And that is more than likely to continue.

The problem is that the idea of PSBs becoming less public sector (forget being privatized) is something that will not go down well with the employees of the banks and their multiple unions. This is the nuisance value that any government wanting to reduce the its stake in PSBs to 33 per cent needs to handle.

The First Narasimham Committee of 1991 had suggested that India should have many regional and local banks. If this suggestion were to be implemented today, many PSBs will have to confine their activities primarily to a certain part of the country. This might also lead to a contraction in their size. The loans they can give out and the deposits they can raise will reduce, at least initially. The same holds true if smaller PSBs are only allowed to do retail banking.

Back in 2000, the Atal Bihari Vajpayee government tried to push through the move and dilute the government stake in PSBs to 33 per cent. And it failed. Why?

Vajpayee's finance minister, Yashwant Sinha, had introduced a bill to reduce the government's stake in PSBs to 33 per cent. It never saw the light of day. In a 2018 interview, Sinha said: 'The parliament and the people were not prepared for such [a] kind of step'.[460] In fact, all these years down the line, we are still grappling with the same issue.

Sinha couldn't push through the bill despite having the support of his prime minister. In another interview in 2018, commenting on the same issue, Sinha said: 'The proposal was sent to the finance commission ... We didn't hear anything about it. There was resistance from within the BJP'.[461]

The story goes that the ministry of law in the Vajpayee government couldn't figure out how the public sector character of PSBs can be maintained after the government holding in them is reduced to 33 per cent.[462]

What this means is that while Sinha and Vajpayee were fine with the idea of government holding in PSBs coming down to 33 per cent, their colleagues – both in the government and the party – clearly were not. Hence, the move, even though it was supported by the prime minister, was scuttled. The Central governments that followed couldn't do anything on this front and the Centre continues to own more than 50 per cent stake in PSBs nearly two decades later.

Vajpayee's government did not have a full majority on its own in the Lok Sabha and had to depend on its allies, some of them mercurial, to continue holding a majority in the parliament. The current Narendra Modi government does not suffer from such a problem. It has the numbers to push for the dilution of the government's stake in PSBs in the parliament. It also, for the lack of a better phrase, does smart floor management in the parliament.

But has the story changed nearly two decades later? Are politicians of this era, the ones who are in power and the ones who are in the Opposition, open to the idea of the government diluting its stake in PSBs to 33 per cent? There is nothing in the public domain that suggests anything like that.

Politicians continue to look at public sector enterprises as family jewels, which should not be sold fully, or even partly for that matter. They continue to love the idea of the government running businesses and owning companies as well as banks.

When it comes to the current BJP government, the Sangh Parivar – to which the party belongs – has generally been against the idea of the government privatizing public sector enterprises. If the government dilutes its stake in PSBs and, at the same time, follows the Axis Bank model, it won't mean privatization of the PSBs. Nevertheless, it would mean the government getting out of the banking business, which may not go down well with the Sangh Parivar.

This is not to say that if any other party was in power, they would have been working towards reducing the government's stake in PSBs. The Congress, which is stuck in a time warp, still thinks of the nationalization of banks in 1969 as an excellent move. While it is something that may have been required in 1969, it is clearly not working five decades later. But as senior Congress leader Jairam Ramesh said in a July 2019 interview with respect to PSBs: 'The government should not bring down its stake below 51 per cent holding'.[463]

Hence, with very little political support, it is highly unlikely that any such decision will be made. Any such decision, at least initially, is likely to be an unpopular one among the people at large. Also, the nuisance value of the employees and trade unions will be at work, in case any change in the character or the area of operation of PSBs is made.

Economic reforms in India – whenever they have happened – have always been reforms by stealth, but that has also stopped in the last decade. India's politicians have never really bothered to explain or sell economic reforms to the people of the country. If economic reforms, in any form, are to become the order of the day, politicians need to start explaining them to the people, to say the very least. Of course, this is difficult, given that no politician wants to take a lead on this front. It is always easier to sell socialism and government giveaways.

To conclude, the government is trying to solve the problem of bad loans primarily through the IBC. While sorting out this mess is important, it's equally important to ensure that something like this does not happen again. How do we prevent that? As the economist Hyman Minsky writes: 'The spectacular panics, debt deflations ... that historically followed a speculative boom as well as the recovery from depressions are of lesser importance in the analysis of instability than the developments over a period characterised by sustained growth that lead to the emergence of fragile and unstable financial structures'.[464]

He is essentially saying that the period of stability should not lead to instability. The indiscriminate lending that happens in a period of stability should be stopped. Or, to put it in simple English, prevention is better than cure.

This argument will never work as long as banks continue to be majorly owned and run by the government. No government will want to pull the plug on fast economic growth – even if it's being fuelled by excessive lending by banks – by asking the banks that it owns to go slow on lending. There is already enough evidence of that on offer.

More importantly, there will always be a temptation to encourage banks to continue to lend when an economic slowdown is around the corner. There will also be a temptation among politicians to favour those crony capitalists close to the party in power.

The next bad money crisis will happen sooner rather than later. As has been the case this time around, we, the taxpayers, will bear the burden of the next crisis as well.

And that is the long and the short of it.

Notes

1. Lok Sabha unstarred question no. 2513, available at http://164.100.47.190/loksabhaquestions/annex/14/AU2513. pdf, (accessed on 23 April 2019).
2. V. Kaul, 'Do Numbers Always Tell the Truth?', *Bangalore Mirror*, 11 April 2018.
3. T.C. Schelling, *Choice and Consequence. Perspectives of an Errant Economist*, Cambridge, Massachusetts: Harvard University Press, 1984.
4. R.H. Thaler, *Misbehaving—The Making of Behavioural Economics*, New York, New Delhi: Penguin Books, 2016.
5. J. Tirole, *Economics for the Common Good*, Princeton and Oxford: Princeton University Press, 2017.
6. J.P. Upadhyay, 'Nirav Modi, Vijay Mallya, and twenty-nine other Indian fugitives owe Rs 40,000 crore', 9 April 2018, www. livemint.com, (accessed on 23 April 2019). Available at https://www.livemint.com/Companies/2rBU4V1jumGfJguL9rdSyO/Nirav-Modi-Vijay-Mallya-and-29-other-Indian-fugitives-owe.html.
7. A.S. Blinder, *After the Music Stopped—The Financial Crisis, the Response, and the Work Ahead*, New York: Penguin Press, 2013.
8. C. Giles, 'The economics forecasters' failing vision', *Financial Times*, 25 November 2008. Accessed on June 6, 2019. Available at https://www.ft.com/content/50007754-ca35-11dd-93e5-000077b07658.
9. Financial Stability Report, Reserve Bank of India, December 2015.

10. H.P. Minsky, *Stabilizing an Unstable Economy*, New York: McGraw-Hill, 2008.
11. L.R. Wray, *Why Minsky Matters: An Introduction to the Work of a Maverick Economist*, Princeton and Oxford: Princeton University Press, 2016.
12. Ibid.
13. Ibid.
14. 'Non-Performing Assets of Financial Institutions', Twenty-Seventh Report, Standing Committee on Finance (2015–16), Sixteenth Lok Sabha, February 2016.
15. B.K. Dadabhoy, *Barons of Banking: Glimpses of Indian Banking History*, Gurgaon, Portfolio, Penguin, 2013.
16. Ibid.
17. Ibid.
18. Ibid.
19. Ibid.
20. Ibid.
21. Ibid.
22. Ibid.
23. Ibid.
24. The Reserve Bank of India, *The Reserve Bank of India*, Vol III (1967–1981), Mumbai: Reserve Bank of India, 2005.
25. Ibid.
26. Ibid.
27. Ibid.
28. Ibid.
29. Ibid.
30. Ibid.
31. I.G. Patel, *Glimpses of Indian Economic Policy: An Insider's View*, New Delhi: Oxford University Press, 2002.
32. Ibid.
33. The Reserve Bank of India, *The Reserve Bank of India*, Vol III (1967-1981), Mumbai: Reserve Bank of India, 2005.
34. Ibid.
35. Patel, 2002
36. The Reserve Bank of India, *The Reserve Bank of India*, Vol III (1967–1981), Mumbai: Reserve Bank of India, 2005.

37. Ibid.
38. Ibid.
39. V. Acharya, 'What Saved the Indian Banking System: State Ownership or State Guarantees?', available at http://pages. stern.nyu.edu/~sternfin/vacharya/public_html/BI%20viral%20 acharya.pdf, (accessed on 27 April 2019).
40. S. Baru, *1991: How P.V. Narasimha Rao Made History*, New Delhi: Aleph Book Company, 2016.
41. Ibid.
42. Ibid.
43. M. Singh, Budget Speech of 1991–92, available at https://www. indiabudget.gov.in/bspeech/bs199192.pdf, (accessed on 30 April 2019).
44. C.P. Chandrasekhar and Jayati Ghosh, 'The Banking Connudrum—Non-performing Assets and Neo liberal Reform', *Economic and Political Weekly*, 31 March 2018, Vol. LIII, No. 13, pp 129–137, (accessed on 29 April, 2019).
45. R.V. Pulley, 'Making the Poor Creditworthy—A Case Study of the Integrated Rural Credit Programme of India', World Bank Discussion Papers, 1989.
46. R. Nilekani, 'The Loan Messiah', *Sunday Magazine,* November 8–14, 1987. Accessed on July 11, 2019. Available at https:// archive.rohininilekani.org/the-loan-messiah/.
47. Ibid.
48. The Reserve Bank of India, *The Reserve Bank of India*, Vol III (1967–1981), Mumbai: Reserve Bank of India, 2005.
49. Ibid.
50. R. Dasgupta, 'Priority Sector Lending—Yesterday, Today and Tomorrow', *Economic and Political Weekly*, 12 October 2002, Volume 37, Issue No. 41, pp. 4239–45, (accessed on 30 April 2019).
51. 'Priority Sector Lending', available at http://shodhganga. inflibnet.ac.in/bitstream/10603/11728/11/11_chapter%204. pdf, (accessed on 30 April 2019).
52. The Reserve Bank of India, *The Reserve Bank of India*, Vol III (1967–1981), Mumbai: Reserve Bank of India, 2005.
53. Ibid.

54. Nilekani, 1987.
55. Pulley, 1989.
56. The committee on the financial system (Chairman: M. Narasimham), 1991.
57. The Reserve Bank of India, *The Reserve Bank of India*, Vol IV (1981–1997), Delhi: Academic Foundation, 2013.
58. Pulley, 1989.
59. V. Mahajan, 'Call for an Inclusive Banking Structure for India by 2019, Fifty Years after Bank Nationalisation', available at https://www.accessdev.org/wp-content/uploads/2017/07/1032-1006-FILE.pdf, (accessed on 30 April 30 2019).
60. H.S. Shylendra, 'Farm loan waivers: a distributional and impact analysis of the agricultural and rural debt relief scheme, 1990', RBI Endowment Unit Working Paper 86, Institute of Rural Management, June 1995.
61. Ibid.
62. R. Sharma, *The Rise and Fall of Nations: Ten Rules of Change in the Post-Crisis World,* London: Penguin, 2016.
63. A. Vasudevan, 'Engineering Banking Sector Recovery and Growth', *Economic and Political Weekly*, 31 March 2018. Vol. LIII, No. 13, pp. 138–143, (accessed on May 2, 2019).
64. Ibid.
65. S. Hede, 'Do States Have Fiscal Space for Farm Loan Waivers?', CARE Ratings, 2 January 2019.
66. J. Tepper and D. Hearn, *The Myth of Capitalism: Monopolies and the Death of Competition,* Hoboken, New Jersey: Wiley, 2019.
67. Y. Mounk, *The People Vs. Democracy: Why Our Freedom is in Danger and How to Save It,* Cambridge, Massachusetts and London: Harvard University Press, 2018.
68. G. Balachandran, *The Reserve Bank of India*, Volume II (1951–1967), Reserve Bank of India, Delhi: Oxford University Press, 1998.
69. Ibid.
70. Ibid.
71. Dadabhoy, 2013.
72. S.L.N. Sinha (ed.), *History of the Reserve Bank of India*, Vol I (1935–1951), Bombay, Reserve Bank of India, 1970.

73. Dadabhoy, 2013.

74. S.L.N. Sinha (ed.), *History of the Reserve Bank of India*, Vol I (1935-1951), Bombay, Reserve Bank of India, 1970.

75. 'An Overview of Development Financial Institutions in India', available at http://shodhganga.inflibnet.ac.in/bitstream/10603/52958/12/11_chapter%203.pdf, (accessed on 4 May 2019).

76. Ibid.

77. G. Balachandran, *The Reserve Bank of India*, Volume II (1951–1967), Reserve Bank of India, Delhi: Oxford University Press, 1998.

78. Ibid.

79. Dadabhoy, 2013.

80. G. Balachandran, *The Reserve Bank of India*, Volume II (1951–1967), Reserve Bank of India, Delhi: Oxford University Press, 1998.

81. Ibid.

82. Ibid.

83. The London Correspondent, 'Britain and the Financing of Commonwealth Economic Development', *The Economic Weekly*, 18 June 1965. Available at https://www.epw.in/system/files/pdf/1955_7/24-25-26/britain_and_the_financing_of_commonwealth_economic_development.pdf, (accessed on 7 May 2019).

84. G. Balachandran, *The Reserve Bank of India*, Volume II (1951–1967), Reserve Bank of India, Delhi: Oxford University Press, 1998.

85. Dadabhoy, 2013.

86. *The Economic Weekly*, 18 June 1965.

87. G. Balachandran, *The Reserve Bank of India*, Volume II (1951–1967), Reserve Bank of India, Delhi: Oxford University Press, 1998.

88. Ibid.

89. Ibid.

90. An Overview of Development Financial Institutions in India. Available at https://shodhganga.inflibnet.ac.in/bitstream/10603/52958/12/11_chapter%203.pdf. Accessed on May 4, 2019.

91. Ha-Joon Chang, *Bad Samaritans: The Guilty Secrets of Rich Nations and the Threat to Global Prosperity*, London: Random House Business Books, 2008.

92. G. Balachandran, *The Reserve Bank of India*, Volume II (1951–1967), Reserve Bank of India, Delhi: Oxford University Press, 1998.

93. Dadabhoy, 2013.

94. Committee on Banking Sector Reforms (Narasimham Committee II) – Action taken on the recommendations, The Reserve Bank of India, available at https://rbidocs.rbi.org.in/rdocs/PublicationReport/Pdfs/24157.pdf, (accessed on 7 May 2019).

95. Reform committees on banking supervision, financial system and performance, available at http://shodhganga.inflibnet.ac.in/bitstream/10603/118728/8/08_chapter%202.pdf, (accessed on 7 May 2019).

96. Ibid.

97. R. Sengupta and H. Vardhan, 'Non-performing Assets in Indian Banks—This Time It Is Different', *Economic and Political Weekly*, 25 March 2017, Vol. LII, No. 12, pp.85–95.

98. Dadabhoy, 2013.

99. M. Pettis, *The Great Rebalancing: Trade, Conflict, and the Perilous Road Ahead for the World Economy*, Princeton and Oxford: Princeton University Press, 2013.

100. Ibid.

101. Tirloe, *Economics for the Common Good*, Princeton: Princeton University Press, 2017.

102. S. Tharoor, *India: From Midnight to Millennium*, New Delhi: Penguin Books India, 1997.

103. Economic Survey 2016–17.

104. R. Rajan, Note to Parliamentary Estimates Committee on Bank NPAs, 6 September 2018.

105. Ibid.

106. Ibid.

107. A. Mukhopadhyay, 'Finding Innovative Solutions to India's NPA Woes', ORF Issue Brief, July 2018. Issue No. 246.

108. Sengupta and Vardhan, 2017.

109. Mukhopadhyay, 2018.
110. Sengupta and Vardhan 2017.
111. Sengupta and Vardhan, 2017, and the Economic Survey of 2014–15.
112. D. Subbarao, *Who Moved My Interest Rate? Leading the Reserve Bank of India through Five Turbulent Years,* Gurgaon: Penguin Random House India, 2016.
113. Ibid.
114. M. Friedman, *Money Mischief: Episodes in Monetary History,* New York: Harcourt Brace, 1994.
115. Subbarao, 2016.
116. Ibid.
117 Press Trust of India, Debt waiver for farmers hiked to Rs 71,680 crore, May 24, 2008. Available at https://www.outlookindia.com/newswire/amp/debt-waiver-for-farmers-hiked-to-rs-71680-crore/6956.
118. ET Bureau, 'Govt unveils Rs 30,700-cr stimulus package', *The Economic Times,* 8 December 2008. Available at //economictimes.indiatimes.com/articleshow/3805950.cms?utm_source=contentofinterest&utm_medium=text&utm_campaign=cppst, (accessed on 14 June 2019).
119. ET Bureau, 'Stimulus-II: India Inc gets more room to grow', *The Economic Times,* 3 January 2009. Available at: //economictimes.indiatimes.com/articleshow/3929013.cms?from=mdr&utm_source=contentofinterest&utm_medium=text&utm_campaign=cppst, (accessed on 14 June 2019).
120. RBI press release, 'RBI Announces Further Monetary Stimulus', 2 January 2009. Available at https://rbi.org.in/scripts/BS_PressReleaseDisplay.aspx?prid=19792, (accessed on 14 June 2019).
121. BS Reporters, 'Pranab unveils third fiscal stimulus package', *Business Standard,* 25 February 2009. Available at https://www.rediff.com/money/2009/feb/25pranab-unveils-third-fiscal-stimulus-package.htm, (accessed on 14 June 2019).
122. P. Mukherjee, *The Coalition Years 1996–12,* New Delhi: Rupa Publications India, 2017.
123. Subbarao, 2016.

124. Economic Survey of 2016–17.
125. Sengupta and Vardhan, 2017.
126. Ibid.
127. T.T. Ram Mohan, 'Twin Balance Sheet Problem—Causes, Consequences, Remedies', *Economic and Political Weekly*, Volume LII, No. 9, pp. 12–13, (accessed on May 15, 2019).
128. Chandrasekhar and Ghosh, March 2018.
129. S. Ganapathy, N. Shah and A. Nainani, *Indian Banks: Miles to Go Before I Sleep*, Macquarie Research, June 2018. Scribd.com/document/39253347/India-Banks-Macquarie.
130. Rajan, September 2018.
131. Ibid.
132. Ibid.
133. Ibid.
134. D. Kahneman, *Thinking Fast and Slow,* London: Penguin Books, 2011.
135. Ibid.
136. R. Gandhi, 'PSBs: At Cross Road', Summit organized by Bengal Chamber of Commerce and Industry, 10 January 10 2015.
137. K. Sehgal, *Coined: The Rich Life of Money and How Its History Has Shaped Us,* London: John Murray (Publishers), 2015.
138. Ibid.
139. Sehgal, 2015
140. D. Davies, *Lying for Money: How Legendary Frauds Reveal the Workings of our World*, London: Profile Books, 2018.
141. Ibid.
142. Sehgal, 2015.
143. Ibid.
144. J. Crabtree, *The Billionaire Raj: A Journey Through India's Gilded Age*. Noida: HarperCollins, 2018.
145. R. Gandhi, 'Banks, Debt Recovery and Regulations: A Synergy', Workshop for Judges of DRATs and Presiding Officers of DRTs conducted by CAFRAL at Leadership Development Academy, Larsen & Toubro Ltd., N-H 4, Lonavala, December 2014.
146. Rajan, November 2014.
147. Rajan, September 2018.

148. Express News Service, 'Bank of Maharashtra reinstates its CEO, executive director after clean chit in fraud case', *The Indian Express*, 3 November 2018. Available at https://indianexpress. com/article/business/banking-and-finance/bank-of-maharashtra-reinstates-its-ceo-executive-director-after-clean-chit-in-fraud-case-5432152/, (accessed on 1 August 2019).

149. Ibid.

150. A. Singh, A. Diwanji and M. Shrivastava, 'Unmasking India's NPA issues – Can the banking sector overcome this phase?', EY, 2015.

151. S.S. Mundra, 'Asset Quality Challenges in India: Diagnosis and Prognosis', at the Edelweiss Credit Conclave held in Mumbai on 28 April 2016.

152. R. Rajan, *I Do What I Do,* Noida: HarperCollins: 2017.

153. Ibid.

154. Crabtree, 2018.

155. R.Rajan, Saving Credit, Third Dr. Verghese Kurien Memorial Lecture at IRMA, Anand, November, 2014). Available at https://www.rbi.org.in/scripts/BS_SpeechesView.aspx?Id=929, (accessed on 27 May 2019).

156. Crabtree, 2018.

157. Ibid.

158. S.S. Mundra, 'Banker–Borrower Interplay: Synergies & Challenges', Bankers–Borrowers–Business Meet, organized by ASSOCHAM, New Delhi, 23 March 2015.

159. S. Gupta, 'National Interest: India Stinc', *The Indian Express*, 15 February 2014. Accessed on August 15, 2019. Available at. https://indianexpress.com/article/opinion/columns/india-stink/.

160. Crabtree, 2018.

161. Ibid.

162. Press Trust of India, 'Worst is over, says Bhatt on SBI's NPAs', 26 May 2010. Available at https://smartinvestor.business-standard. com/market/read-29622-readdet-Worst_is_over_says_Bhatt_on_SBIs_NPAs.htm#.XN-x4OszbOQ, (accessed on 18 May 2019).

163. 'SBI's asset quality worrying as bad loans double in Q3', *The Hindu Business Line*, 13 February 2012, (accessed on May 6, 2019. Available at https://www.thehindubusinessline.com/money-and-banking/sbis-asset-quality-worrying-as-bad-loans-double-in-q3/article20397341.ece).

164. Press Trust of India, 'SBI Group Q1 net dips 78%, but says worst of NPAs behind it', 13 August 2016. Available at https://www.dailypioneer.com/2016/business/sbi-group-q1-net-dips-78-but-says-worst-of-npas-behind-it.html, (accessed on 18 May 2019).

165. D. Unnikrishnan, 'Exclusive: Worst is over on NPAs, but a few chunky accounts remain, says SBI's Arundhati Bhattacharya', Firstpost, 22 February 2017. Available at https://www.firstpost.com/business/exclusive-worst-is-over-on-npas-but-a-few-chunky-accounts-remain-says-sbis-arundhati-bhattacharya-3296026.html, (accessed on 2 June 2019).

166. Crabtree, 2018.

167. A. Gupta and P. Kumar, 'House of Debt', Credit Suisse, 2 August 2012.

168. Crabtree, 2018.

169. Ibid.

170. Ibid.

171. Ibid.

172. Ibid.

173. R. Rajan, 'Strong Sustainable Growth for the Indian Economy', FIBAC, 24 August 2015.

174. A. Gupta, K. Shah and P. Kumar, 'House of Debt', Credit Suisse, 21 October 2015.

175. A. Gupta, K. Shah and P. Kumar, 'India Corporate Health Tracker', Credit Suisse, 16 February 2017.

176. A. Gupta, K. Shah and P. Kumar, 'India Corporate Health Tracker', Credit Suisse, 20 February 2019.

177. Lok Sabha Starred Question No 76, Answered on 14 December 2018.

178. K. Kant, 'A fourth of India's top 1,000 listed companies of FY14 in trouble now', *Business Standard*, 17 May 2019, (accessed on 31 May 2019. Available at https://www.business-standard.com/

article/markets/a-fourth-of-india-s-top-1-000-listed-companies-of-fy14-in-trouble-now-119051601445_1.html).

179. Economic Survey 2016-17, The Festering Twin Balance Sheet Problem, February 2017. Available at https://www.indiabudget. gov.in/budget2017-2018/es2016-17/echap04.pdf, (accessed on 2 January 2020).

180. G. Akerlof and R. Shiller, *Phishing for Phools: The Economics of Manipulation and Deception*, Princeton and Oxford: Princeton University Press, 2015.

181. Ibid.

182. Ibid.

183. V. Acharya, 'Some ways to decisively resolve bank stressed assets', Indian Banks' Association Banking Technology Conference, Mumbai, 21 February 2017.

184. M.Doshi, 'Does India need a bad bank to clean up the bad loan mess', Bloomberg–Quint, 6 October 2016, available at https://www.youtube.com/watch?v=NkT6_UMGJJ8, (accessed on 20 May 2019).

185. Crabtree, 2018.

186. Acharya, 2017.

187. R. Rajan, 'Issues in Banking Today', Confederation of Indian Industry's (CII) first Banking Summit, Mumbai, 11 February 2016.

188. Crabtree, 2018.

189. Rajan, February 2016.

190. P. Agarwal and R. Bahl, 'For banks, no respite from bad loans this year', CRISIL Ratings, 12 May 2015.

191. A. Agarwal, S. Kariwala and S. Iyer, 'A Growing Need for Indian TARP', Morgan Stanley Asia Insight, 8 June 2015.

192. Press Information Bureau, Govt Lays Down Four Year Long Plan for Bank Capitilisation; this will Give a Major Boost of for Investment and Growth, 31 July 2015. Available at https://pib. gov.in/newsite/printrelease.aspx?relid=124107, (accessed on 2 January 2020).

193 C. V. Nageswar and S. K. Ghosh, The economics of bank recapitalisation bonds, 31 October 2017. Available at https://www.livemint.com/Opinion/6qGyDfArvbofgYCBWAA4gO/

The-economics-of-bank-recapitalisation-bonds.html. Accessed on February 6, 2020.

194 Economic Survey of 2019–20.

195 Ibid.

196. A. Iyer, 'LIC-owned IDBI Bank is continuing to struggle with its load of bad loans', *Mint*, 14 August 2019, (accessed on June 4, 2019).

197. R. Rajan, 'Saving Credit', The third Dr Verghese Kurien Memorial Lecture at IRMA, Anand, 25 November 2014. Available at https://rbi.org.in/scripts/BS_SpeechesView.aspx?Id=929, (accessed on 13 May 2019).

198. Chapter VI, Asset Quality of PSBs, Report No. 28, 2017. Available at https://cag.gov.in/sites/default/files/audit_report_files/Chapter_6_-_Asset_Quality_Position_of_PSBs_of_Report_No.28_of_2017_-_Performance_audit_Union_Government_Recapitalisation_of_Public_Sector_Banks_Reports_of_Ministry_of_Finance.pdf, (accessed on 22 May 2019).

199. Data sourced from Rajya Sabha, Unstarred Question No. 1854, Answered on 1 September 2017. Available at http://164.100.47.5/qsearch/QResult.aspx, (accessed on 22 May 2019).

200. Global and Domestic Steel—Pressing Issues and Way Ahead, FICCI, 2017. Available at http://ficci.in/spdocument/20888/Steel-Report-2017.pdf, (accessed on 22 May 2019).

201. Ibid.

202. H. Hazlitt, *Economics in One Lesson*, New York: Three Rivers Press, 1979.

203. National Bureau, 'Government imposes minimum import price on 173 steel items', *The Hindu*, 7 February 2016, (accessed on 9 June 2019).

204. S. Asthana, '5 things you need to know about bank write-offs', 12 February 2016. Available at https://www.business-standard.com/article/finance/5-things-you-need-to-know-about-bank-write-offs-116021200192_1.html, (accessed on 13 May 2019).

205. 'Banking sector in India – Issues, challenges and the way forward including non-performing assets/stressed assets in banks/financial institutions', Standing Committee on Finance, 16th Lok Sabha, August 2018.

206. Reserve Bank of India, Framework for Revitalising Distressed Assets in the Economy - Refinancing of Project Loans, Sale of NPA and Other Regulatory Measures, February 2014. Available at https://www.rbi.org.in/Scripts/BS_CircularIndexDisplay. aspx?Id=8756, (accessed on 2 January 2020).

207. Sharma, 2016.

208. A. Subramanian, *Of Counsel: The Challenges of the Modi–Jaitley Economy*, Gurgaon: Penguin Random House India, 2018.

209. Financial Absconders Abroad, Lok Sabha Question No. 1551, answered on 19 December 2018.

210. First Information Report filed by the CBI against Nirav Modi and his co-conspirators. Available at http://cbi.gov.in/firs/2018/2018_ pdf/2018_bsnfc_mumbai_firs/RC0772018E0001.pdf, (accessed on 11 June 2019).

211. Losses incurred by PSBs, Lok Sabha Question No. 218, answered on 9 March 2018.

212. Report of John J. Carney, Examiner, United States Bankruptcy Code, Southern District Court of New York. 25 August 2018.

213. Ibid.

214. Ibid.

215. Ibid.

216. Functioning of Corporate Companies, Lok Sabha Question No. 4644, answered on 23 March 2018.

217. Carney, August 2018.

218. RBI Master Circular on Frauds – Classification and Reporting, Available at https://www.rbi.org.in/CommonPerson/english/ Scripts/Notification.aspx?Id=578, (accessed on 2 January 2020).

219. U. Patel, 'Banking Regulatory Powers Should Be Ownership Neutral', Gujarat National Law University, 14 March 2018.

220. A. Kazmin and L. Barber, 'The Fall of Vijay Mallya', *Financial Times*, 5 May 2016. Available at https://www.ft.com/ content/85252402-1249-11e6-839f-2922947098f0, (accessed on 14 June 2019).

221. Rajya Sabha Unstarred Question No. 2133, Recovering of Outstanding Dues of Banks, answered on 21 March 2017.

222. Crabtree, 2018.

223. K. Nag, 'The Rise, Fall and Escape of Vijay Mallya', *The Hindu Business Line*, 25 September 2018. Available at https://www. thehindubusinessline.com/opinion/columns/the-rise-fall-and-escape-of-vijay-mallya/article25040919.ece, (accessed on 25 June 2019).

224. Kazmin and Barber, May 2016.

225. Crabtree, 2018.

222. Press Trust of India, 'Vijay Mallya resigns from Rajya Sabha', 2 May 2016, Available at https://www.thehindu.com/news/national/Vijay-Mallya-resigns-from-Rajya-Sabha/article14297219.ece, (accessed on 1 August 2019).

227. Kazmin and Barber, May 2016.

228. Crabtree, 2018.

229. H. Timmons, 'Indian Tycoon Spreads His Wings in Aviation', *The New York Times*, 21 June 2007. Available at https://www. nytimes.com/2007/06/21/business/worldbusiness/21air.html, (accessed on 6 July 2019).

230. P.R. Sanjai, 'Kingfisher puts on hold new international flights', *Mint*, 12 October 2008. Available at https://www.livemint.com/Companies/5JpVPy0c2t43A0yJGETBfO/Kingfisher-puts-on-hold-new-international-flights.html, (accessed on 7 July 2019).

231. Kazmin and Barber, May 2016.

232. Ibid.

233. S.Gupta, 'If you flaunt while owing a lot, it suggests you don't care: Raghuram Rajan', Business Standard, 28 January 2016. Available at https://www.business-standard.com/article/finance/if-you-flaunt-while-owing-a-lot-it-suggests-you-don-t-care-raghuram-rajan-116012600132_1.html, (accessed on 2 January 2020).

234. Nag, September 2018.

235. Ibid.

236. Crabtree, 2018.

237. IBBI Quarterly Newsletter (July to September 2019). Available at https://ibbi.gov.in/publication.

238. R. Nair and S.S. Dhanjal, 'Former Bhushan Steel MD Neeraj Singhal arrested', *Mint*, 10 August 2018. Available at: https://www.

livemint.com/Companies/DjNsjYmu5twHXxyK836KAM/
Former-Bhushan-Steel-MD-Neeraj-Singhal-arrested.html,
(accessed on 24 July 2019).

239. M. Bhalla, 'SFIO arrests Bhushan Steel's former CFO Nitin Johri on charges of financial fraud', *The Economic Times*, 4 May 2019. Available at https://economictimes.indiatimes.com/industry/indl-goods/svs/steel/sfio-arrests-bhushan-steels-former-cfo-nitin-johri-on-charges-of-financial-fraud/articleshow/69166567.cms?from=mdr, (accessed on 25 July 2019).

240. A. Sethi, 'NPA crisis: The rise and fall of Bhushan Steel into the great Indian debt trap', *Hindustan Times*, 7 August 2017. Available at https://www.hindustantimes.com/business-news/npa-crisis-the-rise-and-fall-of-bhushan-steel-in-the-great-indian-debt-trap/story-GHrvRRFIBsMLXKJzbqvaFN.html, (accessed on 26 July 2019).

241. Ibid.

242. N. John, 'Billions to Bust', *Business Today*, 7 October 2018. Available at https://www.businesstoday.in/magazine/cover-story/billions-to-bust/story/282440.html, (accessed on 28 July 2019).

243. Sethi, August 2017.

244. Ibid.

245. John, October 2017.

246. Subramanian, 2018

247. Ibid.

248. Ibid.

249. RBI Financial Stability Report June 2012.

250. A. Subramaniam and J. Felman, India's Great Slowdown: What Happened? What's the Way Out?, CID Faculty Working Paper No. 369 December 2019, Working Papers, Center for International Development at Harvard University. Available at https://www.hks.harvard.edu/centers/cid/publications/faculty-working-papers/india-great-slowdown, (accessed on 30 December 2019).

251. Ibid.

252. Ibid.

253. Subramanian, 2018.
254. A. Iyer, 'The gravity of Altico Capital's default and what it tells us about realty sector', 17 September 2019. Available at https://www.livemint.com/market/mark-to-market/the-gravity-of-altico-capital-s-default-and-what-it-tells-us-about-realty-sector-1568656406655.html, (accessed on 31 December 2019).
255. R. Rajan, Saving Credit, Third Dr. Verghese Kurien Memorial Lecture at IRMA, Anand, November, 2014. Available at https://www.rbi.org.in/scripts/BS_SpeechesView.aspx?Id=929, (accessed on 27 May 2019).
256. Ibid.
257. R. Rajan, 'Resolving Stress in the Banking System', RBI governor's speech at the ASSOCHAM Interactive Meet with Industry and Trade, Bengaluru, 22 June 2016.
258. Ibid.
259. Ibid.
260. Report of the High-Level Task Force on Public Credit Registry for India, 6 June 2018. Available at https://rbi.org.in/scripts/PublicationReportDetails.aspx?ID=895, (accessed on 17 June 2019).
261. Rajan, November 2014.
262. Rajan, June 2016.
263. Ibid.
264. Indradhanush press release. Released on August 14, 2015. Available at https://pib.gov.in/newsite/printrelease.aspx?relid=126074, (accessed on 16 July 2019).
265. Ibid.
266. Rajan, November 2014.
267. Economic Survey 2016–17.
268. M. Sabnavis and M. Sachdeva, 'Addressing NPAs of Banks: PARA-the last frontier?', February 2017, CARE Ratings.
269. Ibid.
270. Ibid.
271. Ibid.
272. R. Rajan, 'Interesting, profitable, and challenging – banking in India today', FICCI-IBA (Federation of Indian Chambers of

Commerce & Industry – Indian Banks' Association) Annual Banking Conference, Mumbai, 16 August 2016.

273. A. Subramanian, *Of Counsel: The Challenges of the Modi–Jaitley Economy*, Gurgaon: Penguin Random House India, 2018.

274. Economic Survey 2016–17.

275. Ibid.

276. Ibid.

277. Rajan, November 2016.

278. R. Rajan, *I Do What I Do*, Noida: HarperCollins Publishers, 2017.

279. Ibid.

280. The example is a slight reworking of an example from the research paper, 'A Macroprudential Approach to Financial Regulation', written by S. Hanson, A.K. Kashyap and J.C. Stein. The paper appeared in the *Journal of Economic Perspectives*, Vol. 25, No. 1, winter 2011, pp. 3–28.

281. V. Acharya, 'A Bank Should Be Something One Can "Bank" Upon', FICCI FLO Mumbai Chapter, 28 April 2017.

282. Press Trust of India, 'India needs fewer and mega banks: Jaitley', 18 February 2019. Available at https://www.livemint.com/industry/banking/india-needs-fewer-and-mega-banks-arun-jaitley-1550486128213.html, (accessed on 31 July 2019).

283. C.M. Christensen, R. Alton, C. Rising and A. Waldeck, 'The Big Idea: The New M&A Playbook', *Harvard Business Review*, March 2011. Available at https://hbr.org/2011/03/the-big-idea-the-new-ma-playbook, (accessed on 25 June 2019).

284. Krishnamurthy, July 2017.

285. Ibid.

286. R. Gandhi, '*Consolidation among Public Sector Banks*', South Banking Conclave, Bangalore, April 2016. Available at https://rbidocs.rbi.org.in/rdocs/Bulletin/PDFs/03SP7DC4DCF1956B496588C1A64DEF4416A4.PDF, (accessed on 31 May 2019).

287. Krishnamurthy, July 2017.

288. Ibid.

289. Ibid.

290. J. Lanchester, *How to Speak Money*, London: WW Norton & Company, 2015.

291. Ibid.

292. Press Trust of India, 'Over 3,400 branches of 26 public sector banks closed or merged in last 5 years', 3 November 2019. Available at https://www.businesstoday.in/sectors/banks/over-3400-branches-of-26-public-sector-banks-closed-or-merged-in-last-5-years/story/388260.html, (accessed on 30 December 2019).

293. Ibid.

294. Ibid.

295. Ibid.

296. Ibid.

297. Gandhi, April 2016.

298. P. Bose, 'FRDI Bill, 2017: Inducing Financial Instability', EPW Engage, 27 December 2017. Available at https://www.epw.in/engage/article/frdi-bill-2017-issues-and-concerns, (accessed on 20 June 2019).

299. Ibid.

300. Ibid.

301. ET Online, 'The Bill that spooked bank customers across India has been withdrawn', 7 August 2018. Available at: //economictimes.indiatimes.com/articleshow/65304709.cms?from=mdr&utm_source=contentofinterest&utm_medium=text&utm_campaign=cppst, (accessed on 20 June 2019).

302. M.S. Sahoo, 'A Journey of Endless Hope', 2nd Annual GRR Live, Singapore, 1 April 2019.

303. A. Gayam, 'The Insolvency and Bankruptcy Code: All you need to know', PRS Legislative Research, 10 May 2016.

304. Sahoo, April 2019.

305. Ibid.

306. D. Kahneman, 2011.

307. Sahoo, April 2019.

308. The Banking Regulation Act of 1949. Available at https://rbidocs.rbi.org.in/rdocs/Publications/PDFs/BANKI15122014.PDF, (accessed on 2 January 2020).

309. Press Release, 'RBI identifies Accounts for Reference by Banks under the Insolvency and Bankruptcy Code (IBC)', Reserve Bank of India, 13 June 2017.

310. T. Thomas, 'Govt's new 330-day deadline may not ease resolution bottlenecks', *Mint*, 29 July 2019. Available at https://www. livemint.com/politics/policy/govt-s-new-330-day-deadline-may-not-ease-resolution-bottlenecks-1564340639674.html, (accessed on 8 August 2019).

311. A.R. Mishra, 'Govt shows steely intent in resolving thorny IBC issues', *Mint*, 30 July 2019. Available at https://www. livemint.com/news/india/govt-shows-steely-intent-in-resolving-thorny-ibc-issues-1564425696756.html, (accessed on 8 August 2019).

312. Crisil Ratings, 'Strengthening the Code', May 2019.

313. Thomas, July 2019.

314. Subramanian, 2018.

315. Crisil Ratings, 'Strengthening the Code', May 2019.

316. Subramanian, 2018.

317. Ibid.

318. V. Mehta, 'BOBCAPS NPA Conference: Key takeaways', BOBCAPS, 1 March 2019.

319. Subramanian, 2018.

320. Ibid.

321. Mehta, 2019.

322. Ibid.

323. A. Harlalka and S. Reis, 'India: The Economics of Morality: The 29A Conundrum', Nishith Desai Associates, 15 February 2019. Available at http://www.mondaq.com/india/x/781264/Insolvency+Bankruptcy/The+Economics+Of+Morality+The+29A+Conundrum, (accessed on 7 July 2019).

324. A. Jaitley, 'Two years of insolvency and Bankruptcy Code (IBC)', 3 January 2019. Available at https://ibbi.gov.in/Two_years_of_insolvency_and_Bankruptcy_Code_IBC_Facebook. pdf, (accessed on 4 July 2019).

325. V. Kelkar and A.Shah, *In Service of the Republic – The Art and Science of Economic Policy*, Gurugram: Penguin Random House, 2019.

326. Ibid.

327. Ibid.

328. IANS, 'NCLT sees violation of Sec 29(A) in Sterling Biotech case', 28 March 2019. Available at //economictimes. indiatimes.com/articleshow/68613820.cms?from=mdr&utm_ source=contentofinterest&utm_medium=text&utm_ campaign=cppst, (accessed on 4 July 2019).

329. D. Basu, 'Spinning loot of public money as success story', *Business Standard*, 25 June 2018. Available at: https://www. business-standard.com/article/opinion/spinning-loot-of-public-money-as-success-story-118062400753_1.html, (accessed on 9 August 2019).

330. Ibid.

331. Report of the High-Level Empowered Committee to address the issues of Stressed Thermal Power Project, November 2018.

332. Ibid.

333. Lok Sabha Unstarred Question No. 580, answered on 13 December 2018.

334. Report of the High-Level Empowered Committee to address the issues of Stressed Thermal Power Project, November 2018.

335. 'Stressed assets in the Indian thermal power sector—Challenges and way forward', Grant Thornton and Assocham. February 2019.

336. A. Chatterjee, 'Stressed power projects await ministry implementation of Cabinet measures', *Financial Express*, 29 June 2019. Available at: https://www.financialexpress.com/economy/ stressed-power-projects-await-ministry-implementation-of-cabinet-measures/1622763/, (accessed on 10 August 2019).

337. Coal Reserves, Lok Sabha Unstarred Question No. 2769, answered on 7 July 2019.

338. K.N Das, 'Coal India struggles to produce half of normal output amid strike', Reuters, 7 January 2015. Available at https://in.reuters.com/article/coal-india-strike/coal-india-struggles-to-produce-half-of-normal-output-amid-strike-idINKBN0KG0MD20150107, (accessed on 10 August 2019).

339. Lok Sabha Starred Question No. 441, answered on 24 July 2019. Available at http://loksabhaph.nic.in/Questions/QResult15. aspx?qref=5489&lsno=17, (accessed on 2 January 2020).

340. P. Bhattacharya, 'Opportunities in a Crisis', *Indian Express*, 29 September 2014. Available at https://indianexpress.com/article/opinion/columns/opportunities-in-a-crisis/, (accessed on 12 May 2019).

341. Mehta, 2019.

342. Press Release, 'Square-One: Discom Debt to Reach Pre-UDAY Levels This Fiscal', Crisil, 6 May 2019. Available at https://www.crisil.com/content/dam/crisil/pr/press-release/2017/12/square-one-discom-debt-to-reach-pre-uday-levels-this-fiscal.pdf, (accessed on 9 July 2019).

343. V. Kaul, *India's Big Government—The Intrusive State and How It is Hurting Us*, Mumbai: Equitymaster Agora Pvt. Ltd., 2017.

344. Press Release, 'UDAY (Ujwal DISCOM Assurance Yojana) for financial turnaround of Power Distribution Companies', Press Information Bureau, Union Cabinet, 5 November 2015. Available at http://pib.nic.in/newsite/PrintRelease.aspx?relid=130261, (accessed on 9 July 2019).

345. Press Release, Crisil, May 2019.

346. Ibid.

347. Grant Thornton and Assocham, February 2018.

348. Dues of Discoms, Rajya Sabha Unstarred Question No. 1235, answered on 2 July 2019.

349. Report of the High-Level Empowered Committee to address the issues of Stressed Thermal Power Project, November 2018.

350. Mehta, 2019.

351. Stressed /Non-performing Assets in Electricity Sector, 37th Report, Standing Committee on Energy, Sixteenth Lok Sabha, March 2018.

352. Ibid.

353. Ibid.

354. Report of the High-Level Empowered Committee to address the issues of Stressed Thermal Power Project, November 2018.

355. Stressed /Non-performing Assets in Electricity Sector, March 2018.

356. Grant Thornton and Assocham, February 2018.

357. Report of the High- Level Empowered Committee to address the issues of Stressed Thermal Power Project, November 2018.

358. Grant Thornton and Assocham, Feruary 2018.

359. Report of the High-Level Empowered Committee to address the issues of Stressed Thermal Power Project, November 2018.

360. Chatterjee, June 2019.

361. Report of the High-Level Empowered Committee to Address the issues of Stressed Thermal Power Project, November 2018.

362. Ibid.

363. Ibid.

364. Chatterjee, June 2019.

365. Ibid.

366. S. Maheshwari and V. Mittal, 'Powering Past Pessimism', Edelweiss Securities, 7 December 2018.

367. Subramanian, 2018, and Mehta, 2019.

368. Mehta, 2019.

369. Ibid.

370. Chatterjee, June 2019.

371. Mehta, 2019.

372. Subramanian, 2018.

373. R. Prithiani and M. Patil, 'The big plunge in thermal power', Crisil, October 2018.

374. Mehta, 2019.

375. Maheshwari and Mittal, December 2018.

376. Grant Thornton and Assocham, February 2018.

377. N.S. Vishwanathan, 'It is not Business as Usual for Lenders and Borrowers', National Institute of Bank Management, Pune. 18 April 2018.

378. S.N. Sharma, 'How RBI's Feb 12 circular changed the way banks dealt with stressed assets', 10 February 2019, *The Economic Times*. Available at https://economictimes.indiatimes.com/industry/banking/finance/banking/how-rbis-feb-12-circular-changed-the-way-banks-dealt-with-stressed-assets/articleshow/67920150.cms?from=mdr, (accessed on 13 August 2019).

379. Ganapathy et al., June 2018.

380. S. Ghosh, 'Supreme Court quashes RBI's 12 February circular on one-day default', 2 April 2019, *Mint*.

381. Vishwanathan, April 2018.

382. Ibid.

383. Ibid.

384. Ibid.
385. Ibid.
386. Ibid.
387. Patel, March 2018.
388. Ghosh, April 2019.
389. Press Trust of India, 'RBI circular a welcome step; provides more freedom to bankers: IBA', 8 June 2019. Available at: https://www.theweek.in/news/biz-tech/2019/06/08/rbi-circular-welcome-step-provides-more-freedom-bankers-iba.html, (accessed on 14 August 2019).
390. Committee on Financial Sector Reforms, *A Hundred Small Steps: Report of the Committee on Financial Sector Reforms*, New Delhi: Sage Publications, 2008.
391. Express Web Desk, 'Raghuram Rajan's policies caused economic slowdown, not demonetisation, says NITI Aayog VC', 3 September 2018. Available at https://indianexpress.com/article/india/niti-aayog-vc-rajiv-kumar-npas-growth-decline-demonetisation-raghuram-rajan-policies-5337942/, (accessed on 27 June 2019).
392. R. Rajan, Note to the Parliamentary Estimates Committee on Bank NPAs, Available at https://www.thehindubusinessline.com/money-and-banking/article24924543.ece/binary/Raghuram%20Rajan%20Parliamentary%20note%20on%20NPAs, (accessed on 2 January 2020).
393. V. Achraya, 'Prompt Corrective Action: An Essential Element of Financial Stability Framework', IIT Bombay, 12 October 2018.
394. Ibid.
395. Reserve Bank of India, Revised Prompt Corrective Action (PCA) Framework for Banks, April 2017. Available at https://www.rbi.org.in/Scripts/NotificationUser.aspx?Id=10921&Mode=0, (accessed on 2 January 2020).
396. A. Mukhopadhyay, 'The Central Bank Autonomy Debate and India's Knife-Edge Credit Crisis', Observer Research Foundation, April 2019.
397. G. Matthew, 'Technical write-off creates non-transparency, brings wrong-doings, says KC Chakrabarty', *The Indian Express*, 7 February 2017.

398. Ibid.
399. Y.V. Reddy, *Advice & Dissent: My Life in Public Services*, Noida: Harper Business, 2017.
400. S.Z. Chinoy and T. Jain, 'India's interim budget tries to strike a balance, but the real story is off-balance sheet' *Financial Express*, 4 February 2019; RBI is a close-call next week, JP Morgan, Available at https://markets.jpmorgan.com/ research/open/url/t59R6MoBP2TZNqA9n4LTG-X02GQ Kt3n6Zc94s6NytW6Ey6ekl0X2nr2RXo5I8ql67b5XJWa0 nInHhPNotg5U70JT10K7vw8mpD-iGje0E-qhPjC1Utbzk-j79PZdzDeNBVlVKJ-OKmJHrAP5JbKMnPraf3RW_PoT_ m8A1Lohu-5yB_6nQOptaPSyecXlbpnt?
401. Reserve Bank of India Press Release, 26 September 2019. Available at https://rbidocs.rbi.org.in/rdocs/PressRelease/ PDFs/PR79251BF26FF99DA466181C66889A14D5C95.PDF, (accessed on 31 December 2019).
402. Press Trust of India, 'PMC Bank issue: Exposure to HDIL at Rs 6,500 crore, or 73 per cent of total loan book, Ex-MD Thomas tells RBI, 29 September 2019. Available at https:// www.financialexpress.com/industry/banking-finance/pmc-bank-issue-exposure-to-hdil-at-rs-6500-crore-or-73-of-total-loan-book-ex-md-thomas-tells-rbi/1721112/, (accessed on 31 December 2019).
403. Letter written by Joy Thomas, MD of PMC Bank. Available at https://www.cnbctv18.com/finance/full-text-of-ex-md-pmc-bank-joy-thomas-letter-to-rbi-4455431.htm, (accessed on 31 December 2019).
404. B. Sapam, Behind HDIL downfall lies a failed slum project that became financial drain, *Mint* 4 October 2019. Available at https://www.livemint.com/industry/infrastructure/rise-and-fall-of-hdil-a-story-of-flashy-cars-and-crisis-ridden-infra-projects-11570193940389.html, (accessed on 31 December 2019).
405. G.S. Mengle, 'Betrayed by a bank: How the collapse of Punjab and Maharashtra Cooperative Bank left thousands in distress', *The Hindu*, 16 November 2019, available at https://www. thehindu.com/business/Industry/betrayed-by-a-bank-how-the-

collapse-of-punjab-and-maharashtra-cooperative-bank-left-thousands-in-distress/article29986064.ece, (accessed on 31 December 2019).

405. R.Yadav, 'PMC case shows why dual regulation doesn't work', *Mint*, 4 December 2019, available at https://www.livemint. com/money/personal-finance/pmc-case-shows-why-dual-regulation-doesn-t-work-11575398109144.html, (accessed on 31 December 2019).

407. A.V. Banerjee, E. Duflo, *Good Economics for Hard Times,* New Delhi: Juggernaut, 2019.

408. R. Shiller, *Narrative Economics,* Princeton: Princeton University Press, 2019.

409. Ibid.

410. Ibid.

411. Banerjee and Duflo, 2019.

412. H.Rosling, O. Rosling and A.R. Rönnlund, *Factfulness: Ten Reasons We're Wrong About the World—and Why Things Are Better Than You Think*, New York: Flatiron Books, 2019.

413. S. Chakravorty, *The Truth About Us,* Gurgaon: Hachette India, 2019.

414. Report of the Committee to Review Governance of Boards of Banks in India, May 2014.

415. Ibid.

416. Ibid.

417. Ibid.

418. Ibid.

419. Ibid.

420. Ibid.

421. D. Choudhury, 'No parent can feed the child permanently', 21 March 2012, *Mint*. Available at https://www.livemint.com/ Opinion/XkRsEz8zUWo59sQtk0a03I/Views--No-parent-can-feed-the-child-permanently.html, (accessed on 20 August 2019).

422. Report of the Committee to Review Governance of Boards of Banks in India, May 2014.

423. Ibid.

424. Ibid.

425. Rajan, 2017.

426. Y.V. Reddy, *Advice & Dissent: My Life in Public Services*, Noida: Harper Business, 2017.

427. Subramanian, 2018.

428. Y. Sinha, Budget Speech of 2000–01, 29 February 2000. Available at https://www.indiabudget.gov.in/doc/bspeech/bs200001.pdf, (accessed on 2 January 2020).

429. R. Rajan, 'The Changing Paradigm of Financial Inclusion' , National Seminar on Equity, Access and Inclusion, Hyderabad, 18 July 2016.

430. Ibid.

431. Ibid.

432. R. Rajan, Interesting, Profitable, and Challenging: Banking in India Today, FICCI-IBA Annual Banking Conference, Mumbai, August 16, 2016. Available at https://www.rbi.org.in/scripts/FS_Speeches.aspx?Id=1015&fn=2, (accessed on 2 January 2020).

433. Ibid.

434. T. Sowell, *Basic Economics: A Common Sense Guide to the Economy*, New York: Basic Books, 2015.

435. S.S.A. Aiyar, *From Narasimha Rao to Narendra Modi: 25 Years of Swaminomics,* New Delhi: Times Books: 2016.

435. Ibid.

437. Rajan, August 2016.

438. Ibid.

439. Reddy, 2017.

440. R. Gandhi, 'Consolidation among PSBs', MINT South Banking Enclave, Bengaluru, 22 April 2016.

441. R. Rajan, 'Competition in the Banking Sector—Opportunities and Challenges', Annual Day Lecture of the Competition Commission of India, 20 May 2014.

442. R. Krishnamurthy, 'PSB Mergers—A Reality Check', *Economic and Political Weekly*, Vol. LII, No. 29, 22 July 2017.

443. Rajan, August 2016.

444. Ibid.

445. U.R. Patel, 'Banking Regulatory Powers Should Be Ownership Neutral', Inaugural Lecture: Centre for Law & Economics, Centre for Banking & Financial Laws, Gujarat National Law University, Gandhinagar, March 2018.

446. Ibid.

447. Report of the Committee to Review Governance of Boards of Banks in India, May 2014.

448. R. Rajan, 'Policy and Evidence', Inaugural Address, Reserve Bank of India at the 10th Statistics Day Conference 2016, Reserve Bank of India, 26 July 2016, Mumbai.

449. Subramanian, 2018.

450. Patel, 2018.

451. K. Narayan, 'More conflict of interest? Mumbai house of Kochhars has Videocon connection', *Indian Express*, 21 June 2018. Available at https://indianexpress.com/article/business/more-conflict-of-interest-mumbai-house-of-chanda-kochhars-has-videocon-connection-icici-bank-5226372/, (accessed on 3 August 2019).

452. S. Shukla and B. Kalesh, 'Reconsider Shikha Sharma's 4th term: RBI to Axis Board', *The Economic Times*, 2 April 2018. Available at https://economictimes.indiatimes.com/industry/banking/finance/banking/reconsider-shikha-sharmas-4th-term-rbi-to-axis-board/articleshow/63573435.cms?from=mdr, (accessed on 16 August 2019).

453. S. Das, RBI trims Rana Kapoor's term as Yes Bank CEO, *The Economic Times*, 20 September, 2019 Available at: //economictimes.indiatimes.com/articleshow/65875341.cms?from=mdr&utm_source=contentofinterest&utm_medium=text&utm_campaign=cppst, (accessed on 2 January 2020).

454. S. Mundy, 'Indian billionaire ordered to step down from Yes Bank', *Financial Times*, 20 September 2018. Available at https://www.ft.com/content/79e18cbc-bca0-11e8-94b2-17176fbf93f5, (accessed on 19 August 2019).

455. Patel, March 2018.

456. S. Jalihal, 'Cashiers, peon among those penalised for bank NPAs in FY18, reveals RTI', *Business Standard*, 13 December 2019. Available at https://www.business-standard.com/article/current-affairs/cashiers-peon-among-those-penalised-for-bank-npas-in-fy18-reveals-rti-119121100370_1.html, (accessed on 30 December 2019).

457. Press Trust of India, 'When HDFC Bank refused loan to Vijay Mallya', 11 July 2019. Available at https://www.livemint, com/industry/banking/when-hdfc-bank-refused-loan-to-vijay-mallya-1562817740179.html, (accessed on 2 January 2020).

458. J. Crabtree, 2018.

459. Ibid.

460. S. Shrinate, 'More skeletons will tumble out if forensic audit of banks is carried out: Yashwant Sinha', *The Economic Times*, 5 April 2018. Available at https://economictimes.indiatimes. com/markets/expert-view/more-skeletons-will-tumble-out-if-forensic-audit-of-banks-is-carried-out-yashwant-sinha/ articleshow/63626823.cms?from=mdr, (accessed on 16 June 2019).

461. S. Punj, 'Vajpayee's finance minister Yashwant Sinha remembers his economics and his way of getting things done', www. dailyo.in, 25 August 2018. Available at https://www.dailyo.in/ business/atal-bihari-vajpayee-yashwant-sinha-finance-minister-liberalisation/story/1/26260.html, (accessed on 20 August 2019).

462. D. Choudhury, 'No parent can feed the child permanently', *Mint*, 21 March 2012, Available at https://www.livemint.com/ Opinion/XkRsEz8zUWo59sQtk0a03I/Views--No-parent-can-feed-the-child-permanently.html, (accessed on 20 August 2019).

463. Press Trust of India, 'Government should not privatise public sector banks: Jairam Ramesh', 19 July 2019. Available at https:// www.financialexpress.com/india-news/government-should-not-privatise-public-sector-banks-jairam-ramesh/1650051/, (accessed on 21 August 2019).

464. Minsky, 2008.

Index

abandoned/shelved/stalled
projects, 68
Acharya, Viral, 108, 183
Adani group, 101
Adani Power, 230, 233
*Advice & Dissent: My Life in
Public Service*, 247, 278
Aggregate Technical and
Commercial (ATC) losses, 223
Agricultural and Rural Debt
Relief Scheme (ARDRS), 34
AIG–largest insurance company,
71
Air Deccan, 149–50
Aiyar, Swaminathan, 277
Akerlof, George, 104
Allahabad Bank, 142, 183
PCA framework, 183
net NPAs, 184
CRAR ratio, 185
All-India Congress Committee
(AICC), 24
All-India Rural Credit Survey
Committee (AIRCS), 21

All-India Rural Financial
Inclusion Survey, 274
Alok Industries, 146, 205, 216
Altico Capital, 162
Ambani, Anil, 157
American economic sanctions,
59
Andhra Bank, 27, 197, 216
Animal Farm, 91
ArcelorMittal India, 207-8
acquisition of Essar Steel,
207, 216
armchair analysis, 92
Arthashastra, 88
Asom Gana Parishad, 34
Asset Quality Review, xiii, 109,
111–12, 155, 172, 235, 242,
245, 249, 288
Asset Reconstruction Companies
(ARCs), 168, 171–72, 178,
212–13
asset reconstruction firms, 213
asset–liability mismatch, 162
average size of a fraud, 4

Axis Bank, 195, 217, 267–68,
    284, 288, 291
Axis Bank model, 267–68, 288,
    291
Axis Bank, bad loan rate, 195

bad loans, xi–xv, xvii, 3–5, 7, 11,
    15, 17–18, 20, 27, 30, 34–35,
    49, 57, 61, 75, 78, 83–86,
    90–93, 94, 99–100, 102–3,
    106–15, 119, 121, 124,
    126–29, 131–32, 137–38,
    152, 155–57, 160–62,
    164–65, 167–73, 175–79,
    181, 185, 188, 192–93,
    195–96, 198, 201, 203, 205,
    210, 218, 234–35, 238–39,
    242, 244–47, 250, 255,
    257, 266–67, 278, 280–81,
    284–85, 288–89, 290
    of Bank of Baroda, 195, 196
    fresh recognition of, 246
    of Dena bank, 195
    of PSBs, 4, 7, 11, 30, 35, 57,
        83f, 92, 108, 155–56, 164,
        171, 173, 244, 245
    rate of recovery of, 130
    of SBI, 18, 99, 192
    serious recognition of, 245
    substandard and doubtful
        asset, 110
    of UCO Bank, 115
    of Vijaya Bank, 195
    written-off, 127–28, 245
bad money hole, 108

Bad Samaritans, 46
Banerjee, Abhijit, 261–63
Bank Investment Company,
    270–72
    idea of, 270
bank lending
    to agriculture, 31
    growth in, 58
    to industry, 57, 59–62, 65,
        79, 136f
    to infrastructure, 65
Bank Nationalisation Act, 1980,
    271, 282
bank nationalization policy, 20
Bank of Baroda, 21, 160, 186,
    195–96
    under-reported bad loans,
        160
    bad loans rate, 195t
Bank of India, PCA framework,
    183
Bank of Maharashtra, PCA
    framework, 183
Banking Companies
    (Acquisition and Transfer
    of Undertakings) Act, 1970,
    282
banking crisis, 28, 57
    multiple causes, 11
Banking Regulation Act 1949,
    190, 204, 282
bankruptcy reform, 215
bankruptcy resolution, 232
banks borrow deposits, 39
banks recapitalization, 172

*Barons of Banking: Glimpses of
Indian Banking History*, 20
Baru, Sanjaya, 28
basic business model of a bank,
    17
*Basic Economics: A Common
Sense Guide to the Economy*,
277
Bharatiya Janata Party (BJP), 34,
    290-91
Bhartiya Mahila Bank, 16, 18,
    99, 191, 193
Bhasin, T.S., 125
Bhatt, O.P., 99
Bhattacharya, Arundhati, 99, 102
Bhattacharya, Partha, 222
Bhushan Steel, xii, 146, 152–54,
    204–5, 208, 214, 216
    recovery rate, 216
    acquisition by Tata Steel, 206
    debts, 153
Black, Eugene R., 43
Blinder, Alan S., 11
Branson, Richard, 148
Bureau of Industrial and
    Financial Reconstruction
    (BIFR), 208
Business Standard, 103

capital market, 96
CARE ratings, 36
cash reserve ratio, 9, 19, 72, 280
CDR mechanism, 84–85
Central Bank of India, 115, 184,
    186–87

advances of, 184
CRAR fall over, 186
PCA framework, 183
Central Bureau of Investigation
    (CBI), 171, 273, 269
Central Repository of
    Information on Large Credits
    (CRILC), 166–67
Central Vigilance Commission
    (CVC), 171, 268–69, 271, 273
Chakrabarty, K.C., 129, 246
Chakrovorty, Sanjoy, 264
Chandra, Naresh, 28
Chandrasekhar, M.G., 138
Chang, Ha-Joon, 46
Chaudhuri, Pratip, 99
Chetty, Shanmukham, 20, 42
Chidambaram, P., 47, 75–76
*Choice and Consequence:
Perspectives of an Errant
Economist*, 5
Choksi, Mehul, 138
Chopra, Priyanka, 5, 143
Coal India, xiii, 219–20, 222
Coalgate scam, 219–23
Coalition Years, The, 77
*Coined: The Rich Life of Money
and How Its History Has
Shaped Us*, 88
Committee on Banking Sector
    Reforms, 47, 273
Committee on Financial Sector
    Reforms, 241
Committee on Financial System,
    32, 47

Commonwealth Development
Finance Company (CDFC),
44
Companies Act, 270–71, 282
competition in banking space,
189
Comptroller and Auditor
General, 169, 171, 273
construction, lending to, 66
Consumer Price Index, 70–71,
73
Controller of Currency, 19
corporate bankruptcy, 168, 201
corporate borrowers, defaults
by, xii
corporate debt restructuring
(CDR), 84, 235
corporate defaulters' liquidation,
209
corporate defaults, xii, 202, 211,
213
corporate insolvency resolution
process (CIRP), 205–11,
215–16, 227, 230
number of CIRPs filed, 211
corporate insolvency, 160, 201,
205, 234
corporate loans under
restructuring, 234
corporate profitability, 59
Corporation Bank, 27, 184, 187,
197, 243, 261
PCA framework, 183
merger with Union Bank of
India, 261

corruption scandals in the coal
and telecom sector, 79
credit deposit ratio, 9
credit risk premium, 121
Credit Suisse, 100, 103, 165
credit-data gap, 166
credit-deposit ratio, 10, 183, 249
CRISIL ratings, 111
crony capitalism, xiii, 177, 240
crony capitalists, 35, 93, 177,
240, 278, 292
crude oil
import dependency of, 118
Indian basket price, 118

Dadabhoy, Bakhtiar K., 20
Das, Satyajit, xvi
Das, Shaktikanta, 240, 243
Davies, Dan, 89
debt delinquency, 89–90
debt forgiveness, jubilee episodes
of, 89
Debt Recovery Tribunals, 130,
169, 211
debt restructuring, 85, 170
debt to equity ratio, 79, 96–97,
161, 218–19
debtors' prisons, 89
Deccan Aviation, 149
default norm, 239
demonetization, 161, 243
Dena Bank, 25, 184, 186–87,
195–97, 235, 261
bad loans rate, 195
CRAR fall over, 186

merged with Bank of Baroda, 261

PCA framework, 183

Deposit Insurance and Credit Guarantee Corporation (DICGC), 200

deposits raised by banks, 134

deposits with the small savings schemes, 250

developmental financial institution (DFI), 41–49, 62, 279

business model of, 48

different proposals for, 43

lending for new industrial, 48

special treatment of, 48

success in Europe, 42

Devi Lal, 33

Dewan Housing Finance Ltd., 161–63, 247

double-digit growth, 59, 79–80

Dravida Munnetra Kazhagam, 34

due diligence, 34, 54, 61, 93–94, 96–97, 162, 168, 176–77, 214, 280

Duflo, Esther, 260–63

echo chamber, 263

economic growth, xii, 13, 15, 23, 28, 58–59, 63–64, 70, 75–77, 79, 160, 176, 204, 292

economic reforms, 59, 191, 266, 290–92

rewards of, 59

economic slowdown, 76, 177, 241, 292

Economic Survey, 59, 80–81, 104, 120, 170, 174–76

Economics for the Common Good, 6

Economics in One Lesson, 125

Economist, The, xi

electricity generation, lending to, 66

Emanuel, Rahm, 265

employee stock options (ESOPs), 281

Enforcement Directorate, 137, 143

Essar Steel, 146, 151, 205, 206–8, 210, 214, 216

defaulted on bank loans, 214

interest coverage ratio, 101

excise duty, 76, 77

Extreme Money: The Masters of the Universe and the Cult of Risk, xvi

fake news, 261–62

family saving, 51

farm loan waiver, 36, 38, 75

Fault Lines: How Hidden Fractures Still Threaten the World Economy, xvi

Felman, Josh, 162

finance, three stages of, 13

financial crisis, xii, xvi, 11–12, 69, 71, 73–75, 78, 80, 149 aftermath of, xii, xvi, 12, 72, 74–75, 212

financial instability hypothesis, 13, 61

financial irregularities, 137, 256

Financial Resolution and Deposit Insurance (FRDI) Bill, 198–99
  'bail-in', 199
  basic idea, 198
  intention of, 198
  objective of, 197

financial stability hypothesis, 13

Financial Stability Report, 12, 154–55, 160

Financial Times, 103, 146

fiscal deficit, 9, 64, 76–77, 251–53

fiscal dominance, 254

fiscal package, 77

fiscal stimuli, 76, 78

fixed deposits, 50–51, 53, 67, 115, 142, 249, 251, 253, 258

Food Corporation of India (FCI), 162, 250–53

food security, 250–52
  budget allocation, 252

food subsidy, 252

foreign exchange crisis, 28, 30

frauds, classifications of, 145

Friedman, Milton, 74

From Narasimha Rao to Narendra Modi: 25 Years of Swaminomics, 277

Gadgil, D.R., 31

Galbraith, John Kenneth, xv

Gandhi, Indira, 23–27

Gandhi, R., 90, 191, 197

Gandhi, Rajiv, 29

Glimpses of Indian Economic History, 24

Global Competitiveness Report, 204

global economic growth, 64

Global Trust Bank (GTB), 106, 190, 259, 265
  merged with Oriental Bank of Commerce, 259, 265

GMR, 101, 103

Good Economics for Hard Times, 261

'goongi gudiya'. *See* Gandhi, Indira

government securities, 9, 251

Goyal, Naresh, 152

Goyal, Piyush, 200

Great Crash 1929, The, xv

Great Depression, xv

Great Rebalancing, The, 50

Gross Domestic Product (GDP), 58–62, 64, 76–77, 79, 117, 172–74, 253–54

Gupta, Ashish, 100, 165

Gupta, Shekhar, 97

GVK, 101, 103

haircut, 199, 206, 217, 231, 233

Haksar, P.N., 25

Harane, Mukesh, 5
Harshad Mehta scam, 50, 53
Harvard Business Review, 190
Hazlitt, Henry, 125
HDFC Bank, 191, 275, 288
healing touch, 185
Hearn, Denise, 36
"hedge" finance, 14
Hegde, Ramakrishna, 147
high concentration risk of banks, 100
Hindu rate of growth, 58
Holland, T.H., 41
home loans outstanding, 159
House of Debt, 100, 102–3
household financial savings, 51–53
    shares of components, 52
Housing Development and Infrastructure Ltd (HDIL), 256–58
    insolvency proceedings, 257
How to Speak Money, 194
Hugo, Victor, 29–30
hygiene factor for political parties, 36

I Do What I Do, 272
ICICI Bank, 48–49, 194, 230, 284, 288
    bad loan rate, 195
    PCA framework, 183
    bad loans, 115

Imperial Bank of India, 19–21.
    See also State Bank of India
In Search of Some Old Wisdom, 13
In Service of the Republic, 215
India growth story, 61
India: From Midnight to Millennium, 58
India's Big Government, 287
Indian Bank, bad loans rate, 18
Indian Banks' Association, 185–86, 240
Indian Companies Act, 42
Indian Express, 97
Indian Overseas Bank, 18, 115, 185–87
    PCA framework, 183
    bad loans rate, 18
    CRAR fall over, 186
Indian Premier League (IPL), 149
Indian Railway Finance Corporation, 252
Indias Big Government, 287
Indradhanush Bank Recapitalization Plan, 112
Indradhanush document, 112
Indradhanush reforms, 112, 168–70, 172
    Banks Board Bureau (BBB), 169
    Debt Recovery Tribunals (DRTs), 168–70
    infuse more capital into the PSBs, 169

steps to de-stress PSBs, 168
Industrial Credit and Investment
    Corporation of India (ICICI),
    44
Industrial Development Bank of
    India (IDBI), xiv, 16–18, 27,
    36, 45–46, 93, 106, 115, 118,
    185–87
    bad loans, 17, 118
    market capitalization of, 118
Industrial Finance Corporation
    of India (IFCI), 41–42,
    44–45, 270
industrial lending
    burst in, 70
    slowdown in, 160
inflation, 58, 60, 70–75, 78, 80
    vs. repo rate, 73
    key measure of, 70
inflow of excessive deposits, 161
Infrastructure Leasing &
    Financial Services (IL&FS),
    161, 163, 247
ING Vysya Bank, 191
Insolvency and Bankruptcy
    Board, 215
Insolvency and Bankruptcy Code
    (IBC), 86, 98, 105, 129–31,
    201, 205, 215, 240
    negative side of, 208
interest coverage ratio, 80–81,
    82, 84, 101–3, 175
interest margin, 119, 249, 250
interest rates on loans, 80

interim budget of 2019–2020,
    174
International Monetary Fund
    (IMF), 29

Jaitley, Arun, 189, 194, 201
James, Michel, 138
Jan Dhan accounts, 283
Janata Dal, 34
Jaypee, 101, 205
Jet Airways, 148, 152
Jha, L.K., 24
JM Financial Asset
    Reconstruction Co.
    (JMFARC), 217
Jobanputra, Ashish Sureshbhai,
    138
Jobanputra, Priti Ashish, 138
Johri, Nikhil, 153
Joint Lenders' Forum (JLF), 166,
    169–71, 177, 238
    main idea behind the, 170
JSW Energy, 229, 233
JSW Steel, 103, 210

Kahneman, Daniel, 87
Kamaraj, K., 26
Kapoor, Rana, 283–84, 288
Kautaliya, 88
Kelkar, Vijay, 215
Keynes, John Maynard, xi
Keynesian expenditure, 64
Khan, Genghis, 105
Kharat, Manoj, 140

King of Good Times. *See* Mallya, Vijay

Kingfisher Airlines, 148, 150

Kingfisher brand, 147, 151

Kingfisher calendars, 147

Kochhar, Chanda, 285, 289

Kochhar, Deepak, 284

Kotak Mahindra Bank, 191

Krishnamachari, T.T., 43, 45

Kumar, Ashwani, 235

Kumar, Prashant, 10

Kumar, Rajiv, 241

labour-intensive exports, 117–19

Lanchester, John, 194

Lanco Infratech, 97, 101, 103, 205

Left Front, 34

Lehman Brothers, xvi, 71

lending by bank, 133*f*

liberalization of 1991, 145

license-quota raj, 29

Life Insurance Corporation (LIC), xiv, 16, 36, 106, 115, 118–19, 216, 268
    acquisition of IDBI Bank, 118
    initial public offerings, 118
    nationalisation of, 25

liquid corporate bond market, 62

listing obligations and disclosure requirements, 269

loan mela, 30–33

loan waiver, 33–34

loans categorization, idea of, 167

Lok Adalats, 130

long-term credit needs of industrial sector, 40

Lying for Money: How Legendary Frauds Reveal the Workings of our World, 89

Mac, Freddie, 71

Madras Industrial Investment Corporation Limited (MIIL), 42

Mae, Fannie, 71

Mallya, Vijay, 7, 11, 98, 137–39, 144, 146–52, 288
    defaulted on bank loan, 7
    elected to the Rajya Sabha, 147
    extradition case, 151
    international flying plans, 149
    over-the-top lifestyle, 151
    poster-boy of this entire era, 152

Mallya, Vittal, 145–47

Marathe, R.P., 93

master circular, 144

Mehta, Jatin, 7, 139

Mehta, Sunil, 240

Mergers of banks
    aftereffects of the, 191

associate banks of SBI with
SBI, 191
Bank of Madura and Sangli
Bank with ICICI Bank,
191
Centurion Bank of Punjab
with HDFC Bank, 191
Dena Bank and Vijaya Bank
with Bank of Baroda, 36,
273
ING Vysya Bank with Kotak
Mahindra Bank, 191
Punjab & Sind Bank with
PNB, 196
rationalization the
workforce, 196
synergy necessary for, 192
Vijaya Bank with Canara
Bank, 196
minimum import price (MIP) on
stell, 123–25
Minsky, Hyman, 12–15, 61, 87,
292
financial instability
hypothesis, 15
*Misbehaving: The Making of
Behavioural Economics*, 5
mismanagement of money by
UTI, 53
Mitra, B.N., 41
modest increase in GDP, 59
Modi, Narendra, 143, 201, 223,
290

Modi, Nirav, 3, 5, 7, 11, 137–39,
140–46, 152, 155, 266, 284,
288
poster boy for corporate
India looting the PSBs, 7
fugitive, 4
defrauded PNB, 266
fraud and default, 4, 288
managed to avoid the
authorities, 144
Rs 12,645.97 crore fraud, 7
scam degenerated into a
Ponzi scheme, 143
Monetary Policy Committee
(MPC), 8, 10–11
monetary policy, operational
effectiveness of, 255
*Money Mischief: Episodes in
Monetary History*, 74
moneylenders, 31, 275–76
professional, 21
agriculturist, 21
Mounk, Yascha, 37–38
Mukherjee, Pranab, 77
Mumbai terror attacks, 76
Mundra, S.S., 94, 96
Mutual funds, 48, 72, 162, 279
*Myth of Capitalism: Monopolies
and the Death of
Competition, The*, 36

Narasimham Committee, xi, 33,
47, 273, 279, 287, 289
Narasimham, M., 33, 47

Narrative Economics, 263

National Asset Management
Company, 232

National Companies Law
Tribunal (NCLT), 201, 205,
211–12, 216–17
pressure on, 213

National Front, 34

National Highways Authority of
India, 252

National Industrial Development
Corporation (NIDC), 45

National Institute of Bank
Management, 276

National Investment and
Infrastructure Fund (NIIF),
230

National Small Savings Fund
(NSSF), 251–53
borrowings from, 252–53

National Thermal Power
Corporation Limited
(NTPC), 229–31, 233

nationalization of banks, 24,
26–27, 291
consequence of, 106
of private banks, 24, 26–27,
30

Nayak Committee, 267–71, 282

Nayak, P.J., 267, 269, 286–88

New Bank of India, 27, 107,
191, 259, 265

New York debt prisons, 89

New York Stock Exchange, xv

*1991: How PV Narasimha Rao
Made History*, 28

NITI Aayog, 240

no free Lunch, 115–24

non-banking financial
companies (NBFCs), 158,
160–62, 198, 288–89

non-food credit, 161, 241–43
growth, 243

non-performing assets (NPAs),
xi, 16–17, 92, 99, 111, 126,
129, 157, 165, 180–85, 197,
205, 240–43, 246, 257
categorization, 126
doubtful assets, 126
growth, xi
loss assets, 127
substandard assets, 126

non-retail and non-agriculture
bank, 272

non-telecom revenue, 158

normal banking transaction, 93

Obama, Barack, 266

Of Counsel, 138, 155–56, 173

oil prices, 149

oil shock of 1979, 28

Oriental Bank of Commerce
(OBC), 27, 186–87, 190, 197,
243
advances of, 184
PCA framework, 183

Orwell, George, 91

ostrich syndrome, 102

outstanding deposits in the
    Indian banking system, 132

Parekh, Ketan scam, 50, 53
Patel, I.G., 24–26, 29
Patel, Urjit, xiii, 145, 238, 243,
    282, 284
People Vs. Democracy, The, 37
per capita income, 59
Pettis, Michael, 50
*Phishing for Phools: The
    Economics of Manipulation
    and Deception*, 104
PMC scam, 256–57, 260–64
    banker-corporate nexus, 257
Poddar, Ramnath, 26
political economy, 27
Ponzi position, 14
Ponzi scheme, 15, 143
Ponzi stage, 82, 87
Ponzi, Charles, 14–15
Poojary, 30, 32
Poojary, Janardhana, 30
Power Finance Corporation
    (PFC), 228, 231, 252
power generation companies,
    interest coverage ratio, 81
power purchase agreements,
    223–26, 228–30, 232
Presidency Banks of Bombay, 19
Price, T. Rowe, 270
priority-sector lending, 31–32,
    280
privatization by stealth, 132

promoter-bank nexus, 240
Prompt Corrective Action (PCA)
    framework, 132, 180–85,
    187–88, 225, 241–44, 283,
    285
public distribution system, 251
Public Sector Asset
    Rehabilitation Agency
    (PARA), 175–79
public sector banks (PSbs)
    bleeding, 111
    capital to risk weighted
        assets ratio (CRAR),
        185–86
    consequences of defaulting
        on loans, 90
    deposits with, 107
    government investment in,
        113
    interest margin of, 250
    lending to industry by, 67,
        69
    lending to infrastructure, 66
    loans to corporates, 102
    outstanding retail loans of,
        135–36
    overall bad loans rate of, 18
    PCA framework, 242
    provisioning for bad loans,
        113
    raised just Rs 2.7 lakh crore
        deposits, 133
    recognition of bad loans by,
        250

reform of, 269
variety of authorities, 172
public sector borrowing
requirement (PBSR), 253
public-private partnerships, 62
Punjab & Sind Bank, 26–27
Punjab and Maharashtra
Cooperative (PMC) Bank,
256
Punjab National Bank (PNB),
3–4, 27, 139–43, 145–46,
191, 196, 266, 284, 288
Nirav Modi scam, 3–4, 143,
146
average size of fraud, 4
filed a complaint with CBI,
139–41
forced merger with New
Bank of India, 191
merger with OBC and United
bank, 27, 197, 265
merger with Punjab & Sindh
Bank, 196
under-reported bad loans,
160
bad loans of, 4
Puri, Aditya, 288

Queen Elizabeth II, 12

Rajagopal, Lagadapati, 97
Rajan, Raghuram, xiii, xvi, xvii,
61, 90, 93–95, 98, 102, 106,
108–10, 120, 151, 164–66,

172, 178, 241–42, 272, 276,
289
Rajya Sabha Ethics Panel, 147
Ramesh, Jairam, 291
Rao, P.V. Narasimha, 29
Rau, B. Rama, 21, 44
RCom, 157
real estate, 93, 96, 125, 157–60,
162, 247, 257–58
big problem looming, 158
unsold inventory, 158–59
recapitalization, 35, 171–73, 244
Reddy, Y.S. Rajasekhara, 97
Reddy, Y.V., 70–, 248, 254, 272,
279
Reliance Industries Ltd. (RIL),
216
Reliance Jio, 157
repo rate, 8–10, 71–75, 79, 255
cutting, 10–11, 50, 73, 189,
249
Reserve Bank of India Act, 130
Resolution Corporation, 198–99
resurgent power, 230
retail lending, growth, 135
Right to Information Act,
268–69, 271
Rise and Fall of Nations: Ten
Rules in the Post-Crisis
World, The, 35
risk threshold, 181–82
Rönnlund, Anna Rosling, 264
Rosling, Hans, 264
Rosling, Ola, 264

Royal Challengers Bangalore,
149. *See also* Mallya, Vijay
Ruia brothers (Shashi and Ravi),
152–53, 214. *See also* Essar
Steel
Rural Banking Enquiry
Committee (RBEC), 21
Rural Electricity Corporation,
231, 252

Saksena, Mohanlal, 20
Sandesara, Chetan Jayantilal, 7,
139, 215
Sandesara, Nitin Jayantilal, 7,
139, 215
Schelling, Thomas, 5
Scheme for Harnessing and
Allocating Koyala (Shakti),
229
secular rate of growth, 58
Securities and Exchange Board
of India (SEBI), 167
Securitisation and
Reconstruction of Financial
Assets and Enforcement
of Securities Interest
(SARFAESI) Act, 98, 130
Sehgal, Kabir, 88–90
senior citizens saving, 51
Serious Fraud Investigation
Office (SFIO), 153–54
severe stress scenario, 155–56,
160–61
Shah, Ajay, 215
Shah, Kush, 102

Sharma, Ruchir, 35, 135
Sharma, Shikha, 284
Shastri, Lal Bahadur, 23
Shaw Wallace, acquisition of,
147
Shekhar, Chandra, 26, 28
Shetty, Gokulnath, 141
Shiller, Robert J., 104, 262–63
short-term funds, access to, 39
Shroff Committee, 46
Shroff, A.D., 46
sick companies, 90
Singal, Brij Bhushan, 152
Singal, Neeraj, 153
Singh, Manmohan, 29, 76–77
Singh, Vishwanath Pratap, 34
Sinha, Yashwant, 273, 290
small savings schemes, rate of
interest, 253
Sorkin, Andrew Ross, xvi
Sowell, Thomas, 92, 276
Special Mention Account (SMA),
167
Specified Undertaking of the
Unit Trust of India (SUUTI),
268
*Stabilizing an Unstable
Economy*, 13
stalled projects (as zombie
projects), 86
State Bank of India (SBI), 4, 16,
18–22, 87, 92–93, 99–100,
191–93, 196
bad loans, 18, 92, 99, 192
birth of, 19–22

engaged Tata Consultancy
  Services, 193
industrial landing, 22
merger with associate banks,
  16, 21, 191, 193
retail lending, 92
subsidiaries of, 22
total advances, 192
under-reported bad loans, 160
State Bank of India Act, 1955,
  282
State Financial Corporations
  Act, 42
statutory liquidity ratio, 9, 48,
  72, 280
Sterling Biotech, 215–16
stimulus package, 76–77
strategic debt restructuring
  (SDR), 167–68, 171, 235
stressed assets, 99
Subbarao, D., 70–75, 78, 164
Subramanian, Arvind, 138,
  155–56, 161–62, 173, 175,
  177–78, 231–32
Sui Gas Transmission Company,
  44
Sukthankar, Paresh, 288
sunk cost fallacy, 87
sustainable structuring for
  stressed assets (S4A), 168,
  171, 235
Swadeshi movement, 40
Syndicate, 23–24, 26–27, 197

Tata Consultancy Services, 193

Tata Power, 230
telecom sector, in a bad shape,
  82
Telugu Desam Party, 34
Tepper, Jonathan, 36
Thaler, Richard H., 5
Tharoor, Shashi, 58
Thinking, Fast and Slow, 87
Thomas, Joy, 257
time-healing factor, 244
Tirole, Jean, 6, 51
Too Big to Fail, xvi
total loans written off vs. total
  loans recovered, 128
Truth About Us, The, 264
twin balance sheet (TBS)
  problem, 104, 176

UCO Bank, 18, 115, 183,
  186–87
  bad loans rate, 18, 115
  CRAR fall over, 186
  CRAR ratio, 185–86
  NPAs, 184–85
  PCA framework, 183
  return on assets, 186–87
Uday, 223–24
Ujwal DISCOM Assurance
  Yojana, 223
Unit Trust of India (UTI), 51, 53,
  267–68
United Bank of India, 183–87
  return on assets, 186–87
  CRAR ratio, 185–86
  advances of, 184

PCA framework, 183
NPAs, 184–85
United Breweries, 146–47,
149–50
United Progressive Alliance
(UPA), 69
US Bankruptcy Code, 213
US-64 scheme, 53
UTI Bank. *See* Axis Bank
UTI Mutual Fund, 268

Vajpayee, Atal Bihari, 26, 274,
290
Vanishing Companies Scam of
1994, 53
Vedanta, 101, 103, 230, 233
Videocon, 101, 103, 284
interest coverage ratio, 101
operating losses, 103
Vijaya Bank, 26–27, 36, 195–96
bad loans rate of, 18, 195
Vishwanathan, N.S., 234, 236

Viswanathan, Ramachandran,
138
voluntary mergers, 191

waiving farm loans, 38
wave of nationalizing India's
private banks, 29
Wealth, Poverty and Politics, 92
WhatsApp University, 7
Who Moved My Interest Rate?,
71
wholesale price index, 70–71, 74
Why Minsky Matters, 14
Whyte & Mackay, 149
World Bank, 30, 33, 43, 202
World War I, 40
World War II, 41, 147
Wray, L. Randall, 14
write-off, 110, 126–30, 178,
180, 245–46

Yes Bank, 284–85, 288

Acknowledgements

As anyone who writes for a living will tell you, figuring out what to write is the more difficult thing; the actual writing, as and when it happens, is relatively easier.

The idea for this book came from my editor, Sachin Sharma. It took me a while to warm up to it. The reason for this was that in the close to eight years that I have been in the freelancing business, I have written extensively on public sector banks and their bad loans. So I didn't want to get down to working on a long documentation of a topic I had already written about at length. Then, one fine day, while I was daydreaming post a heavy lunch, the title for the book (*Bad Money*) came to me. And that got me excited and I began looking forward to writing it. Thanks, Sachin, for the idea. Also, apologies for missing several deadlines. But I guess you are already used to it.

While only my name is credited as the author of this book, there are a host of people who helped me write it.

My father, Vir Krishen, read the manuscript and pointed out many mistakes in it – everything from grammatical errors to typos, to factual mistakes to logical fallacies – and saved me from a lot of embarrassment in the process. Thank you, Papa.

Nupur Pavan Bang, as has been the case with my previous four books, took out time from her busy schedule, and read and critiqued this book as well. The readability of the book improved tremendously thanks to her detailed feedback. I can't thank her enough for that.

Preeti Harkare was the first to read bits and pieces of the book, and told me that I was headed in the right direction. She also read the book once I had completed it, and was very particular about the commas and the way I used them. Thank you, Preeti.

S.Subramanian was quick to read the book and offered many detailed suggestions for me to incorporate in the book. I managed to incorporate some, but not all of them primarily due to space issues and time constraints. Thank you, Subbu.

Shaheen Jamil, who is the only person I know who reads as much or perhaps even more than I do, read *Bad Money* quite enthusiastically and pointed out many small mistakes in it. He also picked out one big howler, which no one else had, and for that I will be forever obliged to him.

Jyotsna Raman edited the book and made it much more readable. I can't thank her enough for that.

Late in the day, Malini Sinha gave me some very good feedback on the structure of the book and what I could possibly do to improve it. Thank you, Malini.

Many of the ideas discussed and detailed in the book were first written as a part of my regular columns in the media. Given this, I would like to thank Vinay Kamat, Sunit Arora and Ajai Srivatsan at *Mint*, Manisha Pande and Atul Chaurasia at Newslaundry, Jaiprakash Gajbhiv at the now defunct *Daily News and Analysis* (*DNA*), Soutik Biswas at BBC India, Brian Carvalho and Kunal Purandare at *Forbes India*, Dinesh Unnikrishnan at Firstpost, Ravi Joshi at *Bangalore Mirror*, Srinivasa Raghotham at *Deccan Herald* and Rajeev Sachan at *Dainik Jagran*.

In the end, the book wouldn't have been possible without the blessings of my parents, Vir Krishen and Nimmi, and the fact that they let me be, at least on most days.

My sister Vividha, did some deft last minute editing, and picked up some big howlers in the book. Thank you for doing that.

To anyone I have inadvertently left out in this list, my sincerest apologies.

The mistakes that remain in the book are mine.

About the Author

Vivek Kaul has worked in senior positions at the *Daily News and Analysis* (DNA) and *The Economic Times*.

He is the author of four books, including the bestselling *Easy Money* trilogy, on the history of money and banking, and how that caused the financial crisis that started in 2008 and is still on.

India's Big Government: The Intrusive State and How It Is Hurting Us, his fourth book, was published in January 2017.

Kaul is a regular columnist for the *Mint*, BBC, *Dainik Jagran*, Firstpost, *Bangalore Mirror* and the *Deccan Herald*. He has also appeared as an economics commentator on the BBC, Mirror Now, CNBC Awaaz and NDTV India. He is a regular guest on 'The Seen and the Unseen', one of India's most popular podcasts.

He speaks regularly on economics and finance and has lectured at IIM Bangalore, IIM Indore, IIM Kozhikode, IIM Vishakhapatnam, NMIMS and the Symbiosis Institute of Media and Communication, among others.

Kaul lives in Mumbai and loves to read crime fiction in his free time.